THE WELLINGTON MONUMENT

Portrait of Alfred Stevens, by Julian Brewer, of Norwich.
Victoria and Albert Museum Library,
photograph in the MacColl Collection.

VICTORIA AND ALBERT MUSEUM

The Wellington Monument

by JOHN PHYSICK

LONDON
HER MAJESTY'S STATIONERY OFFICE
1970

Preface

Outstanding among the sculptural achievements of Victorian England was Alfred Stevens's towering monument to the Duke of Wellington in St. Paul's Cathedral. Not only does the Victoria and Albert Museum possess many of the artist's preliminary drawings, but also his quarter-size competition model, and a full scale plaster version as well.

Although designed in 1857, the monument was not completed until 1912; the papers of D. S. MacColl in the Museum's Library provide the history of the final achievement.

The author is indebted to the Dean and Chapter of St. Paul's, and their Librarian, Mr. A. R. B. Fuller; to the Librarian of the Royal Institute of British Architects, for permission to use material in their possession; and also he is grateful for the advice and help given by his colleague, Mr. Harold Barkley.

Contents

List of Illustrations

I

Prelude

In 1857, Alfred Stevens, an almost unknown man of forty, submitted a design for the national memorial in St. Paul's Cathedral to the Duke of Wellington. He concealed his identity by using the motto 'I know of but one art'. Although awarded the commission, Stevens died nearly twenty years later, a worried man, beset by financial difficulties, with his supreme masterpiece still incomplete. This unhappy outcome was as much his own fault, as it was that of the government officials who have been accused of harrying and humiliating him, and of the art-world which applauded their action. The almost unbelievable history of controversy, secrecy, suspicion and criticism which attended the British government's tribute to the Duke, lasted for nearly sixty years.

The whole state of official and semi-official sculpture in this country throughout the 19th century was, indeed, confused and unhappy; Wellington, and Nelson as well, came out of it particularly badly, in spite of—and probably because of—the high ideals and determined endeavours to produce the best possible to their memory. The story begins during the eighteen-thirties, and many threads are interwoven during the remainder of the century— the same sculptors compete or complain, the same government officials appear and reappear attended by one crisis or another, the same arguments develop, and the same criticism, 'it is not suitable', is voiced.

During the autumn of 1836 an equestrian statue of George III (Plate 1) was unveiled by his son Ernest, Duke of Cumberland,[1] in Cockspur Street, London, not far from the National Gallery. This statue had been suggested as early as 1822, but difficulties over its site, and other matters, delayed its execution for a considerable time.[2] The result was much criticised, especially for the fact that its sculptor, Matthew Cotes Wyatt,[3] had not won the commission through competition, but had been the choice of a committee.

However, shortly after the unveiling, the City of London decided that it would like to erect, near the Mansion House, a statue of the Duke of Wellington. This decision was taken largely at the instigation of one of the Common Councillors, Thomas Bridge Simpson, who was a great admirer of the figure of George III. Simpson wrote directly to Matthew Wyatt, and asked if he would be willing to undertake the Wellington. Wyatt agreed to accept the work, and a subscription list was opened. Not everyone was in favour of Wyatt, however, and Sir Francis Chantrey's name was put forward as a rival artist. At a committee meeting to consider the proposal, the choice of sculptor was forced to a vote; both Wyatt and Chantrey came out with the same number each,

---

[1] Became King of Hanover on the death of his elder brother William IV in 1837.

[2] Just before its unveiling the statue was mysteriously and maliciously damaged—'the mischief was *not* accidental, it *could not* be accidental; this was confirmed by the most scientific men of the country,' said Sir Frederick Trench, quoted by Rupert Gunnis, *Dictionary of British Sculptors, 1660–1851*, 1953, p. 447.

[3] Matthew Cotes Wyatt (1777–1862), son of the architect James Wyatt. Was employed at Belvoir Castle by the Duke of Rutland; carved the monument in St. George's Chapel, Windsor, to Princess Charlotte of Wales, and his marble dog 'Bashaw' is now in the Department of Architecture and Sculpture, Victoria and Albert Museum, A.4–1960.

so the Lord Mayor gave his casting vote in favour of Chantrey.[1]

Sir Francis went at once to work, on what was to prove to be his last important commission. He was given £3,000 on signing the contract in February 1839; a further £2,000 when he had completed the preliminary model, and at this time he received the required amount of metal, worth £1,520, which had been donated by the government. Chantrey was to be given a further £4,000 when the statue was completed at the arranged date in 1843, but in 1841 he died. The group was finished by his assistant Henry Weekes, and by 1844 it was in position outside the Royal Exchange (Plate 2), when it was unveiled on Waterloo Day, 18th June. The work was not received with tumultuous enthusiasm, and the *Art-Union* in August thought it a grievous failure, and was of the opinion that the citizens of London 'begin to look for another fire as a boon'. Nevertheless, the City fathers were proud of it, and at a meeting Thomas Simpson was formally thanked for having suggested a statue of Wellington and also for his 'zeal and activity in assisting to carry it to a successful issue'.

Simpson had been zealous and active elsewhere at the same time. Having been voted down on the issue of Wyatt as the sculptor of the City statue, he immediately proposed that there should be yet another figure of the Duke, not in the City, but in the western outskirts of London—a proposal which led to the greatest sculptural fiasco of the 19th century, attended by almost an excess of press coverage.

By the beginning of 1838 a committee of 62 members had been formed to consider this suggestion by Simpson, and a working sub-committee was appointed under the chairmanship of the Duke of Rutland. Its

PLATE 1. *Statue of George III, in Cockspur Street, London, by Matthew Cotes Wyatt. Photograph:* Author.

members were the Marquess of Londonderry, Viscount Beresford, Viscount Hill, John Wilson Croker, Stephen Rumbold Lushington, and Sir Frederick Trench.[2] This sub-committee undertook all the preliminary work,

---

[1] Sir Francis Legatt Chantrey, R.A. (1781–1841), one of the most successful sculptors of England during the early 19th century. Carved many monuments including the widely popular and sentimental 'Sleeping Children' in Lichfield Cathedral. Bequeathed his fortune to the Royal Academy.

[2] 5th Duke of Rutland (1778–1857); 3rd Marquess of Londonderry (1778–1854); Viscount Beresford (1768–1854); Rowland, 1st Viscount Hill (1772–1842); John Wilson Croker (1780–1857), politician, one-time Secretary to the Admiralty; Stephen Rumbold Lushington, P.C. (1776–1868), son-in-law of the 1st Lord Harris; General Sir Frederick Trench, K.C.H. (1775–1859).

and, after considering various sites for the statue, came to the conclusion that somewhere at Hyde Park Corner near Apsley House would be the best position for it, and it was suggested that the sculpture should be placed on the triumphal arch recently erected at the top of Constitution Hill by Decimus Burton.[1] Before a firm decision could be reached, however, the permission of Queen Victoria had to be obtained. Accordingly, the Duke of Rutland entered into negotiations with the Treasury in order to gain government approval before he approached the Queen.

In the meantime, argument had broken out over the choice of a sculptor. The suggestion that the arch might be used had first been made by John Wilson Croker. He had also walked round London looking at its recent sculpture, and had come to the conclusion that Wyatt's statue of George III in Cockspur Street was the best. Consequently, when the sub-committee was considering whom to turn to for its Wellington statue, Wyatt's name came up, and he was asked whether he would accept the commission. This he agreed to do.

In June 1838, the Duke of Rutland had an audience of the Queen at which she gave her permission for the statue to be placed on top of the arch at Constitution Hill. Rutland at once called a meeting of the full Wellington Memorial Committee at which the Queen's sanction was to be the principal business on the agenda, although there was also to be some 'ulterior business'. What this was, was not specified. Of the 62 members only 26 turned up at the meeting. After being told the good news about the arch, the Duke of Rutland went on to the surprise matter of choosing the sculptor. Only Matthew Cotes Wyatt was proposed, and consequently his appointment to provide a

PLATE 2. *Statue of the Duke of Wellington, outside the Royal Exchange, London, by Sir Francis Chantrey. Photograph:* Author.

design for the statue was confirmed by the meeting which resolved that he was 'in every respect eminently qualified to be entrusted with the execution of the proposed equestrian statue'.[2]

When this resolution was made public, many people were dismayed at the selection of Wyatt, and also the manner in which it had been made. The *Art-Union* foresaw that this country would have no cause to be proud of its tribute to Wellington. Shortly after the meeting the Duke of Rutland, on 22nd June 1838, received a joint letter from the Marquess of

---

[1] Decimus Burton (1800–81). Designed the screen at Hyde Park Corner (*c.* 1825), and the Constitution Hill arch (*c.* 1828). His designs are in the Victoria and Albert Museum, Department of Prints and Drawings. Another, in the R.I.B.A., was exhibited in the Bicentenary Exhibition of the Royal Academy, 1968.

[2] Unless otherwise stated the documents quoted relevant to the Wyatt statue are in *Correspondence on the Wellington Testimonial* and *Copy of the report from the Sub-Committee* both published by order of the House of Commons, June and July 1846.

Anglesey, the Marquess of Tavistock, the Duke of Buccleuch, Lord Lynedoch, the Duke of Richmond, Viscount Hill, the Duke of Northumberland, the Bishop of London and Nicholas Ridley-Colborne,[1] all full members of the committee. In this letter they asked the Duke to call another meeting as they had 'reason to believe that great dissatisfaction prevails among the subscribers'. Two days later Rutland replied that he saw no reason to do as requested just because several members had not attended the meeting, and now wished that they had done so.

Anglesey and his fellow signatories were not appeased by this. They told Rutland, on 30th July, that they were unwilling to say anything 'in disparagement of Mr. M. Wyatt, but we really do feel that the selection of him . . . without full notice and deliberation, excluding all competition . . . bears on the face of it an appearance of favour which we ought not to sanction.'

Rutland remained unmoved; a week later he informed Anglesey that at the original meeting Lord Londonderry had proposed Wyatt, and this had been seconded by the Duke of Cambridge.[2] Wyatt had now been told of the committee's choice, and was hard at work in preparing a preliminary design for its consideration. Anglesey was still not satisfied; he and his friends produced a letter which was sent to various newspapers for publication, in which they stated that they regretted Rutland's decision, and were of the opinion that as Wyatt was at work it precluded 'any further discussion or consideration, and closed the door against all competition', but it certainly had not been made clear that the main purpose of the meeting had been to select a sculptor, otherwise more than 26 people would have attended. Anglesey wanted to make it quite clear that they were not objecting to Wyatt as a sculptor, but only to the method of his selection. Protest would have been made if Chantrey, Westmacott,[3] or any other sculptor had been selected in the same way. The letter went on to state that it had been learnt that Sir Frederick Trench had approached Wyatt before the meeting, and Wyatt alone; obviously the meeting had been called to give formal approval to a decision taken in advance, by Rutland, Trench, Croker, and the other sub-committee members.

Shortly after the publication of this protest by Anglesey, the *Morning Post* printed an attack on him and the other dissentients in 'strong, if not uncivil terms'. Anglesey made enquiries and found that this had been published by the newspaper upon directions from Trench. As a result, a meeting was called at Lord William Bentinck's house in St. James's, attended by Anglesey, Northumberland, Tavistock, Richmond, Buccleuch, Palmerston,[4] and others, and a letter was sent to the Prime Minister, Melbourne, asking Her Majesty's Government to suspend any decision upon the arch and statue that it might have come to. Melbourne agreed to the request on 26th August. Upon receiving the Prime Minister's letter, Anglesey sent a copy of it to the Duke of Rutland. The latter was infuriated and told Anglesey that he was pained that those who had never attended any of the committee meetings should now be finding fault, and he wrote also to Melbourne stating that he was concerned about this 'breakaway action', and that he found 'it somewhat singular that you

---

[1] 1st Marquess of Anglesey (1768–1854), Field Marshal wounded at Waterloo; Marquess of Tavistock (1788–1861), succeeded as 7th Duke of Bedford, 1839; 5th Duke of Buccleuch (1806–84); Lord Lynedoch (1748–1843), General; 5th Duke of Richmond (1791–1860), married to a daughter of the Marquess of Anglesey; 3rd Duke of Northumberland (1785–1847); Charles James Blomfield, Bishop of London (1786–1857); Nicholas Ridley-Colborne (1779–1854), created Baron Colborne, 15th May 1839.

[2] Adolphus Frederick, Duke of Cambridge (1774–1850), seventh son of George III.

[3] Sir Richard Westmacott, R.A. (1775–1856), a successful sculptor with a large practice in church monuments.

[4] 3rd Viscount Palmerston (1784–1865), Foreign Secretary.

[Melbourne] should have written . . . without previous intimation to myself.' Melbourne's reply, from Windsor Castle, was that he did not want to take either side in the dispute, but as there was so much difference of opinion, he felt that there should be time for things to be sorted out.

Whilst this argument over the selection of Wyatt was developing, there had been further activity concerning the use of the arch. On 22nd June 1838 Croker wrote to Thomas Spring-Rice,[1] Chancellor of the Exchequer, expressing his surprise over the amount of disagreement concerning the sculptor; no-one was forced to accept what Wyatt offered, and Croker enclosed a sketch of the arch with a suggestion for an equestrian statue, which had been drawn for him by Decimus Burton. During July, a few weeks later, a wooden outline of such a statue appeared on top of the arch itself, taking London by surprise, and causing a good deal of derisive comment. Croker wrote angrily to Spring-Rice, on 10th August, complaining that he had been very surprised to hear about this silhouette, which he presumed had been based upon the sketch which he had sent to Spring-Rice privately. This had been intended only to show the appearance of the arch surmounted by an equestrian statue, but Croker now recalled that Spring-Rice had once said, 'If I were malicious, I would get a wooden silhouette . . . put on top of the arch, and I think all London would rise in arms.'

Spring-Rice was not slow to tell Croker that he had not realized that the sketch had been a private matter between them. After all, it had been drawn by Decimus Burton, who was the government's architect. Croker should feel assured that if he sent a 'correct representation of your Colossal Equestrian Statue, my model shall be dethroned, and shall give place to yours . . . At all events, we must both keep our

good humour.' Croker was still testy, however, and wanted to know why the Chancellor had not asked his committee, in the first place, for its own version of the statue, and had used a design which the Chancellor had 'already laughed at'; Croker added that in spite of the outline's enormous imperfections, it had produced a general opinion that an equestrian statue on top of the arch would look very fine, and that 'the only doubts that have reached me are as to size. The committee had already decided on one much smaller.' Obviously Croker was rather out of touch with general public opinion, and also with the plans of the Duke of Rutland, who had decided that Wyatt's group was going to be the largest equestrian statue ever made.

Whilst Croker and Spring-Rice were quarrelling, the Commissioner of Woods and Forests (predecessor of today's Minister of Public Building and Works), who was responsible for the arch, received a letter from G. J. Pennington of the Treasury informing him that, as a result of various letters between the Duke of Rutland and Viscount Melbourne,[2] the Treasury had agreed to the statue being placed upon the arch, adding that it was the responsibility of the Office of Woods and Forests to see that there was no damage as a result. However, as a consequence of the various arguments then raging, this permission was shortly afterwards put aside.

Unperturbed by all this, Wyatt was working away on his designs.[3] On Christmas Eve, 1838, Rutland sent him an invitation to visit Belvoir Castle, 'for the party next week, for if the Duke of Wellington should come, it will be important for you to be here, & at all Events Mr. Croker, & Sir Frederick [Trench] will be here'. Wellington himself had first heard of the proposed statue during the previous June,

[1] Thomas Spring-Rice, 1st Lord Monteagle (1790–1866), Chancellor of the Exchequer, 1835–9.

[2] 2nd Viscount Melbourne (1779–1848).
[3] A correspondent to *The Times*, 24th August 1882, said that the small plaster model by Wyatt was then in the Royal United Services Institution.

when Rutland visited him at Apsley House to let him know of the suggestion.

The situation remained fairly static until the beginning of May 1839. In that month Melbourne was told by Rutland that Wyatt's statue was to represent the Duke on the eve of 18th June 1815, towards the close of the Battle of Waterloo, and that the Duke had been very obliging, and had sat for Wyatt in the clothes he had worn on that occasion. Rutland, however, did not receive any encouragement from the Prime Minister who, on 12th June, could not agree to any plan for the statue until the whole matter had been considered again by 'a full meeting of the committee, and, if necessary, at a general meeting of the subscribers'.

Presumably Rutland soon smothered any remaining opposition, for on 8th August, he heard from the Treasury that permission to use the arch was not now withheld, and he was asked to ensure that his sub-committee worked closely with the Office of Woods and Forests. Consequently, at the end of the month Rutland wrote to the Chief Commissioner requesting that Decimus Burton should get in touch with Wyatt to discuss what alterations would be needed to the arch. A month later, in September 1839, Burton was required by the Office of Woods and Forests to produce an estimate of how much it would cost to place the statue in position.

Now that permission had been received, Rutland, his sub-committee, and Wyatt were able speedily to carry on with their plans. On 23rd October a Mr. Porrett of the Tower of London, sent a request to the Ordnance Storekeeper at Woolwich:

'My friend Mr Wyatt the Sculptor and Architect who has to execute a Collossal [sic] Equestrian Statue of the Duke of Wellington is desirous of ascertaining whether any Brass cannon could be obtained from Ordnance, to form a portion of the Mass of which the Cast will be formed, he is particularly desirous if

possible to have some that were taken at Waterloo or in any of the Duke's Battles. I am not sufficiently acquainted with the Store of these Articles at Woolwich to be able to give him the information he requires, but if you would have the goodness to afford it to him you will much oblige me.'[1]

Wyatt, assisted by his son James,[2] carried on with the making of their huge plaster model.[3] Years later it was said in Parliament that the Duke had not sat for the sculptors, and that the head had been modelled on a bust by Joseph Nollekens; but a letter in the Victoria and Albert Museum Library, sent in confidence to Wyatt by Croker, states:

'I begin to fear that you may never have another sitting from the great Duke—at least one that would be of much use to you in improving the resemblance of the countenance;—for his face seems to me visibly altered —slightly in form, but more in surface and expression. I shall however, as occasion may present, see whether it be possible, *or worth while*, to have another sitting for the bust. Let me know how you feel on this point, for if you are quite satisfied I had rather not importune His Grace. One thing is certain that no time should be lost in finishing the head as high as you can carry it.'

Croker then continued with some criticisms of the model itself:

'I wish to suggest to you to consider whether the arm with the truncheon (which, I doubt, might better be a spy glass)[4] should not be a

---

[1] Letter in Wyatt papers, Victoria and Albert Museum Library.

[2] James Wyatt, the Younger (1808–93).

[3] There are various drawings by James Wyatt in the Department of Prints and Drawings, Victoria and Albert Museum. *The Times*, 10th May 1884, reported that the large model was still in some outbuildings in a yard attached to Dudley Grove House, Paddington, not far from the old G.W.R. station, and opposite the 'Dudley Arms'.

[4] Wyatt, in fact, altered this to a small telescope in the executed statue.

little more elevated than in the drawing;—for the sake of the composition, it ought to be visible clear of the horse's neck, & for the sake of the sentiment, the elevation might express the celebrated *mot* attributed to the Duke "Up & at them." I mention this, this early, as perhaps your iron framework may include the right arm. I begin to doubt and more than doubt about the little cloak—in point of fact the evening of the day of Waterloo was, I believe, fine & I dare say the Duke did not wear the cloak at the close of battle, but that is of no great importance—indeed I might say none at all—but my chief objection is that it give a clumsiness to the statue, which at *that great height*, where feature & expression will be lost & outline alone observable, will be a great defect.—When you are near enough to distinguish the details of face & the indication of the figure under the folds, drapery is of no great consequence—but objects to be seen at a great distance cannot be too light in form. I am also of the opinion that to break the uniformity of surface of so large a mass advantage should be taken of every accident of ornamental decoration in the dress of the figure & the housings of the horse—Now the cloak will have a very contrary effect & will I fear be like throwing a "wet blanket" over the work.

I venture to offer you these suggestions, to which you will give such consideration as they seem to deserve and I [*some words illegible due to a fold*] . . . because I had been one of those who in the first instance favoured the cloak, which on more mature consideration I am now disposed to discard.'

By the beginning of 1842 the two Wyatts were in a position to show something of the vastness of their sculpture. On 9th January Matthew Wyatt wrote to Sir Frederick Trench suggesting that the King of Prussia[1] be asked to visit the studio as 'His Majesty is the greatest patron of the Arts in Europe, as Baron Buelow tells me,' and the *Art-Union* was able to inform its incredulous readers that each of the horse's ears was over two feet long, and that a mounted rider could safely pass beneath the creature, so high was it off the ground. Such a vast creation consumed an enormous amount of metal and there was (again according to the *Art-Union*), a halt in casting, during January 1843, due to a shortage of metal. From about this time onwards London read about, and waited for, the great day when the statue should be revealed—which was planned to be on Waterloo Day, 1846.

A year before this, on 8th June 1845, Decimus Burton tardily produced his estimate for the cost of raising the statue on to the arch, which he thought would cost something in the region of £2,000. He had not submitted this estimate earlier, as he had hopefully remained under the impression that the project had been abandoned. As it was obviously very much alive, Burton sent several objections to the Earl of Lincoln,[2] then Chief Commissioner of Woods and Forests. The statue, said to be the largest in the world, was going to be far too tall for his arch. He had originally planned a quadriga (Plate 3), which was to be quite low in height. If Rutland went ahead with his scheme, Burton's arch would be reduced to the role of an insignificant pedestal. Another of his criticisms was that such a statue should be placed parallel with the road through the arch, not across it.

Lord Lincoln told the Duke of Rutland about Burton's objections, and added a few of his own. Perhaps Rutland did not know that on one side of the arch was a police station, and in the other, a park-keeper's house. Consequently, there were twelve chimneys, and apart from the nuisance of smoke pouring over the statue, the walls carrying the flues would have to be strengthened, and the accommodation

[1] Friedrich Wilhelm IV (1795–1861).

[2] Henry, Earl of Lincoln (1811–64), succeeded his father as 5th Duke of Newcastle-under-Lyne in 1851. He was Chief Commissioner of Woods and Forests from 1846 to 1851.

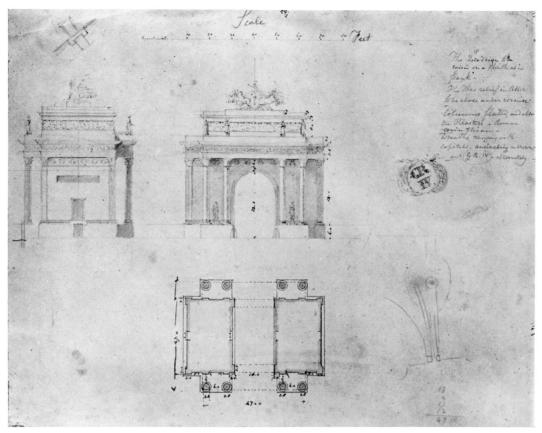

PLATE 3. *Design for the Constitution Hill Arch, by Decimus Burton, showing a Quadriga. Victoria and Albert Museum, Department of Prints and Drawings, E.2336–1910.*

probably abandoned. This would mean extra expense for the Treasury, which had not been sanctioned as part of the original proposal.

At this point in his plans, Rutland was not going to have any nonsense from the Office of Woods and Forests, and asked Lincoln why smoke should suddenly create a nuisance, when Burton had always planned a sculptural group. He saw absolutely no reason to modify his plans, as 'the Committee may be permitted to observe, that when a figure was placed by some unknown agency upon the arch, three years since (as was then supposed for the purpose of burlesque) its effect was grand and imposing'.

On 30th June, Lincoln told Rutland that although he much regretted the Duke's determination, he could not very well refuse access to the arch, and requested Burton to make the necessary arrangements with Wyatt. Burton immediately protested again about the unsuitability of his arch for the purpose, but to no avail, as Wyatt asked on 3rd December 1845 for possession of the arch so that his workmen could begin on certain essential preliminaries. Burton once again protested to the Office of Woods, but nothing was done, in spite of obvious misgivings by the Office as well.[1]

By 4th April 1846, Wyatt had designed the

[1] Burton felt so strongly about this that his will contained a provision for £2,000 to be spent in removing the statue. H. M. Colvin, *A Biographical Dictionary of English Architects*, 1954, p. 109.

supports for the statue, and was of the opinion that the occupants of the arch would hardly be disturbed. As he understood that there were never more than three fires in use, he proposed to carry the smoke through metal tubes while the work was in progress. During this period, he was of the opinion that the police and the park-keeper could share accommodation on whichever side of the arch happened at the time to be convenient. Rutland sent this news to Viscount Canning,[1] now the Chief Commissioner of Woods and Forests, who, in his turn passed it on to Decimus Burton; the latter thought that the arrangements were sensible, and presumed that Rutland's committee would pay for any damage.

As by 24th April Rutland had not heard anything from the government, he asked Canning if he might carry on, but was told that he would have to wait for confirmation of the arrangements from the Treasury. Canning lamented the determination of Rutland to persevere with the scheme in spite of continued opposition, and he announced that he 'would gladly escape from any share, however humble, of the condemnation which, I venture to think, awaits those who have had any hand in such an erection'.

Canning, unwilling to take any action, had not, in fact, yet asked the Treasury for its blessing, as he did not do this until 25th April, at the same time repeating his views expressed to Rutland. The Treasury, however, gave its sanction on 29th April, which was passed to Rutland by A. Milne of the Office of Woods and Forests, with the stipulation that all work was to be supervised by Burton.

The task of strengthening the arch was well in hand by the middle of May, when Rutland received a surprising letter from Canning in the name of the government:

'. . . the remonstrances which reach Her Majesty's Government are so many and so

strong, the representations of its architect, Mr. Burton . . . are so earnest, and the opinion of every other architect, artist, or competent authority who has been consulted on the subject is so decided, that Her Majesty's Government feels called upon not only to make a final effort to induce the subscribers to reconsider the project . . . but to do all that lies in their power to facilitate a change in design.'

Canning then proposed two new sites for the statue—either in Waterloo Place between the Athenaeum and the United Services Club, or on Horse Guards Parade, and he promised to ask Parliament for any extra money that a change to either of these sites would require. '*If . . . their proposal should not be accepted, Her Majesty's Government will at least have the satisfaction of knowing that they have done everything in their power . . . to place the statue in a position more worthy of it . . . and more creditable to public taste.*'

Rutland was not to be deflected from his aim, and refused to consider any new suggestion, merely replying that he was determined to have the statue up on Waterloo Day of that year. What an extraordinary and ineffectual position for the government to be forced into. Why did not it insist that this colossal statue was far to clumsy for the arch, and refuse it there before it was too late?

Time was, indeed, running short. It was now the beginning of June, and Waterloo Day was on the 18th of the month. On 12th June Rutland told Wyatt that the Dinner which Lord Londonderry had proposed to give to the sub-committee was abandoned as Londonderry had not told his wife; he had just learnt that Londonderry House was '*bespoke* on that evening for a great assembly which the Marchioness proposes to give'. However, Rutland continued, 'this is of minor Importance to the great Point of the Erection of the group on that important Day. It seemed to me when I was last at Dudley House that the

---

[1] Charles, Viscount Canning (1812–62), created Earl Canning in 1859.

Doubts on that Point had vanished and I trust that nothing has occurred to bring on a renewal of them. I should on my own account deeply regret not viewing the work in its proper Position, for I remain on the 18th almost entirely with that view and I shall lose the high satisfaction which your Triumph will give me, for if you do not succeed in placing the group on the Arch on the 18th, the Committee understand that on the very first day after it, on which the object is practicable, it is to be accomplished.'[1]

Waterloo Day came and went, and the arch was inviolate, but not for long, as on 23rd June, Burton was told by A. Milne that the Commissioners had received an undertaking from the sub-committee that it would bear the whole expense of strengthening the arch, as well as the restoration of all works disturbed, and also for providing temporary accommodation for the police and park-keeper if necessary; consequently the Commissioners of Woods and Forests had 'by letter to the Duke of Rutland of this day's date given to the Sub-Committee the temporary possession of the Arch'.[2] So the government had capitulated. Rutland's triumph was not complete, however, for the government had stipulated a trial exposure of the statue for only three weeks.[3]

This conditional victory led to disagreement among the sub-committee about the degree of display which should attend the statue's elevation. Obviously, one could not drag the largest statue in the world through the streets of London, and erect it at a busy crossroads, in secrecy. The statue would make its journey on

28th September, it was decided; on the 18th of the month Rutland wrote to Wyatt:

'I return to you the Copy of Lord Londonderry's letter to me, which I received (by mistake) yesterday. I own that I do not see the subject in the same Light as does Lord Londonderry. It is at all Events most uncertain whether we shall be permitted to have the Statue on the Arch beyond the proposed period of publick Trial. Then if we make a great Parade on the occasion of fixing the Statue on the Arch and in three weeks after we are called upon to make it retrace its steps to the Ground we should run the risk of being laughed at. The true occasion on which to make a Demonstration will be when (as I hope may be the Case) the admiring and approving eye of the Queen, the Government, & the Public shall call for its permanent establishment on the Arch. I write to Ld Londonderry & tell him what are my opinions but I add that I shall readily put them in my Pocket, if my colleagues of the Sub-Committee are of the opinion that it would be better to make a Parade on the Day of the Erection of the Statue, for *Trial*. By all means the outstanding Subscriptions should be called in. Be so good as to consult Sir Fred Trench on the best mode of ensuring that object. It can only be done by Advertisements in the newspapers. It is lamentable that there should be any large Sum (I do not know the Amount) outstanding.'[4]

By now, London was reaching a pitch of excitement and anticipation concerning the mammoth. The *Illustrated London News*, allowed a peep into the Wyatts' studio and foundry, engraved views of the work, as well as illustrations of how it was assumed the statue would look upon the arch, and these had been appearing in that periodical for some weeks. Readers were told how Wyatt had used more than 100 tons of plaster in the model, that

[1] Letter in Wyatt papers, Victoria and Albert Museum Library.

[2] *Ibid.*

[3] '. . . the Queen is of the opinion that if she is considered individually she is bound by her word, and must allow the Statue to go up, however bad the appearance of it will be . . . It would . . . be better . . . that the Prince should not go to Town to give an opinion of the figure, when up.' Queen Victoria to Lord John Russell, 7th August 1846, *Letters of Queen Victoria*, edited by A. C. Benson and Viscount Esher, Volume 2, 1907, pp. 112, 113.

[4] Letter among the Wyatt papers, Victoria and Albert Museum Library.

the group was fashioned on a turntable itself weighing several tons, and that the sculptors had been forced to construct a travelling floor, which could be adjusted at any height to allow them to reach all parts of the statue. The *Illustrated London News* estimated that there were more than 40 tons of metal in horse and rider, which had been cast in several pieces, and then bolted and fused together; and it gave such dimensions as the length of each ear being 2 feet 4 inches, or that the horse's girth was 22 feet 8 inches. 'In consequence of the colossal size of the group, there were, for some time, upwards of thirty men employed at once upon the bronze; and in case of any work being required to be done within the figure of the rider, the head was removed, to allow the workmen to descend through the neck . . . The roof of the Foundry has already been removed, and in three or four days, the colossal group will be lifted entire out of the pit with shears, and placed upon a carriage, designed and constructed for conveying the great group to its final destination—the triumphal arch at Hyde Park Corner . . . We may at present add that the sculptor's contract with the Committee by whom the funds have been raised, was fixed at £30,000; but the cost will be somewhat short of this sum. Messrs. Grissell and Peto have contracted to convey the group from the sculptor's, and raise it upon the arch for the sum of £2,000.'

Since the spring, large numbers of visitors had visited Wyatt to gaze upon the wonderful work, and in the Museum Library is a letter from the Duchess of Kent, Queen Victoria's mother, dated 25th March 1846, in which she regretted having to postpone her visit for a few days.

On 27th September the statue was moved from Wyatt's foundry at Dudley Grove House, in the Harrow Road. To allow of this, the roof had to be taken off, and one outside wall demolished. The statue was placed in its special car. This weighed 20 tons, and had cast-iron

wheels ten feet in diameter. The statue nestled within it on the horse's belly, with its feet only slightly off the ground. This was to ensure that the centre of gravity of the whole structure was kept as low down as possible in order to avoid the risk of the statue overturning. Needless to say, there were many who forecast that the combined weight of more than 60 tons would sink into the ground, disrupt underground sewers, or do other damage.

The Duke of Rutland had, for once, been over-ruled, as on the following day London turned out to witness what must have been one of the strangest public spectacles of the 19th century—a great military parade for a statue—even though it was in honour of the Iron Duke (who had decided to go to Walmer Castle, and keep out of the way).

A grandstand had been built at Wyatt's studio. Here the committee and many others, including the Duke of Cambridge, the Hereditary Grand Duke of Mecklenburg-Strelitz, came to see the statue begin its journey. At 9.30 in the morning, the military arrived, and half-an-hour later 100 Fusilier Guards pulled the carriage into the Harrow Road, where it took a further hour to turn it into the right direction. Twenty-nine horses, with their heads wreathed with laurel (supplied by Mr. Goding, a brewer) were then attached, under the direction of a drayman Matthias Butcher, who wore his Waterloo medal. During this period of preliminary activity several daguerreotypes were made by Antoine Claudet, the photographer.

As the clock of Paddington Church struck noon, the procession set off on its journey to the playing of 'See the Conquering Hero Comes' by one of the military bands. Leading were a detachment of the Life Guards and their regimental band. After them came two troops of Life Guards, pioneers of the Fusilier Guards, and then the statue, on either side of which were twenty Life Guards. Behind the carriage marched another hundred Fusilier Guards whose duty was to steady, or restrain, the carriage should it become necessary. Bringing up the rear of the cortège were the band and a hundred Fusilier Guards, the band and two hundred Grenadier Guards, the band and one hundred Coldstream Guards, and right at the end, a troop of the 2nd Life Guards.

It took the procession an hour and a half to reach Apsley House; this allowed for a 'breathing time' for the horses when they reached Upper Seymour Street, and shafts breaking, first at Dudley House, Park Lane, and again in Hamilton Place. The only mishap reported was a gas-lamp broken when the carriage rammed it at the junction of Oxford Street and the Edgware Road. The various members of the committee had intended to accompany their statue, but at the last moment they changed their minds, and went to Apsley House by side streets.

A great crowd lined the whole route, but it was at its thickest at Hyde Park Corner, hoping to see the statue raised; even invalids, said *Punch*, of St. George's Hospital crowded its roof, looking like 'patients on a monument'. At Apsley House, in the absence of Wellington,[1] Lord Charles Wellesley acted as host to Queen Adelaide,[2] the Princess of Prussia,[3] the Duke and Duchess of Cambridge, the Grand Duke and Duchess of Mecklenburg-Strelitz,[4] Prince George[5] and Princess Mary[6] of Cam-

bridge, and many others, including the Mr. Simpson who had had the idea for it all in 1838.

By a quarter-to-four of that afternoon, the statue was in position among the forest of scaffolding obscuring the arch and, though late, all was ready to start lifting. Queen Adelaide sent across to ask if it was worthwhile waiting, but the decision was that hoisting would begin on the following day; so the Queen went home to Marlborough House. During the evening the area was crowded with sightseers, and Mr. Goding's men were treated to a supper of 'roast beef, geese, &c.'

Early the next morning, Wednesday, 29th September, riggers from Woolwich Dockyard began to raise the statue. This took all day, during which time Queen Adelaide returned to the balcony of Apsley House, and even the Prime Minister[7] felt sufficiently curious to pay Wyatt a visit on the site. The statue was finally bolted in place by 1 o'clock of the following afternoon, Thursday, and was 'destined, we trust', trumpeted the *Illustrated London News* 'for centuries, to commemorate the bravery of the British Hero; the skill of the British Artist; and the gratitude of the British Nation.'

But was it going to be allowed to do this? The statue was only on probation for three weeks (perhaps this was not known to the *Illustrated London News*), and ranged against it was *Punch*, then only about five years old. From the beginning, *Punch* was relentless in its attacks on the sculpture, and also on one of the committee members in particular, Sir Frederick Trench (Plates 4, 5):

'As the Duke of Wellington was looking the other day out of Apsley House, and saw the Achilles on one side of him, and the Monster Statue on the other, he was heard to sing, in a voice of the utmost feeling,—"How happy I could be with neither."'

---

[1] I am Dead . . . in conformity with that principle of conduct, when the Queen Dowager, the Princess of Prussia . . . came to my house in October to see the Statue moved into Piccadilly . . . I did not attend to receive them; I went off to Walmer Castle.' Letter to Angela Burdett-Coutts, 28th November 1846, *Wellington and his Friends*, edited by the 7th Duke of Wellington, 1965, pp. 236, 237.

[2] Adelaide of Saxe-Meiningen (1792–1849), widow of William IV.

[3] Augusta of Saxe-Weimar (1811–90), wife of Wilhelm I of Prussia.

[4] Georg (1779–1860), Marie of Hesse-Kassel (1796–1880).

[5] Prince George of Cambridge (1819–1904), succeeded his father in 1850, as 2nd Duke of Cambridge, Commander-in-Chief, 1856–95.

[6] Princess Mary of Cambridge (1833–97), married the Duke of Teck, and was the mother of Queen Mary.

[7] Lord John Russell (1792–1878), created Earl Russell in 1861.

PLATE 4. *Distant view of London (taken from Putney Heath). From* Punch, *Volume 11, 1846, page 51.*

There is considerable difficulty experienced in collecting the opinions of the public on the monstrous affair. The general expression on the countenance of everyone who looks up at it seems to say . . . "I've no opinion of it." We have been at some pains to get correct reports of the public sentiment, but we have been unable to catch anything more decisive than "Well, I never!" with an occasional "Did you ever?" . . . One of the most frequent ebullitions of sentiment that the Statue has elicited, consisted of the two monosyllables "Oh! My!" uttered in a state of profound bewilderment. We, of course, are quite unable to decide whether this is intended to convey a favourable judgment, and a shriek of "Lawk!" which we have repeatedly heard from persons

looking at the Statue, is equally difficult of translation.'

Punch also published a cartoon by John Leech in which Queen Victoria says, 'Well, Mr. Punch . . . if you think the Statue ought to come down, why down it shall come!'

Nevertheless in spite of *Punch* and all the other critics, it did not prove quite so easy to remove the statue, even though all the scaffolding was still in position.

While his greatest work was being laughed at, Matthew Wyatt had other troubles. On 12th October he wrote to the Marquess of Londonderry:[1]

'I beg to acknowledge with thanks your Lordships two letters of the 7th & of the 10 Ins.: the manner in which your Lordship

[1] Letter in Wyatt papers, Victoria and Albert Museum Library.

PLATE 5. *The Wellington Statue and the Arch. From* Punch, *Volume 11, 1846, page 51.*

expresses yourself is truly gratifying to me & I think there is little doubt but the letter to Ld. Morpeth will have due weight as far as his Lordship is concerned. Whether it will be in the other quarters I am doubtful. I regret very much that the Committee was held on Wednesday last the 7th when it was impossible for your Lordship to be present. Mr Bury summoned me to attend at the Meeting at 12 O Clock. I was there a few minutes before that time I found the Accounts had already been gone into: and all that remained to be done appeared to be to query me over the balance but I confess I was very much surprized and vexed to find that it was considered necessary to keep back a considerable portion of it until the matter of the Arch is finally settled, not having at all contemplated such an arrangement it forced me to break engagements which I had made. However the Duke of Rutland & Mr Lushington promised that immediately after the 10. of next month there should be a meeting called for the purpose of settling with me, that a longer notice should be given in hopes of more of the members attending. It appears that fund in hand amounts

to £9000 & there is about £1000 not collected but owing by such men as are considered sure. The sum I recieved [*sic*] was £6400 leaving with what is outstanding about £3600. What it can have been thought necessary to retain so large a sum I certainly cannot think. I consider that I have fulfilled my contract nay much more than fulfilled it for the statue. I have made measures full twice the surface of what I had undertaken to produce & that I did because I knew that some of my friends on the Committee wished that it should be the largest in existence, & I also knew that the effect would be better upon that bulky arch. It is with great pride & pleasure that I find that I have done is approved & I must be satisfied with the consciousness of having done my duty by the Committee & having earned their good opinion, but as to pecuniary profits they are little indeed if any. I am not speaking in the voice of complaint nor with the remotest view of this circumstance being in any way altered but at the same time I do wish that it should not be supposed that I have grown rich by so ardous [*sic*] and expensive a work. The labor difficulty & cost of which the world knows nothing about. I ought to apologize for troubling yr. Lordship with so long a letter & so much about my self. I beg now to say that it will afford me very great pleasure if I can be of any use to yr Lordship & that I will avail myself of yr Lordships kind invitation to Wynyard one day between the 20th. & 30th. The day I will apprize yr Lordship of as soon as the scaffold is sufficiently removed for the statue to be seen . . .'

In December the blow fell; Queen Victoria was paying a visit to Arundel Castle, and from there came:

'Lord Morpeth[1] presents his compts. to Mr. Wyatt, and begs to acquaint him that it has been irrevocably decided by Her Majesty and the Government that the Equestrian Statue of the Duke of Wellington should be removed from the Arch.'[2]

So far, during all the controversy of the last few years, the Duke of Wellington himself had remained quite aloof, an attitude he maintained over any statue of himself. He told a friend, Angela Burdett-Coutts, that when he had been approached about the sculpture he had agreed to give sittings for it, 'but beyond that I could have no relation with the undertaking; and that I must desire to be considered as *Dead*!'[3]

He was, not unnaturally, upset by the hostile reception given to the statue when it was seen in position, and the subsequent decision to remove it:

'I am very much annoyed by the course which the Queen has taken . . . She certainly gave her consent . . . The Queen came to town on Saturday the 7th of November with Prince Albert purposely to desire that the statue should be taken down. Lord Morpeth wrote to me on the 9th . . . to tell me that he was about to give such Orders. I don't think that the Queen's Course will be approved in this affair. But that is Her Business, not mine!'[4]

A few days later the Duke told Miss Burdett-Coutts that he was not going to express any opinion on the statue until a decision on its future had been made, in case it was felt that he had exerted some influence. At this time it was reported that the Duke had let it be known that if the statue were taken down it would appear to the public that he had, for some reason or another, fallen from the Queen's favour. As he told John Croker, 'they must be idiots to suppose it possible that a man who is working day and night, without any object in view except the public benefit, will not be sensible of a disgrace inflicted upon him by the Sovereign and Government whom he is serving. The ridicule will be felt if nothing else . . .'[5] (Years afterwards, in 1883, it was reported in Parliament that Wellington had told Lord John Russell, that if the statue were removed then he would have to consider resigning not only his commission, but his peerage as well.) In fact, the Duke wrote to Queen Victoria a few months later and told her that he apprehended that he might find it impossible to perform the duties with which he had been entrusted.

For the moment, the statue remained; Wyatt was asked when the scaffolding was to be removed,[6] and Lord Morpeth, still hoping for another site for the statue, wrote:

'I remember when I was at your house last summer, I saw a drawing for a proposed pedestal of the Duke of Wellington, I am not

---

[1] Viscount Morpeth (1802–64), succeeded his father as 7th Earl of Carlisle in 1848, Chief Commissioner of Woods and Forests from 1846 to 1850.

[2] In the Wyatt papers, Victoria and Albert Museum Library.

[3] Letter to Angela Burdett-Coutts, 28th November 1846. *Wellington and his Friends*, 1965, pp. 236, 237.

[4] Letter to Angela Burdett-Coutts, *loc. cit.*

[5] *Letters of Queen Victoria*, edited by A. C. Benson and Viscount Esher, Volume 2, 1907, page 146, note 1.

[6] '[The weather has been such (deleted)] There has been no change in the weather as to render it impracticable to

able to give you any assurance as to it being adopted, but as I must see more than one design for it I should be much pleased if you would like to send it to me for inspection, with the estimate of the probable cost.'

There was quite a lot of activity behind the scenes and among members of both Houses of Parliament in order to find a face-saving solu-

tion. By 10th July 1847 Lord George Bentinck was able to write to Croker:[1]

'A private communication and negotiation had previously taken place between Lord John and me, the result of which was that Lord John engaged "that the statue should remain . . . unless the Duke intimated to Lord John that its removal would give him more pleasure" and that "*the Duke's declining to give any opinion is to be construed as dissent*".

This, of course, concludes the business. I have written to the Duke of Wellington acquainting him of this . . .'

The immediate problem was solved, when two days afterward, on 12th July, Queen Victoria once again made up her mind. On that day she sent to Lord Palmerston:

'The Queen has been informed by Lord John Russell that the Duke of Wellington is apprehensive that the removal of his statue from the Arch to another pedestal might be construed as a mark of displeasure on her part. Although the Queen had hoped that her esteem and friendship for the Duke was so well known to the public in general as not to render such a construction possible, and although she had thought that another pedestal would have been more suitable for *this* statue, and that the Arch might have been more becomingly ornamented in honour of the Duke than by the statue *now* upon it, she has given immediate direction that the Statue should remain in its present situation, and only regrets that this monument should be so unworthy of

---

make any attempt to remove the huge traversing carriage and to take down the Scaffolding without great danger to the men employed [to say nothing about a very great and useless out lay (*deleted*)] When there is I will communicate with you further on the subject.' Draft of a letter to the Duke of Rutland, Victoria and Albert Museum Library.

[1] *The Croker Papers 1808–1857*, edited by Bernard Pool, 1967, p. 213.

PLATE 7. *The Wellington Arch, Hyde Park Corner. Showing the Arrangements made for lowering the Equestrian Statue. From a photograph by Bedford Lemere, reproduced in* The Builder, *10th February 1883, page 185.*

the great personage to whose honour it has been erected.'[1]

Thus, after nearly a year of indecision, the statue was to remain (Plate 6). There was another attempt to remove it after the Duke's death in 1852, but it was then considered that public opinion would not permit of such a slight to the recently dead hero. The opportunity came, at long last, in 1883, when Hyde Park Corner was re-designed. This necessitated the demolition of Burton's arch, so that it could be rebuilt on a different axis, and further down Constitution Hill—but even this opportunity was mis-handled.

After more than thirty years an entirely new generation had grown up and become accustomed to the great hulking horse and its rider, and the quivering copper plumes on Wellington's hat which gave strange noises in high winds, and the statue was regarded with something like affection. But down it had to come in spite of opposition. During the first three months of 1883, it descended through the centre of the arch, which was demolished at the same time (Plates 7, 8). By March it was on the ground, and had been hauled to a vacant space opposite to Apsley House.[2]

What on earth was to be done with it now? The government appointed a committee to find out whether there was any suitable site in London. Members of this committee were the 2nd Duke of Wellington, Viscount Hardinge,[3]

---

[1] *Letters of Queen Victoria*, Volume 2, 1907, pp. 146, 147.

[2] The Chief Commissioner and the Secretary stood still and looked at one another in wonder. It was just before daybreak and exactly opposite Apsley House.

'Thank you again, Gentlemen,' repeated the sharp metallic voice.

'Where *does* it come from?' asked the Chief Commissioner, in a frightened whisper.

'From me,' was the immediate answer. 'From F. M. the Duke of Wellington.'

('Golden words from a man of metal. From a MS. preserved in the Office of Works.' *Punch*, 12th May 1883, p. 221.)

The method of lowering the statue is fully described in *The Builder*, 27th January, p. 122, and 10th February 1883, p. 187.

[3] 2nd Field Marshal Viscount Hardinge (1822–94).

PLATE 8. *Removal of the Wellington Statue, Hyde Park Corner (sketched 27th Feb.). From the* Illustrated London News, *10th March 1883, page 240.*

PLATE 8. *Removal of the Wellington Statue, Hyde Park Corner (sketched 27th Feb.). From the* Illustrated London News, *10th March 1883, page 240.*

Sir Frederic Leighton,[1] James Fergusson,[2] Edgar Boehm,[3] and A. B. Mitford,[4] Permanent Secretary to the Office of Works. They met at Apsley House on 25th April, and their report was published on 1st May 1883:

'Mr. Mitford informed the Committee that various sites had been suggested, of which the chief were: the Apsley House site, the Horse Guards site, Chelsea Hospital, Primrose Hill, the Tower of London, an exchange of sites with the Achilles in Hyde Park, Knightsbridge Barracks.

Having regard to the unsuitableness of some of the sites and the distance of others, the Committee considered that the discussion might be narrowed to the first two of these sites— namely the Apsley House site, and the Horse Guards.

The Committee felt that in considering the question due regard must be had for the memory of the illustrious warrior whom the statue commemorates. Even had it been for other reasons altogether appropriate they would have had hesitation in recommending its retention in the present place on the grounds of colossal size. They are of the opinion that while it is desirable to place it in some position befitting the military achievements of the Duke of Wellington, it would be out of harmony with its surroundings at Hyde Park Corner.

They recommend, therefore, that the statue should be placed upon a suitable pedestal upon a site immediately within the present railings of St. James's Park, facing the Horse Guards, and upon the central axis of the archway of that building.'

Not long after this report a large wooden model of the statue appeared in St. James's Park. Even the trees could not hide, or sub-due, this 30-ft high construction. Public feeling was not favourable, and eventually it was decided that there was nowhere in London suitable for such a 'Colossus', and the com-mittee advocated its destruction, the metal to

[1] President of the Royal Academy.

[2] James Fergusson, F.R.S. (1808–86), writer upon architecture, Inspector of Public Building and Monuments.

[3] Sir Joseph Edgar Boehm, Bart, R.A. (1834–90).

[4] Algernon Bertram Mitford (assumed additional sur-name, Freeman, when he succeeded to the estates of his cousin, the Earl of Redesdale, in 1886), created Baron Redesdale in 1902, G.C.V.O., K.C.B. (1837–1916).

PLATE 9. *Statue of the Duke of Wellington, Hyde Park Corner, by Sir Edgar Boehm. Photograph:* National Monuments Record.

be used for a new and smaller statue at Hyde Park Corner.[1] A competition was held for a new figure, and this was won by Boehm, one of the members of the committee who had suggested the destruction of the original work (Plate 9).

The army, however, did not welcome the proposal. It was felt that as a large part of the original cost had been paid for by the military, then the army should now have the statue. The Prince of Wales was in favour of this, and thought it should be re-erected somewhere at Aldershot. To this the government agreed provided that public funds would not have to find more than £6,000.

Thus, on 19th May 1884, the statue was handed over to the military authorities, who cut it into small pieces to facilitate transportation to Hampshire. At the end of February 1885, the Prince of Wales and the Duke of Cambridge inspected several sites at Aldershot and eventually selected one near All Saints Garrison Church, where there was a small hill, not far from the Royal Pavilion. There the statue was taken on yet another specially made carriage by the Woolwich craftsmen; the route was circuitous in order to avoid weak bridges thought unable to bear the sudden weight. The statue had been re-assembled by mid-August 1885, when, at a large parade, the Prince of Wales handed it over to the safe-keeping of the army, as he said, 'in perpetuity'.

So languishes today, hidden by trees, on military scrubland, Matthew Cotes Wyatt's largest work, to Wellington, which like that of Chantrey before him, and Stevens's after-

[1] Marcus Stone suggested that the statue should be melted down and the metal used to construct an enlarged version of the Duke's monument in St. Paul's, which might be erected in front of Apsley House. *The Times,* 30th July 1883.

wards, was to prove his last major sculptural achievement (Plate 10).

The fate of the national memorial to Lord Nelson, on the other hand, is happier, although its history is equally one of criticism and indecision lasting for nearly thirty years. It was not until 1838 that a competition was held to select a design for the memorial. One hundred and fifty artists sent in their proposals; the first prize went to William Railton's project for a Corinthian column, and E. H. Baily received the second prize for a figure of the admiral.

PLATE 10. *The Duke of Wellington, by Matthew Cotes Wyatt, at Aldershot. Photograph:* Author.

However, none of the designs was considered suitable, and the government decided that the drawings and models should be returned to their designers, to be resubmitted, if they wished, to a new competition in mid-1839. Railton again was the winner, but Baily was commissioned to carve the statue on top of the column. Although the public had not responded enthusiastically with subscriptions, and the fund stood only at about £17,000, it was decided that a start had to be made on the erection of the monument. For the moment, though, the bas-reliefs on the base, and the four large lions at the corners (to be by J. G. Lough) were to be omitted. By the end of 1843 the column and statue were finished—and remained, surrounded by hoardings, in a state of desolation for another twenty years (Plate 11). The large bronze reliefs were executed from *c.* 1849 onwards, the first in position being that representing the death of Nelson by J. E. Carew (1785?–1860), on the south side. However, someone told the Office of Works that they had not been cast according to the specification which required $3\frac{1}{2}$ tons of bronze. A Mr. Fincham, Clerk of the Works, was sent to investigate, and found that Carew's relief (Plate 12), contained only 2 tons $11\frac{1}{4}$ cwt., the rest of the weight being made up of iron, other metals, and plaster. The founders were prosecuted, found guilty and during the summer of 1853 sent to the Queen's Prison for periods ranging from 1 to 3 months.[1]

In the end Lough did not sculpt the lions, but a minor artist, Thomas Milnes, did so instead. These were rejected and are now at Saltaire in Yorkshire; subsequently a painter, Sir Edwin Landseer, R.A., was given the commission in 1858, amid loud protests from sculptors. Landseer did not execute the work quickly, as he seems to have preferred painting instead, but by the mid-1860s one lion was ready for casting. This was undertaken by Baron Marochetti who, from Landseer's one model produced four casts, and asked for

---

[1] The allegation of using inferior metal during the casting of the effigy of Wellington and the other bronze portions of the St. Paul's Cathedral monument was made in 1873 —see p. 95.

PLATE 11. *The Nelson Column, Trafalgar Square, c. 1844. From a calotype negative by William Henry Fox Talbot, Science Museum.*

£11,000 for his effort. The lions were un-veiled in January 1867.

Probably England's most successful sculptor during the second quarter of the 19th century was John Gibson, R.A. (1790–1866). During his youth in Liverpool he had been apprenticed to a firm of sculptors, S. & F. Franceys,[1] but soon decided that he could do better for him-self and moved to London. There he met John

Flaxman, who encouraged him to go to study sculpture in Rome. He arrived in 1817 and studied under both Canova and Thorwaldsen, then the leading figures in European sculpture. Finding that by remaining in Rome he would meet more people and receive more commis-sions than he would if he returned to London, Gibson decided to stay for the rest of his life. His 'Tinted Venus'[2] caused a sensation when publicly shown at the 1862 Exhibition at South Kensington.

Success convinced Gibson that English sculptors were handicapped by inadequate

[1] Several of Gibson's designs dating from this period are in the Department of Prints and Drawings, Victoria and Albert Museum.

[2] Owen Jones designed a special pavilion for the statue in the Exhibition, and his drawings for this are in the Department of Prints and Drawings.

C

ENGLAND EXPECTS EVERY MAN WILL DO HIS DUTY

training, and he was of the opinion that the 'prospect for advancing high sculpture in England seems . . . far distant'. It was necessary to have a Roman education under a great master for at least ten years.

In March, 1857, he wrote to Earl Stanhope:

'In the year 1844 I visited England after an absence of twenty-seven years. The late Sir Robert Peel sent for me, I waited upon him, and he said that the government had some idea

PLATE 12. *Bronze alto-relievo, by [J. E.] Carew, for the Nelson Monument, Trafalgar Square.— The Death of Nelson. The first instalment of the artistic embellishment of the pedestal of the Nelson Column has just been placed on the side facing Whitehall. From the* Illustrated London News. *15th December 1849, page 393.*

PLATE 13. *Portrait of Carlo, Baron Marochetti, by Camille Silvy. Victoria and Albert Museum Library, Photograph Collection.*

contributes nothing towards the training of their students . . . I have visited England a few times since, and the above are still my sentiments. Every young sculptor in England bungles his way as he can; nor do they visit, generally speaking, each other's studios, which at Rome is the universal practice, and more, they point out each other's errors while their models are still in clay.'[1]

The constant criticism which attended official works, coupled often with jealousy, was linked also with an insular dislike of foreigners working in England. One man in particular aroused the greatest of antipathy; he was Carlo, Baron Marochetti (1805-67) (Plate 13). Marochetti, a Piedmontese, had won repute with his equestrian statue of Emmanuel Philibert of Savoy. This he presented to the city of Turin, and was rewarded with a barony by the King of Sardinia. He then worked in Paris for a while, where he was patronised by Louis-Philippe and the French court, and after the 1848 Revolution Marochetti turned up in London and at once found favour with Queen Victoria and Prince Albert, as well as with some members of the government. The success of the Baron in Royal circles afforded little pleasure to the sculptors of this country. Certain official commissions were given to him, and the fact that no announcement was made of them until after they were finished infuriated native artists.

One such instance was the monument to be erected at Scutari after the Crimean War (Plate 14). The first that the sculptors of England knew of this 'job' as they called it, was an announcement that the commission had been awarded to Marochetti, who, now it was finished, asked for payment of £17,000. Much abuse was poured on the monument and on its sculptor. *The Art Journal* stated that 'the Scutari job has not been without its redeeming

---

of sending students to Rome, and he wished me to give him what information I could upon such a subject . . . I was entirely ignorant of the state of sculpture in England, but since my arrival I had been examining the public monuments, and that I could see the defects of style and feebleness which prevailed in the best of them . . . The English Government spends large sums to erect public monuments, but

[1] *The Biography of John Gibson, R.A., Sculptor, Rome,* by T. Matthews, 1911, p. 104.

PLATE 14. *Angel of the Scutari Monument, by Baron Marochetti, at the Crystal Palace. From the* Illustrated London News, *17th May 1856, page 525.*

incidents. While it disgraced our Arts—which it affects to represent—abroad, and wronged our sculptors—whom it affects to ignore—at home, it has brought the feeling of national injustice and national oversight ... to a point of sensitiveness that must find vent in determined expression. ... The Scutari job was so monstrous, that it startled even the parliamentary conscience, familiarised with monsters as that conscience is ... The monument did, however, grow up in the dark—and may, by the by, owe a portion of its deformities to that unwholesome condition. No hint that such a creation was in progress did the public receive, by any of its organs, till the work had been shipped away, to proclaim to the East, in its inflated language, that we have no sculptor of our own in England—and that same public was requested, in an off-hand manner to pay for the proclamation. The sum of £17,500 was coolly demanded for a declaration of British Art-incompetency ... But the whole of this Scutari monument is extremely curious. When the monster job was first produced in Parliament, a feeling of surprise—judging by our own sensations, we should incline to say panic—seems to have paralysed the Houses.'

The Art Journal continued with an account of the sculptures for the decoration of the new Houses of Parliament. £1,200 was paid for each of the first two figures commissioned, 'but then, the Commissioners began to feel that, as they were dealing only with their own countrymen, the estimate was too liberal—and the price to be paid for the remaining works was reduced to £1,000 each (Plates 15, 16). For *twelve* statues then, by English sculptors, chosen as a result of a general competition ... statues designed at once for the artistic and historic illustration of our great national palace—the price paid was £12,400. For the one Scutari monument, got up no-one knows how, and given to a foreign sculptor no-one can tell us why, the remuneration demanded from Parliament without explanation, and granted

PLATE 15. *Statue of Lord Mansfield, by E. H. Baily, for St. Stephen's Hall of the new Houses of Parliament. From the* Illustrated London News, *2nd February 1856, page 121.*

with scarcely an inquiry—is, we repeat, £17,500.'[1]

The matter was taken up in the House of Lords by the Earl of Harrington, who wanted to know who had authorised the work, who had chosen Marochetti, who was paying, and why had there been no general competition? He stated that it was widely felt that undue influence had been the reason for the Baron's selection. For the government, Lord Panmure replied that the monument was to be erected by 'public wish', the money being voted by the Commons, and in choosing Baron Marochetti, they had been guided by his reputation. The leading sculptors had nothing to complain about, as over and over again they had declined to enter for public works. He [Lord Panmure] took upon himself the responsibility of Baron Marochetti's appointment.[2]

The champion for the moment of British sculpture, *The Art Journal*, had a lot to say about Panmure's answer, stating that as far as it knew there were only two sculptors who declined to enter competitions, John Gibson and Marochetti, and although it was debatable whether the latter could be considered British, he very naturally believed success to be all the more certain if there was no competition against him. E. H. Baily wrote in a letter to *The Times* on the subject, that he knew of no English sculptor (other than Gibson) who had ever declined to compete.[3]

[1] The sculptors for the statues in St. Stephen's Hall included W. Calder Marshall, J. H. Foley, John Bell, E. H. Baily, Patrick MacDowell, J. E. Carew, and William Theed the Younger.

[2] *Daily News*, 9th July 1856.

[3] 'Can Lord Panmure, Lord Harrington, or any other noble lord, say there was any want of response by the British artists for the Nelson Testimonial? Or can it be said that British artists declined to compete for either the erection of the Parliament houses, or, more recently, for their decoration? Did they not cordially reply to the invitation of the City in the cases of the Peel and Wellington competitions? And lastly, did not two British sculptors out of four selected (one being a foreigner and the other Mr. Gibson) submit designs for the Government Wellington Monument . . .? I, for one, never heard of the Scutari

PLATE 16. *Statue of Lord Somers, by William Calder Marshall, for St. Stephen's Hall of the new Houses of Parliament. From the* Illustrated London News, *2nd February 1856, page 121.*

Monument until I read in the public papers that it was completed, and I may say that, had I been applied to, I should have most readily met the views of the government . . .'

Concurrently with the argument about the Scutari monument, Marochetti was the centre of another controversy. In 1851 his gigantic equestrian statue in plaster of Richard Coeur de Lion had been exhibited at the Great Exhibition (Plate 17). It had, in Marochetti's opinion, been unsuitably sited outside the western end of the exhibition building, in the cab-stand area. When the exhibition was over Marochetti devoted himself to finding sufficient money to pay for the group to be cast in bronze. Queen Victoria and Prince Albert headed the subscription list, a fact that caused *The Art Journal* to view the proposal with suspicion, as it felt that the statue was destined to be erected in a prominent, but unsuitable site. Sites suggested, in fact, by Marochetti and his backers were in Hyde Park, to commemorate the Exhibition, or in the area of Exhibition Road in South Kensington.

Eventually, after a trial exposure outside Westminster Hall, that was the position decided upon, in spite, inevitably, of criticism. Parliament voted the baron £1,650 towards the cost, which led the press to suggest that it would be better for everyone if Parliament granted Marochetti an annual salary of £2,000 or £3,000 and 'take whatever the baron is pleased to give the country in return'. When cast, the statue was given to a 'grateful' country, and accepted by the Office of Works as a public monument in 1861, when it was reported that the baron was already at work on a companion statue on an adjacent site, of Edward the Black Prince. Though on 12th January 1861, *The Art Journal* considered Richard Coeur de Lion as 'one of the worst eyesores of London', it has since become a popular group, and certainly came into its own during the Second World War when, after a bomb had bent the upraised sword, the statue was often illustrated as a symbol of the resistance of Londoners against German bombing.

Nevertheless, in spite of this public unpopularity, Marochetti continued to enjoy success.

He knew what his patrons wanted, whether a flamboyant and flattering bust, or a monument with angels whose feathered wings swept the ground. After the death of Prince Albert in 1861, he was chosen to carve the recumbent effigies for the Royal Mausoleum at Windsor, of Queen Victoria and Albert. Later, however, his statue of the Prince Consort for the monument in Kensington Gardens, was rejected, just before his own death in 1867.

PLATE 17. *The model by Baron Marochetti for his equestrian statue of Richard Coeur de Lion. From a calotype photograph made when the model was exhibited outside the 1851 Exhibition Building in Hyde Park. Victoria and Albert Museum Library,* Jury Report *of the Exhibition.*

II

The Monument's Inception and the Competition—1855–7

The Duke of Wellington died during 1852, and was given a lavish state funeral in St. Paul's Cathedral, after his body had been carried through London on what must have been the largest bronze gun-carriage[1] ever made. Parliament had voted the sum of £100,000 (by today's values an immense sum) for expenses, of which some £77,000 were spent. The Duke was eventually buried in the Cathedral crypt, near Lord Nelson, in a large porphyry sarcophagus,[2] but it was soon felt that something more immediately apparent in the form of a magnificent monument in the cathedral was desirable.

With the remaining £23,000 at his disposal, Sir William Molesworth, First Commissioner of Works,[3] made overtures to four sculptors; Edward Hodges Baily, John Gibson, John Foley, and Baron Marochetti were invited to prepare designs—each of them was told who the other three competitors were. Gibson, who lived in Rome, declined on that account, but he held strong views, anyway, against competitions—'nothing but evil consequences must arise to the arts of our country from the prevailing custom of entrusting the decision of matters of this kind to a committee composed of a certain number of members collected from different classes of the community, the major part of whom have no knowledge or connexion with the arts . . . the greatest sculptors will generally not enter into competition because they are constantly employed, nor will they compete with young men unknown to fame'.[4]

Baily and Foley both accepted, but Marochetti, 'who seems to have preferred relying on his private influence'[5] declined. The Baron wrote to Molesworth on 22nd November 1854, saying how flattered he was to have been asked 'to engage in a competition in which success would be only less painful than failure. If, however, the proposed competition should not produce the desired result, and if, in such an event, I should be judged worthy of employment on this work, I should with pride bestow on it the utmost efforts of my art . . .'[6]

After Baily and Foley had sent in their designs there was a period of official silence. On 15th May 1855, Foley asked to withdraw, since he inferred from the delay that his design was not suitable. There was no reply from Molesworth, and three days later Foley wrote again: 'Mr. J. H. Foley presents his compliments to Sir William Molesworth—he has heard with surprise and deep concern that the government is but waiting for Mr. Baily to *pass the Bankruptcy Court* in order to give him the commission. . . . He is loath to believe such to be the case or to feel that he has been made the instrument of a project which would deprive Mr. Baily's creditors of their due.'[7]

But Molesworth did not approve of either of the designs, and although both sculptors

---

[1] Original designs for the gun-carriage by Richard Redgrave, C.B., R.A., are in the Department of Prints and Drawings, Victoria and Albert Museum.

[2] The Duke's body was not placed in the sarcophagus until six years later. A document signed by the principal witnesses was inserted into the Chapter Minutes of St. Paul's; this was dated 15th April 1858.

[3] Sir William Molesworth, 8th Baronet (1810–55).

[4] *The Biography of John Gibson, R.A., Sculptor, Rome,* by T. Matthews, 1911, p. 145.

[5] *Art Journal,* October 1856.

[6] Public Record Office, Works 6.

[7] *Loc. cit.*

offered to make any modifications he suggested, he let them know on 31st May, that it was his 'painful duty' to advise the government to go no further with the matter. When Baily and Foley offered to make entirely fresh designs, they were told that the matter was now closed.

Rumour insisted that Molesworth really intended to give the commission to Marochetti. Perhaps this rumour was ill-founded, but in view of what happened over the Scutari monument, it might have been all too probable. Baily was justifiably annoyed, both at the out-of-hand rejection of his design, and these reports, and took up the cudgels with Molesworth and his successor, Sir Benjamin Hall. His argument was that he would not 'enter into any competition in which it was understood that the authority summoning it retained within his own breast any right or condition not apparent on the face of the challenge which invited me. *That* is not competition, in any reasonable sense of the word, for which it may ultimately be declared that there was no prize. . . . The original call to compete was a commission given amongst four artists. . . . The field of the commission was subsequently narrowed to two sculptors, by the failure of the other two to compete. To give away the commission now to any other than the sculptors invited and accepting,—above all, to either of the two sculptors who declined the invitation, —would be a wrong of many kinds . . .'

Molesworth was adamant, but eventually offered to pay both Baily and Foley their reasonable expenses. The angry Baily refused to name a sum, but Foley asked for £150, so Molesworth awarded them £150 each.[1] Baily, seeing that nothing further in the way of a commission would be forthcoming accepted this under protest. 'I deny,' he told Sir Benjamin Hall,[2] 'the authority of Sir William

Molesworth, or any one else, to commute my right under the agreement for £150, or any other sum,—or to convert that right into anything else *than* the right itself. I refused then— and I now again refuse—to consider the money as a satisfaction for my claim. If I am compelled to put up with it, as all I have been able to get from Sir William Molesworth or yourself, to represent my right, the right nevertheless remains—in the character of a wrong.'

There matters rested for nearly a year, until in May 1856 Sir Benjamin Hall announced in the Commons that it was the government's intention to erect a monument to the Duke of Wellington in St. Paul's, and that not four but several sculptors would be invited to compete to establish what the talent of England could produce. The previously proposed monument was to have been erected for £5,000 but on this occasion £20,000 would be available.

The proposal was generally welcomed, though *The Art Journal* 'devoutly prayed' that there might be no interest covertly at work to prejudice the competition, as no event at that time was so pregnant with good (or evil) to British sculpture. Unfortunately, *The Art Journal's* prayers were most certainly not answered.

The sculptors of England vented their feelings in an open letter published in the *Daily News* of 31st May 1856 addressed to Sir Benjamin Hall:

'We, the undersigned, British sculptors, feel assured that we shall not be deemed intrusive or officious in addressing the following statement to a minister of the crown charged with the supervision of the public monuments in this country.

We have observed with regret that frequent attempts have been lately made by the most influential organ of the daily press to disparage the ability of British sculptors, and to defend as an inevitable necessity a recourse to foreign artists. It is, moreover, reported that a large

[1] There was some correspondence as to whether Baily or his creditors should receive the money. On 23rd June 1855, the Treasury was asked to pay both Baily and Foley (P.R.O.).

[2] Sir Benjamin Hall, Bart. (1802–67), 1st Baron Llanover.

sum of money is about to be devoted to a monument to the Duke of Wellington, and another sum to a memorial at Scutari to the brave men who have fallen in the late war; and, in the present temper of the public mind, and in the disposition of some who exercise the patronage of the country, we are not without apprehension that due justice will fail to be done to the English sculptor.

We desire to guard ourselves against the imputation of an illiberal jealousy of the foreigner. Art is a universal language, and the artist should find himself a native of every great city of the world. There has never been a time when the English courts and the English people have not received with ready welcome the foreign painter, architect and sculptor. May it be thus always. But we claim for native talent that it should be sought for and appreciated. It is not true that there is a dearth of genius amongst the sculptors of England. There are works of indisputable excellence from the hands of living artists that attest the contrary. What is lamentably true is this—that means have rarely been adopted for committing public works to the men of the greatest merit amongst us. We would humbly suggest that if the patronage of the nation were exercised with more care and discrimination, and with a genuine desire to discover the worthiest on whom to bestow it, the public monuments of England would no longer be appealed to as displaying in so many instances a painful mediocrity.

None can feel more deeply than ourselves the degradation which the sculpture of England has suffered during the last 50 years, from the erection in our Metropolitan Cathedral, the Abbey and Guildhall, of the large puerilities and distressing allegories which deface the walls of those buildings. But let it be borne in mind, that while large sums were being lavished upon such productions as these, Flaxman and Banks were alive, needy and seeking employment. Men who were neglected year after year

by the government and the municipal authorities of that time are now the boast of every Englishman, and are acknowledged to have earned an European reputation.

To approach somewhat nearer our own time, we would point to a fact of no little significance. A sculptor of the name of Watson[1] recently died; he was an industrious artist, and a competitor for most of the public monuments erected in his day. He never obtained a commission; but the rejected models which he exhibited on such occasions, are now sought with avidity, and studied by living artists.

Whether the same unfortunate method of selection still attends upon us, we must leave others to decide. We must observe, however, that there is an increasing indisposition among artists of acknowledged merit, to enter into any public competition. It is felt that a proposal for a general competition is no security against an incompetent or partial judge.

To combat this indisposition, to foster the genius of the country, to secure for our greatest monuments, the artists of the greatest power, we would finally submit, 1. That in every competition, a public exhibition of the models of all the competitors should precede the selection of any one of them; and 2. That such selections should be made by a committee so constituted that the body of artists as well as the public in a general way may confide in them.

To a public competition so conducted we cheerfully invite every artist resident in the United Kingdom, and we rest confident that,

---

[1] Musgrave Lewthwaite Watson (1804–47). He became a pupil at the Royal Academy Schools in 1823, and after a period in Italy was employed by Chantrey, Behnes and Baily. In his *Dictionary of British Sculptors* Rupert Gunnis states that 'had he lived he would assuredly have been one of the greater sculptors of the nineteenth century'. The Battle of St. Vincent relief on the base of Nelson's Column is by him, but was not finished when he died. In the Museum's Library is *The Life and Works of Musgrave Lewthwaite Watson* by H. Lonsdale, 1866, which is illustrated by 12 original photographs of Watson's sculpture.

patronage being liberally and wisely exercised, there will no longer be an impression abroad, in this country, that the English sculptor is unequal to the celebration of English heroism.

We have the honour, with respect, to subscribe ourselves—E. H. Baily, R.A.; P. Mac-Dowell, R.A.; W. Calder Marshall, R.A.; J. H. Foley, A.R.A.; H. Weekes; J. Evan Thomas; F. M. Miller; Thomas Thornycroft; Alfred Hone; Timothy Butler; William Behnes; Matthew Noble; John Hancock; Alex. Munro; Edward B. Stephens; J. Sherwood Westmacott; Joseph Durham; J. Edwards; Frederick Thrupp; Edward Davis; Thomas Earle; W. F. Woodington.'

The signatories to this letter were all well-known and successful, or up-and-coming younger sculptors, although some of them have by today slipped into obscurity.[1]

Edward Hodges Baily, R.A. (1788–1867), had been a pupil of John Flaxman and had become the chief modeller for the royal goldsmiths, Rundell and Bridge. Later he carved some figures for George IV, some of which are now on the façade of the National Gallery in Trafalgar Square. Baily gained 2nd Prize in the controversial competition for Nelson's monument, and exhibited at the Royal Academy for more than fifty years. Patrick MacDowell, R.A. (1799–1870), began life as an apprentice to a coach-maker, but became a student at the Royal Academy Schools. Elected R.A. in 1846, among his last works was the group representing Europe on the Albert Memorial in Kensington Gardens, a group which Queen Victoria had asked John Gibson to execute, but which he had declined. William Calder Marshall, R.A. (1813–94) was elected R.A. in 1852, exhibiting between 1835 and 1891. 'Agriculture' on the Albert Memorial was carved by him. John Henry Foley, R.A. (1818–74) was an extremely successful sculptor, elected

R.A. in 1858. When Marochetti, who had been asked to carve the figure of Prince Albert for his Memorial, died in 1867 without producing an acceptable design, Foley was then selected to undertake the work. Henry Weekes, R.A. (1807–77), became a full Academician in 1862. He had been a pupil of Sir Francis Chantrey, and completed many of the latter's works after his death in 1841. A successful carver of portrait-busts, Weekes at the time of this letter had just completed the memorial to the poet Shelley in Christchurch Priory, Hampshire.

John Evan Thomas (1809–73) was a Welshman who exhibited at the Royal Academy between 1838 and 1870. Felix Martin Miller (b. 1820), an orphan whose ability in sculpture had been encouraged by Henry Weekes and J. H. Foley, exhibited at the Academy from 1842 to 1880. Thomas Thornycroft (1815–1885), was first apprenticed to a surgeon, but soon became the pupil of the sculptor John Francis, whose daughter Mary, also a sculptor, became Thornycroft's wife. Thornycroft produced several statues of Prince Albert, carved 'Commerce' on the Consort's memorial, and was the author of the bronze group representing Boadicea at Westminster. Alfred Hone was a minor exhibitor of portrait busts between 1836 and 1852. Timothy Butler (b. 1806), also a popular sculptor of portrait busts, exhibited a large number of them between 1828 and 1879. He also designed lamp standards for the Victoria Embankment.

William Behnes (1795–1864) exhibited at the Academy from 1815 to 1863, and was one of the successful sculptors of the mid-19th century, producing many busts and monuments. Although appointed Sculptor in Ordinary to Queen Victoria, he was unlucky in financial affairs and, becoming bankrupt, died in poverty. Matthew Noble (1818–76), like Thornycroft, had once been a pupil of John Francis. At the time of this letter he had just won the competition for a statue of the Duke of Wellington

[1] These details are based on the entries in Rupert Gunnis's *Dictionary of British Sculptors 1660–1851*, 1953.

at Manchester, a success which had been widely criticised (Plate 18). John Hancock (1825–69) was a minor exhibitor at the Academy for a number of years. Alexander Munro (1825–71) a young Scot, had been encouraged by his father's employer, the Duchess of Sutherland. A producer of portrait busts, he carved figures for the Houses of Parliament then being re-built, and specialised in sentimental groups of children, one of which is in Chilham church, Kent. Probably the only claim for recognition today by Edward Bowring Stephens, A.R.A. (1815–82) is in the story that, when he was elected an Associate in 1864, it was only be-cause he had been confused with Alfred Stevens.[1] He exhibited at the Academy between 1838 and 1883.

James Sherwood Westmacott (1823–88?) was a member of the well-known family of sculptors, being a nephew of Sir Richard Westmacott, R.A., and a cousin of Richard Westmacott the Younger, R.A. He carved some of the decorative figures for the House of Lords. Joseph Durham, A.R.A. (1814–77), had also been a pupil of John Francis, and then an assistant to E. H. Baily. A prodigious worker, he exhibited between 1835 and 1878. He pro-duced the undistinguished group commemor-ating the 1851 Exhibition which now stands to the south of the Royal Albert Hall. John Edwards (1814–83), a Welshman, who had studied at the Royal Academy Schools, ex-hibited from 1838 to 1878.

Frederick Thrupp (1812–95), exhibited be-tween 1832 and 1880, was the sculptor of Wordsworth's statue in Westminster Abbey, the commission for which, it was claimed, Thrupp had received through influence and favouritism. Edward Davis (1813–78), a pupil of E. H. Baily, also attended the Royal Academy Schools, exhibiting for more than

PLATE 18. *The design for the memorial to the Duke of Wellington in Manchester, by Matthew Noble. From the* Illustrated London News, *21st July 1855, page 76.*

forty years. Thomas Earle (1810–76), son of a Yorkshire sculptor, also studied at the Academy Schools, and was employed by Sir Francis Chantrey. He exhibited for thirty years from 1843. William Frederick Wooding-ton, A.R.A. (1806–93), had to wait until 1876 before he was elected an Associate. He was responsible for the relief 'The Battle of the Nile' on the base of Nelson's Column in Trafalgar Square. He also carved decorative figures for the House of Lords.

It is perhaps surprising that other successful men did not sign this joint letter—sculptors

---

[1] 'Stevens suffered much in his lifetime, but worse to him than any financial creditors would be the identifying of him with the Exeter sculptor or stone-cutter.' *The Architect*, 1897.

such as J. G. Lough, Richard Westmacott the Younger, John Thomas, E. G. Papworth, or John Bell.

Sir Benjamin Hall outlined his proposals for the competitors in a Minute to the Treasury on 28th July, and asked for approval for the sum of £20,000 to be allocated for the monument and prize-money. There was no reply, but on 5th August he wrote again, this time asking for the Treasury's immediate approval because, if there was much more delay, then there would not be enough time for foreign sculptors to receive the conditions and prepare their models. The Treasury's sanction reached Sir Benjamin on 19th August.[1]

On 8th September, 1856, the newspapers carried the following advertisement:

WELLINGTON MONUMENT

The COMMISSIONERS of HER MAJESTY'S WORKS and PUBLIC BUILDINGS give notice that it is the intention of Her Majesty's Government to ERECT a MONUMENT in ST. PAUL'S CATHEDRAL, London to the memory of the late Duke of Wellington, and that the Commissioners are prepared to receive DESIGNS for the same from artists of all countries.

A drawing, showing the ground plan of the Cathedral and the site of the proposed MONUMENT, together with a statement of the premiums and other particulars, will be forwarded to artists on application by letter addressed to me at this office.

ALFRED AUSTIN, Secretary.

Office of her Majesty's Works and Public Buildings, Whitehall, London. Sept. 6. 1856

These conditions were as follows:[2]

'Persons desirous of competing must send in Models one-fourth of the size of the intended monument, which is not to exceed at the base

13 feet by 9 feet. Every Model sent in is to be inscribed with a Motto; and an Envelope, with the same Motto on the outside, containing the name of the Competitor, must be addressed to the First Commissioner of Her Majesty's Works and Public Buildings, Whitehall, London.

Each Competitor is to state the exact sum for which he will be prepared, if required to erect the Monument; and such sum must include all expenses, and not exceed £20,000 sterling.

The Monument to be made of Marble, Stone, Bronze, or Granite, or any of these materials combined; but if any Competitor shall be desirous of using any material other than Carrara Marble, the Model must be tinted in those parts in which any other material is used, with the colour of such material.

The Models by Artists residing within the United Kingdom, must be delivered in London, on or before the 1st of June, 1857; those by Artists residing abroad, on or before the 25th of June 1857. The Models are to be addressed to the First Commissioner, and delivered, carriage free, at Westminster Hall, or some other public place to be hereafter determined, and duly advertised, where it is intended that they shall be exhibited in July 1857.

The Commissioner will not be answerable for any damage or accident that may happen to the Models.

The following Premiums will be given for the Nine most approved Designs

			£
For the First			700
,,	,,	Second	500
,,	,,	Third	300
,,	,,	Fourth	200
,,	,,	Fifth	
,,	,,	Sixth	
,,	,,	Seventh	100
,,	,,	Eighth	
,,	,,	Ninth	

---

[1] Public Record Office, Works 6.
[2] British Museum Library.

If, however, the Artist to whom the highest Premium may be awarded, shall be employed to execute his Design, he will not be entitled to receive any Premium. The Models in respect of which Premiums may be awarded, are to remain the property of the Government.'

So now it was known; the monument was to be beneath the easternmost arch on the north of the nave, and sculptors had nearly ten months to make their models, some of the fears about the competition were allayed by the announcement that the models would be publicly exhibited, although whether the exhibition would take place before or after the selection by the judges, was not stipulated. But there were many who had doubts; for one thing, the names of the judges were not announced, and for another the last clause seemed to imply that the design of the first Premium winner need not of right be the monument which would ultimately be erected. There were also objections that the competition should be open to non-British sculptors, while not all were happy with the site. Many people lost sight of the fact that, with two equestrian statues of the Duke in London already (at Hyde Park Corner and outside the Royal Exchange), this monument was a sepulchral memorial; some considered that a statue at the Horse Guards or elsewhere would be preferable.[1] The terms of the competition were in wide-spread demand and on 17th September the Foreign Office asked urgently for a further 150 copies so that they could be sent abroad.[2]

The Secretary of the Sculptors' Institute, Edward Stephens, put several questions about the proposed work to the First Commissioner.

[1] *Daily News*, 10th September 1856. 'Sir, I see that the Board of Works has given notice of the intention . . . to erect a monument to the late Duke of Wellington in St. Paul's Cathedral. Allow me to suggest that instead of placing the monument in St. Paul's, it should be placed on the piece of ground at the south-east angle . . . as a proper pendant to the Statue of Sir Robert Peel on the other side . . . 'Countryman.'

[2] Public Record Office, Works 6.

Not being entirely satisfied with the answers, Stephens had a selection of their correspondence published in the *Morning Post*. Sir Benjamin Hall retaliated on 10th December 1856, by asking the newspaper's editor to publish on his behalf all the letters, which was done two days later.

'Mr. Stephens, the secretary of the Sculptors' Institute, having thought proper to publish a part only of the correspondence which had taken place with this department, notwithstanding the desire expressed that if the correspondence was published, the letter No. 5 might form part of it, the First Commissioner hopes you will be so good as to give insertion to the accompanying letters.

I am, etc. Alfred Austin, Secretary.

No. 1.
32, Sackville-street, Piccadilly.
October 25, 1856.
Sir,

I am requested by members of the Sculptors' Institute to address you on the subject of the monument which her Majesty's Government intend to erect in St. Paul's Cathedral to the memory of the late Duke of Wellington.

In considering the published terms relating to the competition the following questions arose, on which they would be most grateful to receive information from you at your earliest convenience:—

1. Will designs which deviate from the stated dimensions be accepted in competition?
2. Are the designs to be publicly exhibited prior to the decision of the judges?
3. The names of the judges?
4. Is the execution of the monument to be entrusted to the author of the best design submitted in competition?

The members of the institute have reason to believe that the confidence arising from a mutual understanding on the above points would materially add to the success of the competition, and they trust that the importance to be attached to them will plead a sufficient apology for calling your attention to the subject. . . .

I have, &c. Edward B. Stephens, Hon. Sec.

No. 2.
Office of Works &c.
October 29, 1856.

Sir,

I am directed by the First Commissioner of her Majesty's Works, &c. to acknowledge the receipt on the 27th of your letter dated the 25th inst., requesting on behalf of the members of the Sculptors' Institute to be informed on certain points in regard to the monument . . .

With regard to your first query, I am to inform you that the directions as to size that the model shall bear in proportion to the monument are set forth most clearly in the specifications, and competitors must not depart from them.

2. No further information can be given on the subject of your second enquiry than that afforded by the specifications.

3. The names of the judges cannot be given, as the selection has not yet been made, and will not be made for some time.

4. There is nothing in the specifications to bind the Government to employ the author of the best design to execute the work, and no positive obligations can be incurred.

I am, &c. G. Russell, Assistant Secretary.

No. 3
32, Sackville-street, Piccadilly.
December 4, 1856.

Sir,

In consequence of many enquiries from sculptors both at home and abroad upon the points which I had the honour to address to you on the 24th of October, relative to the Government Wellington memorial for St. Paul's, and as to the best means of answering all enquiries,

I have been directed by members of the Sculptors' Institute, at a general meeting, to forward for publication (to which it is presumed you will see no objection) the correspondence, with the accompanying letter.

I have, &c. Edw. B. Stephens, Hon. Sec.
To Sir B. Hall, Bart., M.P.,
First Commissioner of Her Majesty's Works, Whitehall.

No. 4.
Government Wellington Memorial.
To the Editor.
Sir,

As the most effectual method of informing the sculptors of the world on matters which are known to be viewed by some of them with anxiety, I am directed by the members of the Sculptors' Institute to ask the favour of an early insertion in your journal of the enclosed correspondence.

The reasons for seeking official information by the four questions to the First Commissioner of her Majesty's Works were:—

Firstly.	The well-known fact that artists for the sake of effect, increase the difficulties of selection by neglecting the instructions as to the size of the model or sketch. It will be seen the reply now states definitely that all models not *strictly* in accordance with the specified scale will be excluded from the competition.
Secondly.	It was thought that by an anterior exhibition public feeling and opinion might be ascertained, the operation of which would possibly be valuable in contributing towards an impartial selection.
Thirdly.	It appeared also of great importance that the judges should be at once publicly known, in order specially that foreign artists might

be fully assured that the tribunal would be of the highest character and position, and consist of those most competent to decide on the relative merits of sketches; and further that the judges knowing that they were to undertake the office would then scrupulously refrain from visiting the studios of competitors, or from allowing themselves to be in any way influenced by artists or their friends.

Fourthly. This question appeared necessary to set at rest a doubt as to whether the author of the best design would be commissioned to execute the monument.

Foreigners, as well as British sculptors, will certainly be discouraged by the anticipation that he who succeeds in producing the best model probably would not be employed to carry out the work.

I have, &c. Edward B. Stephens, Hon. Sec.

No. 5.

Office of Works &c.

December 6, 1856

Sir,

I am directed by the First Commissioner of her Majesty's Works, &c., to state that you are at perfect liberty to publish your letter, dated October 25, and the answer to that letter, dated October 29, and that you will take the same course with regard to your last letter, dated December 4, if you think proper to do so; but in that event the First Commissioner desires me to say that he does not consider that he has given any grounds for your statement that the artist who succeeds in producing the best model will probably not be employed to carry out the work.

He desires further to remark that he considers it would be most inconvenient to nominate the judges until such time as the models shall have been sent in for exhibition. The First Commissioner hopes that when the judges shall have been appointed, the selection will be such as to secure the approbation of your profession and the public at large.

In your letter of the 4th instant you speak of models and sketches. In order that sculptors may not be misled by the publication of that letter, I am directed to state that no sketches will be received. The specification sent out is clear upon this point, and indicates distinctly that models alone are to be sent in, which models must be exactly quarter size of the monument intended to be erected.[1]

Should you publish the correspondence, the First Commissioner desires that this letter may form part of it.

I am, &c. Alfred Austin, Secretary.'

It was this last letter that the Sculptors' Institute had not published; the wrangle between the sculptors and the Office of Works, was not conducive to harmony, but was taken up by the newspapers. *The Art Journal* considered that the wording of the clause about the size was not the same thing as one fourth scale, which presumably was what was intended; thus the base of the model should not be larger than three feet three inches by two feet three inches.

To keep the fire of controversy glowing, *Lloyd's* on 21st December expressed the view that the correspondence between the sculptors and the Government clearly indicated bad faith on the Government's side. If this were not so, why should Sir Benjamin Hall refuse to name the judges, and why should he decline to state

---

[1] John Bell (1812–95), in fact, sent in sketches as well, and after the announcement of the awards, he wrote to *The Builder*, 29th August 1857, '. . . I sent in two careful little drawings, presenting the monument *in* the arch, neither of which, I understand, was looked at'.

John Gibson's model was passed over by the judges because it was fractionally too large. See No. 76 in the *Catalogue* of the exhibition of models in Westminster Hall on p. 166. Quoted in Gibson's biography is his opinion that his model attracted little notice because of the simplicity of its design.

whether the models would be publicly exhibited before the mysterious jury reached its decision. Obviously the competition was rigged, and British sculptors should not enter it. *Lloyd's* sarcastically pronounced that only foreign artists should compete. Why? 'Long live Marochetti! and down with your Bailys and Foleys and Munros! A baron who uses a chisel, must be a better sculptor—it stands to reason—than any plain Mr. Besides, the sculptor of the Cœur de Lion so seldom gets a commission.[1] It is therefore an act of common justice to recognise his undoubted merits, by assuring him some national work. All people know how terribly the baron has been neglected in England, and how immeasurably above all British sculptors he undoubtedly is. But why not do the thing openly, Sir Benjamin Hall? If you really intend a fair and wide competition among the artists of all nations why decline to give the names of the judges? If you have faith in the opinion of the anonymous jury you intend to appoint, why be afraid of declaring at once that you will put the models to the test of public opinion first? These two points, as put in your reply to British sculptors, have an un-English complexion that it is dangerous for a man in office to wear.'[2]

Sir Benjamin Hall appears to have ignored this final challenge of 1856, and quiet reigned for the next few months. Presumably this was because the sculptors concerned were busy preparing their models for submission at Westminster Hall by 1st June 1857. But in May turmoil broke out again as a result of the following paragraph which appeared in *The Times*:

'Baron Marochetti is at present engaged on a colossal monument to the Duke of Wellington, which will be raised in St. Paul's, if the design meets with the approval of the government. An imitative door of bronze is to be placed between two of the interior pilasters, and on the steps leading to it will sit a gigantic figure of Victory, with outspread wings, supposed to be the constant companion of the hero, even to the tomb. Above the door will stand an equestrian figure of the duke, while on pedestals on each side of the steps will be seated two figures symbolising civil and military honour. The nude figure of Victory, hereafter to be dressed, is now nearly finished, and a grandeur of design by no means common in our public monuments is already indicated.'[3]

This brief report put the cat among the pigeons. Appearing only two or three days before the models were due at Westminster, it described Marochetti's design in such detail for the judges, still un-named, inevitably to know who had created it, in spite of the fact that every entry had to be submitted under the anonymity of a motto. *Lloyd's* on 14th June insisted either that Marochetti should be barred from the competition as he had violated one of the rules, or else that all the other competitors should at once be announced as well. The name of the Prince Consort was for the first time openly mentioned in connection with the Baron's project—'We fancy we can trace the hand of

___

[1] This was probably a sarcastic comment on the Baron's efforts to raise money for this statue, and to find supporters who would be influential enough to ensure a prominent site for it.

[2] *The Art Journal*, May 1857.

[3] *Lloyd's*, 31st May 1857: 'The Iron Duke—in Bronze. Our national art-patrons like their pictures from abroad. It would appear that we have no sculptors in England worth a national commission. Baily is an Englishman, to be sure; so is Munro; so is Foley—but then compare them with— say Baron Marochetti—how dwarfed are they? . . . We find the following paragraph in the *Times* [quoted above] . . . Now, of course, the baron's work will be accepted, for has not this sagacious nobleman already enjoyed the satisfaction of obtaining patronage over the heads of mere English sculptors?' In 1859, Marochetti exhibited the 'Victory' in the garden of Apsley House, and in a letter to *The Times* said that it had been intended for the Duke's monument. He had not taken 'part in the competition proposed by Sir William Molesworth . . . or in the general one opened by Sir B. Hall, mainly because in both cases the model was to be small', and he preferred to work on a large scale. Why then, should he prepare a model if he was convinced that he would be asked to execute the permanent work?

Prince Albert in the chiselling.' The next issue of *The Art Journal* was also condemnatory; it found it surprising that *The Times* should have published such a report at a time when as that newspaper, in common with everybody else, must have been fully aware that even as it was issued anonymous models were arriving at Westminster from all over Europe and America. Moreover, *The Times* had described the Baron's work as the 'colossal monument', not as a model. Did this mean that the Baron was so sure of himself as actually to be at work on a 'coming event—foreknown and pre-arranged'? This was probably correct; as the report appeared so very soon before the models had to be at Westminster, and *The Times* seemed to indicate that Marochetti's work on his project was by no means finished, it would seem that the Baron was certain ultimately that he would be chosen and thus had the time to work at his own pace. But *The Art Journal* hoped that a course so atrocious had not been contemplated; and shortly afterwards it became known that Marochetti had withdrawn. This, however, was not the end of Marochetti's connection with the proposed monument, for he reappears amid the confusion of the following year, 1858.

Eighty-three models duly arrived at Westminster Hall. As they came in they were numbered, especial care being taken to ensure that those from abroad were well mixed among the English entries. This subterfuge, however, was rather defeated as many of the foreign models were easily recognised as such by their mottoes. Sculptors were left to set up their own work. Eight expert modellers were employed, however, by the First Commissioner of Works to assemble those models from overseas which were not accompanied by their authors. Some of these designs consisted of nearly one hundred parts. Inside the hall the models were arranged in three rows on platforms covered with crimson cloth, and from the beginning of July, before the judges' selection was announced, the exhibition was open to the general public who came in large numbers to see what were frequently described as examples of the confectioner's art (Plate 19).

So there were all the models, hopefully displayed, each with its Wellington, and some with Copenhagen, lions, Britannia and 'Prosperity, Strength, Order, Civil Virtue, Justice, Temperance, Prudence, Decision, Constancy, Valour, Protective Force, Truth, Duty, Honour, Energy, Loyalty, Law, Anarchy, Military Genius, Wisdom, Legislation, Diplomacy, Science, Despotism, Military Service, Veneration, and Industry. Of these, some have the symbol, as Justice, the balance, and Strength, the sword; but where they have not, the figures might, in many cases, be shuffled together and stand for one another. The figure of Temperance that might serve as well for a figure of Prudence, and the figure of Valour that might change places with that of Military Genius, are not necessarily the one or the other, —and not, therefore, the Temperance or the Valour of any true Art-poetry.'[1]

[1] *The Art Journal*, September 1857, p. 291.

PLATE 19. '*A Peep into Westminster Hall.*' *Caricatures of the models entered for the Wellington Memorial Competition. From* Punch, *Volume 33, 1857, pages 68, 69.*

III

The Decision—1857

A *Critical and Descriptive Catalogue* was published, which together with criticisms from various journals is given as an Appendix: *The Art Journal* was not in favour of many; *The Builder* was happiest with the more architectural type of monuments; while nothing, not even anything in a gothic style, pleased *The Ecclesiologist*, which could 'only hope that the memory of Wellington and the interior of our metropolitan cathedral may be spared the infliction of any of these either insipid and mediocre, or flagrantly preposterous, designs'.[1]

Although the Public Record Office has a list of the mottoes among the papers relating to the monument from the Office of Works, there does not appear to be a list of the names of the competing artists; secrecy must have been maintained to the end, so that most of the sculptors will now never be known.

The Office of Works list of the models exhibited records that three more boxes were disregarded, as they contained drawings, and in a fourth box lay a clay model so broken that it was beyond repair.

The awards were announced on 7th August 1857. The judges were the Marquess of Lansdowne, Dean Milman, Lord Overstone, Sir Edward Cust, W. E. Gladstone, and C. R. Cockerell, the Architect to St. Paul's,[2] and their report read as follows:

[1] *The Ecclesiologist*, August 1857.
[2] Henry, 3rd Marquess of Lansdowne, K.G. (1780–1863); Henry Hart Milman (1791–1868); Samuel James Loyd (1796–1883), 1st Lord Overstone; General Sir Edward Cust (1794–1878); William Ewart Gladstone (1808–98); Charles Robert Cockerell, R.A. (1788–1863).

'To the Right Hon. Sir B. Hall, Bart. M.P., First Commissioner of Her Majesty's Works and Public Buildings.

Sir,—In the execution of the duty devolved upon us, we beg to recommend that the prizes should be allotted to the models corresponding with the following numbers:—

Premium	No.	Motto
First	80	Most greatly lived this Star of England: Fortune made his Sword.
Second	56	Avon.
Third	36	'Passed away.'
Fourth	10	Arno.
Equal	12	'Tis not my profit that leads mine honour. Mine honour it.'
	18	I know of but one art.
	20	Finis coronat opus.
	21	A design in clay resembles life, A stucco copy resembles death. The execution in marble, however, is the resurrection of the work of art.
	63	Let us guard our honour in arts as in arms.

We have thus endeavoured to adjudge the prizes we have been instructed to distribute (in the scale of which we have not thought ourselves at liberty to make any change), in the order which appeared to us to be that of the relative degree of merit in the models, such models falling within the prescribed conditions as to the space to be occupied and the cost to be incurred.

PLATE 20. *Design by Giovanni Dupré, of Florence, which won the 4th prize in the Wellington Memorial Competition. From the* Illustrated London News, *12th September 1857, page 277.*

In so doing we have not considered ourselves bound to take into exclusive consideration the peculiar fitness and adaptation to that spot in St. Paul's Cathedral which appears to be in contemplation for the erection of the proposed monument, which might possibly have led to some difference in the selection.

We cannot at the same time forbear suggesting that, before any design is finally adopted by the Government, it would be desirable, considering the peculiarity of the situation contemplated, and that it essentially differs from that of all other monuments now existing in the cathedral, the opinion of some experienced artists should be called for, who would be better judges of the local effect than we consider ourselves to be; more especially as Mr. Cockerell, the only one of the appointed judges professionally connected with the arts; though we have derived from him valuable assistance and information in the progress of the examination, has declined on that account taking a part in the ultimate decision.

We may be permitted to add that it is with much regret that we have found ourselves precluded from admitting into the competition some of the models, from the circumstance of their having exceeded the limits as to space, distinctly laid down in the prescribed conditions.

Lansdowne	Edwd. Cust
H. H. Milman	W. E. Gladstone
Overstone	

6, Palace-yard, Aug. 7, 1857.'

The authors of the models to which prizes were awarded were (80) W. Calder Marshall, R.A. (Plate 30); (56) W. F. Woodington (Plate 27); (36) Edgar G. Papworth (Plate 26); (10) Giovanni Dupré of Florence (Plates 20, 21); (12) Mariano Folcini and Ulisse Cambi of Florence (Plate 22); (18) Alfred Stevens (Plates 23, 34–39); (20) Matthew Noble (Plate 24); (21) Ernst Julius Hähnel of Dresden (Plate 25); and (63) Thomas Thornycroft (Plate 28), and they were told of the decision on 8th August.[1]

The expectant world at last knew the long-awaited result of the Wellington Monument competition. It had been won by William Calder Marshall, R.A. No-one, however, was satisfied, probably because four foreigners were named, and partly because the only competent judge on the panel had disassociated himself from his colleagues' choice. Moreover,

[1] Among the unsuccessful competitors were E. H. Baily, John Gibson, John Bell, Joseph Durham, John Lawlor, and John Thomas (see Appendix).

PLATE 21. *Photograph of the model by Mariano Folcini and Ulisse Cambi, of Florence, affixed in a pamphlet in the British Museum Library.*

the judges now said that competent people should be called in to adjudicate on possibly another winner, and very surprisingly admitted that in reaching their decision they had not given special consideration to the suitability of the models for the site for which they were designed.

Understandably the art-world of this country boiled over. *The Builder* protested that Cockerell, who after all had been one of those who had chosen the site, had evaded the task of making the final selection, while as for the others, the journal was sure that the 'practice of such appointments tends to keep up the fallacy that anyone is able to judge a work of art'.

As a result of this article in *The Builder* Cockerell defended his action in a long letter:[1]

'I have to acknowledge and to thank you for the interpretation you have been pleased to put upon my retirement from the adjudication of the prizes in the fine art competition for the Wellington Monument, which, as you justly suggest, was grounded, first, on my doubts as to my own competency, though a well-known amateur of sculpture, to give judgment on an art not professionally my own; and, secondly, on my doubts as to the efficiency of a tribunal, on a technical and professional subject, without the aid of technical and professional counsel, so as to give satisfaction to the artists concerned and to the public generally,—for my isolated appointment on that commission, cannot fairly be urged as supplying the professional element.

At the same time, as you have inferred, I deemed it my duty to the occasion, to my office as surveyor to St. Paul's Cathedral during more than thirty-two years, and as the original suggestor of the site adopted for the erection of that national monument, to offer every service and advice in my power to the commissioners in that character, with reference to the harmonies of the cathedral architecture and of the special locality, though I have no judgment on the relative merits of the designs. These scruples were submitted to my distinguished colleagues with all the zeal and loyalty I owe to the cause of art; but circum-

[1] *The Builder*, 22nd August 1857.

stances prevented their acting upon them, I deemed it my duty to retire . . .'

Within a few days people were asking, 'What is the actual result of the competition?'[1] In spite of the judges' statements that another site might be chosen for the monument, a wooden arch, to the same scale of the models, was made so that it could be placed over them. This, naturally, led to another question—Why was this not done in the first place for all the models? If it was now right to experiment with the chosen few to judge their relationship with the architecture, surely it was just as right that every other competitor should have the same advantage (although it was recognised, that some of the models were too unsuitable to be taken seriously). Opinion held that as the judges had not taken every factor laid down in the competition into account, then their decision must be void. 'Indeed, the conditions (taken in relation to the report of the reward) evidently put many of the competitors on a false scent, who were thrown out by the very fact of attending to those conditions which the judges at the last moment repudiated. The report of the award says that if the judges had specially considered the models according to the site which they were bound to do (as the conditions were equally binding on the judges as on the competitors) they (the judges) should probably have made a different decision.'

The Art Journal[2] analysed the composition of the selection committee. It could well believe the rumours that Sir Benjamin Hall had been hard put to it to find any judges at all. The First Commissioner, it was considered, was at fault in choosing unqualified judges. Lord Lansdowne must have been there to represent the Cabinet, but surely that supposition which assigned the whole range of human

PLATE 22. *Design by Mariano Folcini and Ulisse Cambi, of Florence, which won a prize of £100 in the Wellington Memorial Competition. From the* Illustrated London News, *12th September 1857, page 277.*

knowledge to a minister of state, was extinct. In Lansdowne's case, however, the government was lucky in a man of his attainments, although, surely, he was too old even to have managed to go round all the models? Dean Milman 'made his way into the commission' by virtue of being the Dean of the cathedral in which the monument was to stand, hardly

---

[1] 'As the matter now stands, the result of the Wellington Competition is as bad as if Baron Marochetti had been called in.' *The Building News*, 4th September 1857.

[2] September 1857.

a necessary qualification. Lord Overstone was a financier, and *The Art Journal* was quite unable to find any reason at all for his being chosen, unless it was his coronet. So far, then, the panel contained a minister of state, a high church dignitary, and an ennobled financier. Instead of an artist coming next, there was a soldier, the strangest appointment of all, that of General Cust. Obviously as Wellington had been a soldier, then Sir Benjamin Hall thought that a soldier would be qualified to chose his monument. Next on the list, said *The Art Journal* was the Right Hon. W. E. Gladstone, undoubtedly there to represent the House of Commons. There were many others perhaps more suitable than Gladstone, but they were not all members of the Privy Council. Lastly, as though an afterthought, was the architect, Cockerell. 'One halfpenny-worth of Art-bread to modify all this quantity of aristocratic sack!' Although Cockerell did not sign the report, he could not shake off some of the responsibility as, said the report, the judges had derived valuable assistance from him.

The Art Journal, like many others, considered that 'if the judges, as they would seem to suggest, have given a prize to some clever work, which, nevertheless, was not a clever Wellington monument to stand under a particular arch in St. Paul's Cathedral, then, they have given it for a cleverness essentially different from that which the competition challenged. Sir Benjamin Hall has asked one question, and they have answered another.' And in conclusion, 'although we think they have fallen into some strange mistakes, yet their award will meet with a considerable amount of acquiescence; and that is perhaps as much as in general such an award can aspire to. Many heartburnings and bitterness there will be,—heavy suspicions of prejudice perhaps, and certainly much sense of wrong; but these things are inseparable from such a competition so entered into. There is, for instance, a work here which is understood to be by Mr. Thomas,

PLATE 23. *Design by Alfred Stevens which won a prize of £100 in the Wellington Memorial Competition. From the* Illustrated London News, *12th September 1857, page 278.*

so remarkable for its talent,—though in our opinion unsuited for this particular purpose ... that it will be difficult to satisfy the sculptor that under any circumstances it should have been overlooked by the judges; and a model by Mr. Physick[1] is one of a class which furnish good evidence of what our school can perform. The resulting question is,—What, now, will the Government do in the matter of this Wellington Monument? It is probable, that no one model which appeared in this collection will be executed as the national work:—certainly, we should apprehend, not the one to which the judges have awarded the first prize. But the minister has the money, and we suppose means to have the monument; and there has been far too much of the power necessary for the execution of such a work displayed in this competition, to make it possible for him now to pass by the talent which he found in Westminster Hall. It seems to us, that the wise course will be, to summon to a final competition from eight to twelve ... of the leading sculptors of England *alone*; in which number, as a matter of right the three great prizemen, in the contest just ended, shall be included. Let these new competitors make models, to the half size,—the prize of the final monument being reduced by such a sum to each as shall greatly diminish the cost of his model,—and on the distinct understanding that one of these shall be selected for execution, with such alterations and modifications as may be agreed on between the government, the Court of Selection, and the sculptor himself. Let the Court of Selection be constituted with a care justly proportioned to the importance of the function which it will have to discharge; and contain a sufficient amount of the Art-element,

PLATE 24. *Design by Matthew Noble which won a prize of £100 in the Wellington Memorial Competition. From the* Illustrated London News, *29th August 1857, page 225.*

---

[1] Probably Edward Gustavus Physick (exhibited 1823–1871); see Rupert Gunnis, *Dictionary of British Sculptors*, page 302; it could, however, have been his son Edward James Physick (born 1829) (see Gunnis, *loc. cit.*). Both exhibited at the Great Exhibition of 1851, Edward James showing the *Rape of Proserpine* (Plate 32), for which he had been awarded the Royal Academy gold medal in 1850.

PLATE 25. *Design by Ernst Julius Hähnel, of Dresden, which won a prize of £100 in the Wellington Memorial Competition. From the* Illustrated London News, *12th September 1857, page 277.*

of such a satisfactory kind as might be represented by unfashionable names.—By such a process, the minister will most certainly arrive at an honourable result in the long-pending matter of the Wellington Monument.'

During the first half of 1858 the First Commissioner, Lord John Manners,[1] had several meetings with F. C. Penrose,[2] then Cathedral Architect, to discuss the site of the proposed monument, and at the same time the prize-winning models were re-examined in an attempt to see which of them, after all, would be the most appropriate; a model of the nave arch was made and placed over each one.[3] These discussions were conducted in privacy. Marshall, Woodington and Papworth wrote a joint letter to Lord John on 7th April 1858, asking whether he had yet come to any decision—and were told that he had not.[4] A correspondent in the *Morning Post* declared quite bluntly that the competition in Westminster Hall had been a sham, and that the government had since secretly commissioned Marochetti to make the monument.[5]

[1] Later the Seventh Duke of Rutland.

[2] Francis Cranmer Penrose (1817–1903).

[3] But see what *The Builder* had noted on 1st August 1857; quoted under the exhibition No. 27, on p. 145.

[4] Public Record Office, Works 6.

[5] John Bell, who had been unsuccessful in the Competition with two models, Nos. 57 and 60, bombarded *The Builder* and *The Building News* during 1857 and 1858, under his own name or the pseudonym 'Epsilon', with letters or articles with such titles as 'Wellington Monument—its site and sculptor', 'The Phases of the Wellington Monument', 'The Wellington Monument and Sarcophagus', and 'Art Plot and the Wellington Monument'. Among other suggestions, Bell advocated that the monument should be made the receptacle of the Duke's remains.

IV

The Second Decision—1858

Not until the middle of June 1858 was an announcement of any sort made. Then Lord John Manners told the House of Commons about his meetings with Penrose. Penrose had chosen No. 18 as the most suitable of the winning models (Plates 34–39), and this had been a relief to Manners as he, quite independently, had come to the same decision. With the design of No. 18 in mind he and Penrose had come to the further conclusion that the original site in the nave, that for which all the models had been designed, was not after all the best suited to the monument. The cathedral authorities were, moreover, not enthusiastic about relinquishing so much space in the body of the church, so in the end it had been decided that the monument should be erected in the South-West Chapel which was used as a Consistory Court. The Dean and Chapter, who may have been less than luke-warm in their enthusiasm for the memorial, had readily agreed that the Consistory Court Chapel could be used for this purpose.

So, at long last the news had broken; Alfred Stevens, almost unknown and no higher than sixth in the competition, had been chosen for the execution of one of the most important sculptural projects of the nineteenth century.[1] It was immediately suggested that a new design would have to be made to suit the

PLATE 26. *Design by E. G. Papworth which won the 3rd Prize in the Wellington Memorial Competition. From the* Illustrated London News, *12th September 1857, page 277.*

---

[1] 'It was said that Stevens was the candidate of the architects as against the sculptors; that his success was due to the influence of the Court, which at that time meant Prince Albert; that he was the representative of the ideas which had already begun to be identified with South Kensington, and so on. Few were found to give credit . . . that the obscure Alfred Stevens was a great artist, and that we had a First Commissioner capable of appreciating talent and with courage to back his opinion.' Sir Walter Armstrong, *Alfred Stevens*, 1881, p. 19.

PLATE 27. *Design by W. F. Woodington which won the 2nd prize in the Wellington Memorial Competition. From the* Illustrated London News, *29th August 1857, page 225.*

to a competitor who had finished so low down in the list. Stevens had assured a Member that he had studied both architecture and sculpture, but there was nothing in the way of great work to his credit. This, it was thought, was no disparagement of Stevens who was still a young man, but it was taking a risk just because his model was considered graceful and elegant, and seen to advantage in Westminster Hall.[1]

At the time of receiving the commission for the monument, Stevens was almost 40 years old, and was not at all well-known; he did not exhibit his work at the Royal Academy and elsewhere.

Born at Blandford Forum in Dorset in 1817, the son of a house and sign painter, he had as a youth assisted his father. His talent, however, was such as to attract the attention of a local parson, the Hon. and Rev. Samuel Best who, in 1833, sent him to study in Italy. Stevens stayed there until 1842, at one period becoming a pupil of the Danish sculptor, Bertel Thorwaldsen.

A few years after returning to England, Stevens was, in 1845, appointed an instructor at the School of Design then at Somerset House. He stayed there until 1847, the year in which he was asked to decorate some of the rooms at 'Deysbrook', near Liverpool. This was followed by the commission to decorate a railway carriage for the King of Denmark, and to design some sculpture for the exterior of St. George's Hall, Liverpool, in 1849.

During the following year he was asked to design such fittings as stoves for Messrs. Hoole of Sheffield, and it was while he was working in that town that he attracted to him some local art students, among them Godfrey Sykes, Reuben Townroe and James Gamble, who

changed site, but Manners was quite sure that Stevens's competition design could be easily adapted if necessary. Other sculptors were to provide decoration for the Chapel, and the whole project was to be under the immediate control of Penrose.

The surprise announcement of Stevens as the modeller of the monument led to a lengthy debate in the House of Commons, concern being expressed that the commission was to go

---

[1] 'The statue of the Duke of Wellington on the top of the arch by Matthew Cotes Wyatt at Hyde Park Corner is a national scandal and reproach; let us beware lest we some day find its twin brother in St. Paul's.' Lord Elcho, *The Times*, 21st June 1858.
    '. . . unquestionably a mistake . . .' *The Art Journal*, September 1857.

later worked on the decoration of the older buildings of the present Victoria and Albert Museum. Another assistant, Hugh Stannus, always referred to Stevens as 'the Master'.[1]

In the years between his work at Sheffield and winning the Wellington Memorial Competition, Stevens designed a seated lion for the railings outside the British Museum, a pavement for St. George's Hall, medals for the Department of Science and Art, and in 1856, entered for the competition held at Westminster Hall, for the proposed rebuilding of the Government Offices in Whitehall.[2]

The chief of the judges in the Wellington competition, the Marquess of Lansdowne, admitted that there was no model for the monument of such commanding merit that the judges were able to recommend it above all others. A statement to this effect had been agreed by his colleagues on the committee, but in order to spare the feelings of all the competitors, they had decided not to include it in their report.

Probably because of this, the change of site, and the uncertainty as to whether Stevens would be competent to carry out his design, it was decided that if he accepted the commission, he must make a *full-size model* of the whole memorial to be placed in the cathedral before starting work on the permanent structure. The sculptor, perhaps unthinkingly, agreed to this, and on 9th September 1858, George Russell, an Assistant Secretary in the Office of Works, informed him officially that the Treasury had sanctioned the work, and that he was now authorised to 'Proceed in the preparation of the model, subject to the following conditions, viz.

1st   That the model shall be placed by you in a proper position in the chapel of the Cathedral formerly used as the Consistory Court of the Diocese, in such a state of finish as will give a correct representation of the monument itself, and that its general proportions shall be in accordance with those of the chapel and the neighbouring parts of the

PLATE 28. *Design by Thomas Thornycroft which won a prize of £100 in the Wellington Memorial Competition. From the* Illustrated London News, *29th August 1857, page 225.*

---

[1] *Alfred Stevens and his Work*, by Hugh Stannus, 1891.

[2] One of the competitors used the motto 'I know of but one art' (No. 135). Susan McMorran in 'Alfred Stevens', R.I.B.A. *Journal*, Volume 71, October 1964, pages 435–40, infers that these drawings—incomplete—were by Stevens. 'No. 135 is Italian . . . As there are only five drawings, and no elevation, it is not easy to pass judgment on the intentions of the artist.' *The Building News*, 12th June 1857, p. 597.

PLATE 29. *Design for the Wellington Monument (No. 68: 'Integrità'), by Mr. John Thomas. From* The Builder, *19th September 1857, page 539.*

Cathedral, to be determined by Mr. Penrose, the surveyor to the Dean and Chapter.

2nd That the entire cost of the monument, if executed according to the model, shall not exceed the sum of £11,000.

3rd That as the model during its preparation will constantly require your time and labour as well as a considerable outlay by you, you shall be paid by this Board from time to time during the first twelve months after the commencement of the work, a sum not exceeding £1,000, and during such further time (if any) as shall be found necessary for its completion a proportionate sum.

4th That the general superintendence of the work shall be placed under Mr. Penrose, and that no payment shall be made to you except upon a certificate from him that the general progress thereof sanctions such a payment.

I am accordingly to request that you will communicate with Mr. Penrose, and proceed with the preparation of the model.

You will observe that you are left by the above conditions, so far as depends upon Her Majesty's Government, entirely unfettered as to the composition of the design.'

Russell sent a copy of this letter to Penrose and asked him if he would act as had been suggested, and to this Penrose readily agreed on the following day.[1]

[1] It was at about this time that Stevens was designing the decoration of the vast cupola of the British Museum Reading Room.

V

Preparation of the Model 1858 to 1870

Stevens promptly agreed to erect the model upon the conditions laid down, but with the proviso:

'I must beg to observe that the nature of the design . . . has already been decided upon by the Chief Commissioner, and that the cost of a monument in accordance with the selected design would be considerably in excess of the sum named above. I should be prepared to complete the work, on which I am about to commence the model, for the sum of £14,000.'[1]

At the outset, Stevens made three mistakes: firstly, his idea of the degree of finish of the model was far more lavish than that of the Office of Works; secondly, he agreed to make the monument for only £14,000,[2] which was £6,000 less than the sum for which the monument had been designed while perhaps not appreciating that this was also to cover the cost of the model; and thirdly, the government obviously had in mind a modification of the monument to fit the reduced cost, but Stevens at no time seems to have considered any alteration to the competition design.

In the meantime W. Calder Marshall and W. F. Woodington, the first and second prizewinners in the competition were, as consolation, asked to prepare designs for suitable reliefs for the decoration of the new Wellington Chapel.

At the beginning of November it occurred to Lord John Manners that he had not yet

PLATE 30. *Design by William Calder Marshall which won the 1st Prize in the Wellington Memorial Competition. From the* Illustrated London News, *29th August 1857, page 225.*

[1] 9th October 1858.

[2] This sum, however, was not inconsiderable for, even if it is estimated that the purchasing power of the pound sterling in 1858 was but five times greater than that of today, then Stevens was to be paid £70,000.

PLATE 31. *W. Calder Marshall's design as it would appear in St. Paul's Cathedral. From* The Building News, *25th September 1857, page 1009.*

obtained the formal permission of the cathedral authorities to use the site of the monument, so he wrote to Dean Milman:

'Altho' no difficulty is, I trust, likely to arise from the absence of any formal communication between the Dean and Chapter and this Department on the subject of the site in the cathedral destined for the Wellington Monument, I feel it be now more respectful to the Body of which you are the head to make an official request to erect, in the first instance, the Model, and subsequently the finished Monument in the Chapel hitherto used as the Consistory Court . . .'

Dean Milman and the Chapter gave their approval on 22nd November.[1]

On 18th November 1858, Penrose visited Stevens, who had acquired a new studio at Haverstock Hill[2] in which to construct the enormous model, and which was to involve him in extensive and costly structural alterations, thereby adding to his financial burdens. The framework of the model was ready and Penrose was of the opinion that Stevens should now receive £400. There was no immediate reaction to this letter by the Office of Works and a few days later, on 26th November, Penrose wrote again to Austin on behalf of Stevens, '. . . Poor Mr. Stevens is in great straits for money. The preparations he has made are necessary even if he should be desired somewhat to modify his design. Could not his £400 be advanced without further delay?'

And even here it may be noticed that Penrose was foreseeing possible economies in the

---

[1] Chapter Minutes, St. Paul's Cathedral Library.

[2] Stevens moved from 7 Canning Place, in Kensington, to York Cottage, Walham Green, in April 1858. Not long afterwards he took 5 Church Road, Haverstock Hill. As the model became larger Stevens was forced to find even more spacious premises, and in 1867 he went to 9 Eton Villas, Haverstock Hill, and converted an adjacent derelict church, into a studio in which to erect the model. (K. R. Towndrow, *Alfred Stevens*, 1939.)

monument, but just before he wrote to Austin he had received a letter from Stevens, which was some two months after Stevens had first heard from the Office of Works. He obviously had been giving more serious thought to the monument and its cost, and hoped that Penrose might present his views to the First Commissioner:

'I have received Mr. Russell's letter relating to the Wellington Monument.

To all the conditions it contains, which have reference to the preparation of the model, I at once agree, but I must beg of you to represent to Lord John Manners that it will be impossible to execute the contemplated design in bronze and marble for £11,000, the sum which Mr. Russell's letter informs me, has been set apart for the work.

As the prices paid for the monuments already existing in St. Paul's have no doubt been taken into consideration in fixing the sum to be paid in the present instance, it might be shown how much the proposed Wellington Monument exceeds those works in size and elaborateness. My design (as you may remember) is made up of great masses of sculpture, combined with a framework of architecture. Any one of these masses would almost equal any two; would far exceed in labour of execution the largest monument at present in St. Paul's.

The framework of architecture, with its friezes and soffits and panels of bronze, is of a kind which we have no example in England, and may in no way be compared with the blocks of masonry cased with marble which form the usual basework of a modern monument. These and other facts that you yourself may be able to supply will, I am sure, convince Lord John Manners that I use but ordinary prudence in declining to pledge myself to complete the proposed monument for £11,000.

I shall be prepared to complete the work for £14,000.'[1]

This letter Penrose sent on to Lord John,[2] stating that Stevens's estimate of £14,000 was a most moderate one. In Penrose's view Stevens should get the extra money regardless of what was being paid to Calder Marshall and Woodington for their consolation reliefs because, after all, the monument itself was going to form the focal point of the new Chapel.

Manners agreed to the extra money being

PLATE 32. *The Rape of Proserpine by Edward James Physick, awarded the Royal Academy Gold Medal in 1850, and exhibited at the 1851 Exhibition in Hyde Park (see p. 45).*

E

[1] Stevens went on holiday to Italy from September 1858 to January 1859.
[2] 30th November 1858.

PLATE 33. *Design by Alfred Stevens for the Wellington Monument. It is drawn on the special sheet lithographed with perspective, elevation, and plan, of the proposed site in St. Paul's, which was issued with the conditions of the competition. Victoria and Albert Museum, Department of Prints and Drawings, No. 1119–1884.*

allocated for Stevens's work, and the sculptor then settled down to prepare his model, which it was presumed would take about a year, and 1859 passed quietly in eager anticipation. Calder Marshall on 21st March of that year told Penrose that he and Woodington were ready to show their designs to Lord John Manners. One of the few dissentient voices was *The Art Journal* which still rumbled occasionally; in April it carried a report that Stevens would soon be able to show his model to 'a select few', but thought that there was still a degree of mystery surrounding the final form that the monument would take. The *Journal*

could not resist bringing Baron Marochetti into the affair again, and at the end of 1859 said:

'The prolonged abiding of Marochetti's "Victory" in the garden of Apsley House, seems to be intended as a persistent chastisement of public taste. And are we to believe that this, after all, with the rest of the design is to be that of the intended monument? . . . Will Mr. Stevens's work be ultimately accepted? Will it not in turn be set aside, and Marochetti's adopted? We are perfectly justified in asking the question, seeing the unhesitating reversal of their own decisions by the committee.'[1]

By the beginning of 1860 Calder Marshall's relief illustrating 'Peace' and that of 'War' by

[1] Marochetti had admitted in a letter to *The Times*, reprinted in *The Art Journal*, that the figure at Apsley House was, in fact, part of his original model for the Wellington Monument.

PLATES 34–37. *Alfred Stevens's model which was exhibited in Westminster Hall, 1857. Height 9 ft. 9 in. Victoria and Albert Museum, Department of Architecture and Sculpture, No. 44–1878.*

PLATE 38. *Detail of Alfred Stevens's model—equestrian group.*

Woodington were nearly at the stage when they could be shown to Penrose, but the year passed with no sign of progress from Stevens. He had told Penrose that he still could not give any date for when it would be ready, but he hoped that by the end of 1860 it would be in an advanced stage, and that while the model was being erected in St. Paul's for inspection, he would be able to work on the surmounting equestrian group. The First Commissioner[1] was asked for more money in November, and he took the opportunity to ask Penrose for a report on the progress of the model, and also for an estimate of how much more time was going to be required by the sculptor, as the year allowed for work on the model had now ended.[2]

Penrose went to see Stevens on 27th November 1860, and on the following day he sent his report to the Office of Works:

'The model consists of an architectural composition, composed of three stories.

In the accompanying rough sketch I have called the lower story (1), the middle story (2), and the upper story (3) (Plate 49).

In the lower story is to be contained the recumbent figure of the Duke of Wellington on a richly sculptured sarcophagus.

The middle story is to have two elaborate groups representing virtues and vices allegorically, and surmounted by the armorial bearings of the late Field Marshal. The upper story was originally intended to have exhibited an equestrial portrait of the Duke of Wellington, but as that was objected to by the Dean of

[1] Lord John Manners had been succeeded as First Commissioner of Works and Public Buildings by William Cowper (later Cowper-Temple, created Baron Mount-Temple in 1880), who held that office from 1860 to 1866.
[2] During 1860, Stevens was continuing with his decoration of Dorchester House, and K. R. Towndrow in *The Works of Alfred Stevens at the Tate Gallery*, 1950, dates as *c.* 1860 the scheme for decorating the east end of Christ Church, Cosway Street, Marylebone, which, although there are designs, was never completed.

PLATE 39. *Detail of Alfred Stevens's model—the recumbent effigy of the Duke of Wellington.*

St. Paul's, he is preparing for a different composition.

Of the lower story little is wanting as to the architecture except the ornaments intended for the pedestals of the columns, and the soffit of the arch or vault over the figure.

The ornamental work of the sarcophagus is in a forward state, but the figure is not yet done.

In the middle story the architectural parts are very nearly complete, and one of the groups of sculpture representing, I believe, Truth

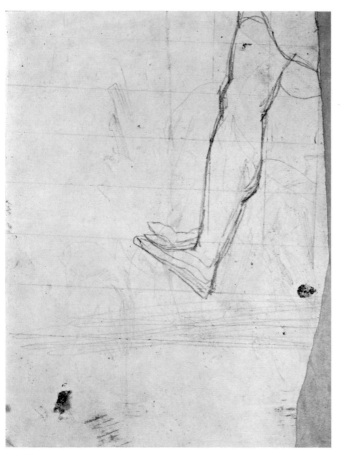

PLATE 40. *Study for the leg of the Duke of Wellington in the equestrian group, by Alfred Stevens. Victoria and Albert Museum, Department of Prints and Drawings, E.2527–1911.*

overcoming Falsehood, is almost two-thirds finished. The heraldic ornaments are not yet done. No advance is yet made with the upper story.

In Mr. Stevens's opinion it will still require seven or eight months to finish the model sufficiently to erect it in the proposed site in St. Paul's Cathedral, but he will use his best endeavours to get it done by the end of June next. It will be necessary to finish it completely in every part on three sides, making, however, if necessary, one of the groups of the middle story do duty for the two groups intended in the finished monument, viz., by repeating the same group.

I believe it was expected both by others and himself that he would have been able to make more progress; but if the great size of the composition is considered, as well as its elaborate nature, it will not be surprising that more time has elapsed than was first thought of.

To enable Mr. Stevens to get the work as forward by the end of June, as he now hopes to do, it will be necessary to supply him with sufficient funds.

The sums already advanced to him have amounted to £1,600 during a space of about two years. Respecting his expenditure, Mr. Stevens writes to me thus:

Nov. 22, 1860

'£500 have been paid on account of a charge of £700 for alterations made in my studio and for setting up the brick and timber framework of my model, and £260 have been expended in rent, leaving a little more than £400 a year for two years of study expenses, that is, assistants and workmen's wages, &c.'

It was arranged in the instructions issued to Mr. Stevens that he was to receive £1,600 during the first twelve months and during such further time (if any) that shall be necessary for the completion of proportionate sum.

Mr. Stevens will, I believe, be willing to guarantee its completion in the manner stated above (subject to his health not failing) for £1,200 in addition to what he has already received, and to enable him to make the proper arrangements for adequately warming his studio and securing the assistance which is necessary for him, he requests to have immediately an instalment of £600.

Looking at the amount of work that the model has already taken, and at the terms of the instructions issued to Mr. Stevens, I cannot think that his request will be thought unreasonable by the First Commissioner, and

PLATE 41. *Head of a cherub —detail of ornament for the monument, by Alfred Stevens. Victoria and Albert Museum, Department of Prints and Drawings, E.2615-1911.*

venture to enclose my certificate of that sum now being due to Mr. Stevens. My statement above of Mr. Stevens being according to the best of my belief willing to guarantee its completion for £1,200 is the result of a conversation with him. I did not ask him for authority to make the offer in his name. It would be best should the First Commissioner concur with it, to obtain Mr. Stevens's sanction for this offer.'

Accordingly, Alfred Austin wrote to Stevens to say that £600 would be forthcoming, and asked if the sculptor would guarantee to finish the model for another £600; on 29th December 1860 Stevens gave this guarantee. He then received the money and at about this time

wrote to Penrose to tell him that he was working on the model as hard as he could.

One interesting point raised by this report of Penrose's, is that Stevens, apparently reconciled to the dismissal of the equestrian figure of Wellington, was making a different group to surmount the monument.

The first half of 1861 went by still with no sign of the model being delivered by Stevens. So on 31st July the Commissioner enquired 'to remind you that the time has long since passed at which you undertook to have a model of the suggested monument . . . ready for inspection and consideration, and I am to inform you that it is necessary that some decision should be arrived at on the subject of that monument without further delay'. On

PLATE 42. *Frieze of four cherub heads—detail of ornament for the monument, by Alfred Stevens. Victoria and Albert Museum, Department of Prints and Drawings, E.2697-1911.*

3rd August Stevens replied that he was working with all possible diligence, and that he would name the date as early as he could. However, there had been an accident to part of the model, which had somewhat delayed things.

The impatience of the Office of Works was stilled for a few more months until 11th November when Stevens was asked again to name the day. However, the sculptor completely ignored this request, and on 6th February 1862, the Office of Works tried again when, reminding Stevens that he had not answered the previous letter, he was asked this time 'immediately' to name an early day when the First Commissioner might see the model. Stevens answered this demand by stating that he found it impossible to fix a date, but he wished to assure the Commissioner that he was giving every hour at his disposal to the work and that, in his opinion, it was progressing satisfactorily. 'It ought to be pointed out to the Chief Commissioner that in a model like the one in question, so large and composed of so many parts, the making of each part is an experiment, and an experiment which often has to be repeated a number of times, hence the difficulty of calculating the time which the finishing of my work may occupy.'[1]

Yet another year, 1862, was gradually slipping away, until the First Commissioner tried again to pin the sculptor down in November.[2] Once more Stevens did not bother to reply, so the Office of Works wrote again, this time rather more strongly than previously, informing Stevens that the First Commissioner 'hoped that you would have exerted yourself to complete the long-delayed model of the Wellington Monument, but that as he has received no communication from you, and no certificate from Mr. Penrose, he is apprehensive that you have not been giving any attention to that work, and he requests to be informed whether anything can be done to secure the completion of the model'. Stevens thought it politic to answer, repeating that he continued to give as much of his attention to the model as circumstances permitted. If the Office of Works would advance him a total of one third of the £14,000 for which he had agreed to make the whole monument (he had already received £2,200), he would, on receipt of a further £2,466 undertake to finish the model within fifteen months.

Rather naturally the Office of Works was taken aback by this somewhat cool request, so

---

[1] However, Stevens did agree that 'it will be quite convenient for me to meet Mr. Cowper and yourself on Saturday'. 22nd May 1862, letter to Penrose, R.I.B.A.

[2] During 1862 Stevens designed a certificate for the 1862 International Exhibition and embarked on the proposal to decorate the interior of St. Paul's Cathedral, another unrealised project which occupied the artist for many years.

they wrote to Penrose to remind him that Stevens had at the outset agreed to do the model for £1,600, that he had by now received £2,200, and now he wanted a further £2,466. What advice had Penrose to offer the Commissioner? Penrose, who was, one suspects, becoming a little tired of this Stevens–Office of Works wrangle, replied at length:

'. . . as it is not questioned that the usage of the profession of sculptors is to receive a payment of one third the price of their works in large commissions, upon the approval of the design, the points to determine, are, firstly, whether Mr. Stevens either by the instructions issued to him, or by his own undertaking is disabled from claiming such general usage: and secondly whether it would be for the advantage of the execution of the model of the Wellington Monument that he should be so much limited in funds, supposing that he has by the instructions accepted by him and by undertaking given prejudiced what would otherwise be his legitimate claim.

I have had a great many conversations with Mr. Stevens on this subject and I believe I am in possession of his views in the matter.

I believe him to have been at the outset more or less sanguine, and that he hoped during the first year to have made more progress than he did, but he certainly never contemplated that it could be completed in a year, or for so small a sum as £1,600. He did not at first observe the construction which might be put upon the words "a proportionate sum during such further time, *if any*", in the instructions which were issued to him, but afterwards when he had drawn £1,600 and was in want of more, he was led from these words to form the erroneous conclusion that Her Majesty's Commissioners wished to get him to execute the model for an inadequate sum.

Under this same impression he gave his undertaking in November 1860 to complete the model for a total sum of £2,800, and felt

PLATE 43. *Sketch designs for the arch of the monument, by Alfred Stevens. Victoria and Albert Museum, Department of Prints and Drawings, E.2638–1911.*

PLATE 44. *Studies for the architecture and orna-ment for the monument, by Alfred Stevens. Victoria and Albert Museum, Department of Prints and Drawings, E.2646–1911.*

himself obliged to obtain funds from other sources by accepting work from other people.

He proceeded, however, with the monu-ment, although he did not give it his undivided attention, and has made very considerable progress; but it has been greatly delayed by want of funds, partly from his health suffering from the difficulties he was in; and the work itself was damaged, especially on one occasion by frost, by which a great deal of time and labour was wasted, and which might have been put out of reach of accident at a moderate expense if he had been able to afford it.

It appears to me that the work must suffer and be indefinitely protracted unless Mr. Stevens is adequately supplied with funds; and there can be little doubt that the general usage of the profession points out the proper scale that should be adopted.

No doubt Mr. Stevens is prepared for £2,800 total payment, to complete the model, but he is not prepared, nor can he give his undivided time to it. When I was desired by the First Commissioner to urge on Mr. Stevens the immediate completion of the model, I found he was in the difficulties I endeavoured to explain, and I strongly recommended him to lay the whole case before the First Commis-sioner, and an interview accordingly took place at the Office of Works. And as Mr. Stevens is now ready to give his undivided attention to the model and to complete it in a given time, I venture to recommend that the sum which would enable Mr. Stevens to do so, namely £2,466 . . . should be paid to him.'

Penrose heard from Stevens at the beginning of February 1863, that Mr. Holford[1] wanted to

[1] Stevens had been commissioned by Sir Robert S. Holford in 1858 to decorate Dorchester House, and to design fireplaces for the same building. Hugh Stannus records that he had been a munificent and patient patron paying in advance for the projected works, some of which were never executed—apparently an unfortunate failing of Stevens's. During 1863 Stevens made a model to show the proposed decoration of the Victoria and Albert Museum, Bombay.

PLATE 45. *Studies for the head of 'Falsehood' and the figure of 'Truth', by Alfred Stevens. Victoria and Albert Museum, Department of Prints and Drawings, D.1234-1907.*

commission some more work from him, but Stevens would not accept if the government gave him an adequate sum of money. Penrose wrote to William Cowper, the First Commissioner, to tell him this and on the following day, 4th February, the Office of Works told Stevens that he would be given his £2,466, if the Treasury approved, and if Stevens undertook to have the model finished within fifteen months. At this time Stevens agreed that Penrose certainly 'had a right to complain', so

perhaps we may assume that the two of them had a heart-to-heart talk.

The sculptor now had some money, and fifteen months in which to concentrate solely on the model, and for a year there were no more letters from the government, Penrose, or from anyone, until 19th February 1864. On that day Alfred Austin told Stevens that 'as the time is approaching when you engaged to have the model of the monument . . . placed in St. Paul's, he [the First Commissioner] requests to be informed when you will be prepared to let him see it, and he thinks it may be advantageous that he should see it in its present unfinished state, rather than that he should be forced to wait until any alterations he may require will occasion you more trouble than they would produce at the moment'.

PLATE 46. *Two studies of a female figure for 'Truth', by Alfred Stevens. Victoria and Albert Museum, Department of Prints and Drawings, D.1188-1907.*

Yet again Stevens chose to ignore the letter, and when the agreed fifteen months had elapsed, a further enquiry from the First Commissioner, on 27th June 1864, was also left unanswered. However, Cowper took the precaution of writing to Penrose as well, asking him to find out what exactly was going on.[1] Stevens, when confronted by the Cathedral architect, begged for a further three months' grace.[2]

On 1st July, after five years of silence on the subject, *The Art Journal* decided that it had been quiet long enough. What progress, it demanded, had been made during these five years? None, it supposed, as not even Penrose appeared to know anything, although it was rumoured that the *model* might be, at last, nearing completion. The nation had been waiting for years to see Nelson's lions,[3] and as with that monument perhaps the next generation would see the Wellington monument placed in position in St. Paul's.

The Office of Works was now justifiably angry at the 'extraordinary delay', and the First Commissioner, on 8th July, minuted his staff to 'tell me the date on which he promised to have the model ready and the period to which this promise referred'. Irritated by Stevens constantly ignoring their letters, the Office of Works wrote on 13th August to remind him that as he had previously 'neglected the common courtesy of answering', would he now do so? Once again the government was completely ignored by the sculptor, and on 21st March 1865, Alfred Austin tried again. He reminded Stevens once more of the promise to finish the

[1] 'The time is nearly approaching [when] Mr. Stevens promised to have the model ready for inspection. A letter has been written to him from this office without obtaining an answer, will you have the goodness to tell me whether you know anything of the stage of progress, for if not, I must again ask him for some information on the subject.' 4th May 1864 (R.I.B.A., Penrose Papers).
[2] '. . . which he considers himself to have lost through illness.' *Ibid.*, 6th May 1864.
[3] It was not until the beginning of 1867 that the lions in Trafalgar Square were unveiled.

model within fifteen months, but the sculptor had now broken his agreement, and had 'treated with contempt the two letters. The First Commissioner feeling sorry that an eminent artist should place himself in such a position, desires to afford you a last opportunity of explanation before taking the serious step which can no longer be deferred', and, on 27th March, the Commissioner wrote a Minute to the effect that he wanted to see what Stevens had managed to produce so far.

This hint of strong government measures stirred Stevens at last into action, and his reply was soon at Whitehall. He appreciated that he had not kept his promise and this troubled him more than he could say. He had underestimated the time his workmen would take, but was hastening on. Feeling perhaps that this letter might not be sufficient to placate Whitehall, Stevens wrote again two days later suggesting that, if it was thought desirable, he would be pleased to go to Whitehall for a meeting with the Commissioner. Yes, replied Whitehall, come at 3 o'clock on the next afternoon.[1] There appears to be no record now of what went on at that meeting, so we do not know what Stevens said to Cowper, but he must have soothed the ruffled feathers, for there was no more correspondence between them for nearly another year, until 27th February 1866, when the Office of Works wrote yet again asking for news of the model. On this occasion Stevens answered, and asked for a further five months for the necessary work 'if I am well enough'.[2]

But Whitehall, by this time, eight years after the model had been started, had had enough of Stevens constantly assuring them

PLATE 47. *Study of a female head, for 'Truth', by Alfred Stevens. Victoria and Albert Museum, Department of Prints and Drawings, D.1245– 1907.*

[1] 28th March 1865 'I shall be glad to see him tomorrow (Wed.) at 3 . . .' Minute by the First Commissioner (Public Record Office, Works 6).

[2] His health had not been good for some time. At the end of 1864, writing to his friend, Alfred Pegler, Stevens was mentioning bilious attacks, and a year later he wrote 'my strength has been a long time coming back to me'. (K. R. Towndrow, *op. cit.*, pp. 199, 210.)

to be patient for just a little while longer. On 23rd March Stevens heard from Alfred Austin that although the First Commissioner was not willing to believe that Stevens was deliberately regardless of his agreements, he must incline to the 'alternatives that you have not found your capacity or your perseverance equal to your conceptions of them, and he wishes to point out that if you indulge in the further delay of five months . . . you will lay yourself open to animadversion, and will contribute to throw discouragement in the way of adoption

PLATE 48. *Valour and Cowardice, original sketch by Alfred Stevens. Victoria and Albert Museum, Department of Architecture and Sculpture, A.7-1912.*

of such public monuments in the future.' Austin continued by saying that if Stevens felt that he was not up to the task, then he should ask for help.

By now *The Art Journal* was again on the warpath. Cowper had mentioned the matter in the House of Commons, which had the effect of publicising the fact that, after all these years of work and waiting, even the model was not yet finished. The *Journal* thought that Stevens was obviously quite indifferent, and that surely there must be some way of exacting a penalty— a private employer would have sued him for damages long before. In April 1866 *The Art Journal* thundered again—'The *Pall Mall Gazette* has dealt with the subject, characterising it as a disreputable job from beginning to end. We have said as much . . . three or four times, since the award was made that placed the work in hands now confessedly incompetent.'

In July of 1866 Penrose went to see Stevens and asked 'if a question should be asked in Parliament relative to the state of the work &c., and the promise made in March last that in about 5 months from that time he would have the model ready to be seen, whether such questions could be answered in a satisfactory manner . . . He assured me that he saw no reason to doubt that he should be ready by that time.'

Penrose suggested a private viewing of the model, but the sculptor was not happy about that, 'and a glimpse which he allowed me of the model showed me that it could not be at present seen properly, as much of the exterior ornament has been stripped off to get at the central core to finish it. I venture to suggest that on Saturday Mr. Stevens considered himself to have 3 more weeks according to the terms of his last promise.'[1] Did Penrose hope that this last statement would now be taken seriously by anyone, or was he naive, and being fooled by Stevens?

After this meeting Stevens wrote a letter of self-justification to Penrose:

'My design is of great size, is made of figures (nine in marble), and elaborately decorated sarcophagus, and a pile of arms, all of bronze,

[1] 23rd July 1866, R.I.B.A., Penrose Papers, letter to Lord John Manners.

with an architectural framework composed of bronze and marble.

Such a work under the most favourable circumstances would take a long time, and models . . . to be afterwards cast in bronze, require to be much more carefully finished than those from which marble copies are to be made.'[1]

Stevens complained about the imposition of having to complete all the architectural parts of the model, which increased the cost and the time used. The reduction of the original amount of money allocated to the project from £20,000 to £14,000 meant that there was barely sufficient money to cover the costs, and in order to live he had been forced to undertake other works, and also he had been ill, and unable to do much for a year.

In his comments upon this letter Penrose noted that Stevens had admitted that casting in bronze was quicker than copying in marble.

In the meantime a member of the House of Lords had taken up the fight. Earl Cadogan wrote to Penrose about Stevens and the monument.[2] It was Cadogan's view that Stevens needed a stronger stimulus to bring him to a sense of what was due to his own professional reputation and to the public, and thus force him to get a move on. Penrose felt that the time had come when he had to write firmly to Stevens, who had been complaining about the tone of the Office of Works letters, and Penrose told him that 'you judge these matters from your own point of view, and feel much aggrieved . . . Try to put yourself in the point of view of the Commissioners of Works, and ask yourself if it is surprising that they should prove somewhat impatient.'[3]

Penrose, who had gradually become more and more involved with both sides, wrote to the First Commissioner (once again Lord John

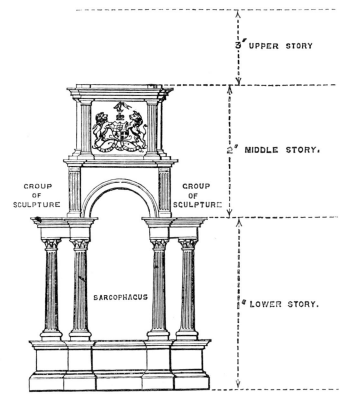

PLATE 49. *Diagram of the monument included in a report to the Office of Works from the Cathedral architect, F. C. Penrose, 28th November 1860. From* Correspondence relative to the Wellington Monument, *Her Majesty's Stationery Office, 1870, Victoria and Albert Museum Library, MacColl Collection.*

Manners) to let him know that Lord Cadogan was being troublesome, and that, as he was not satisfied with the state of the monument, Cadogan intended to ask a question in the Lords. Penrose added that he felt 'the real cause of the delay to be this—Mr. Stevens on receiving the instructions . . . to prepare a model for a monument to cost £14,000 failed to see that a simpler design was expected from him than the small model which he had produced in competition with a view to £20,000'.[4]

---

[1] R.I.B.A., Penrose papers.
[2] 12th March, 15th June 1866. R.I.B.A., *ibid.*
[3] 15th June 1866. R.I.B.A., *ibid.*

[4] 23rd June 1866. R.I.B.A., *ibid.*

F

PLATE 50. *The full-size model of the monument in Alfred Stevens's studio, with a painted 'St. Paul's Cathedral' background. The indicated equestrian group shows that Stevens had not abandoned the idea. He had, by this stage, decided to add pediments beneath the two major sculptural groups, and to place them on heightened pedestals. Victoria and Albert Museum Library, photograph in the MacColl Collection.*

Stevens had been, no doubt, over-sanguine as to his rate of progress, and at first too shy in asking for sufficient funds to be advanced to him—he had, therefore, all along been struggling against the tide. That this unfavourable current had been of Stevens's own choosing did not alter the fact of the great lapse of time. However, as Stevens was creating an entirely original work, he had necessarily to carry out most of the work himself, and consequently much depended upon his health.

The next step was taken when the First Commissioner went to Stevens's studio to see the model. He told Penrose, on 22nd August 1866, that he was well satisfied with it, although it was still very incomplete.[1] Stevens was still anxious to have the equestrian group, so the Commissioner asked Penrose for his opinion on the probable effect on the whole composition, as well as an estimate of the extra cost. If there was no possibility of the equestrian figure, then what else could be suggested? On 10th January 1867, Penrose learned that Lord John had decided against the equestrian group after all, but, although no start had actually been made on the monument, there was now no chance of it being abandoned on that score. Manners hoped that eventually Stevens would come along with a suitable alternative to the horse and rider, though, if he did not, then Manners did not think that the lack would be disastrous.[2]

Stevens had been working slowly on the model, but at last, still in January 1867, Penrose was able to inform Manners that the model had been completed to such an extent that some idea of the general design could be obtained (Plates 50–55), and that perhaps Stevens ought now to be authorised to proceed with the construction of the actual monument itself. Penrose also pointed out that should Stevens be told to go ahead, then he would need some more money. The work was to be so large

[1] R.I.B.A., Penrose papers.
[2] R.I.B.A., *ibid.*

that Stevens was going to have a very heavy initial outlay of money for marble, bronze and workmen.

The Dean of St. Paul's went to see the model and had no objection to the design provided there was no horse on top. He told Manners in a very tepid comment, 'The recumbent figure of the Duke is fine, though perhaps not very original. At all events, since you relieved the Cathedral itself from the incumbrance of so large a structure, and, with great judgement, suggested the chapel which it is to occupy, I do not look upon the object with the same apprehension which I must confess I felt at one time.'

Stevens having learnt from Penrose that a further £2,800 was to be available, promptly asked for it, with another £1,400 five months later, and another similar sum five months after that. The First Commissioner on 12th March agreed to the first £2,800, and to the further instalments provided that Penrose certified the work on the monument itself, and that further payments were justified.

So, at long, long last, almost ten years after the competition in Westminster Hall, Stevens was to be allowed to start on the Duke's memorial. Ten years had been lost in indecision and futile expenditure of time and money on the preparation of a full-sized model which faithfully reproduced the quarter-sized monument used in the competition. This was now not to be used for the purpose of its construction—that is, in St. Paul's Cathedral, to see how it looked, as had been the original intention; Stevens had wasted so much of his now precious time in the preparation of the model in such elaborate detail that it would have been quite a problem to move it from the studio to St. Paul's and to erect it in the Chapel.[1]

Stevens had told Penrose in February 1867, that if he were paid £10,000, that is £2,800 at

[1] K. R. Towndrow, *op. cit.*, p. 215, states that the large model was photographed in May 1867, by Joseph Cundall.

PLATE 51. *The full-size model in Alfred Stevens's studio. This shows that Stevens was then proposing to incorporate two supporters of the Duke's arms (see Plate 56). Victoria and Albert Museum Library, photograph in the MacColl Collection.*

PLATES 52–55. *The full-size model of the sarcophagus and base. Height 10 feet. Victoria and Albert Museum, Department of Architecture and Sculpture, No. 321–1878.*

once, and three half-yearly instalments of £2,000, with a final payment of £1,560 when the work was complete, he would then have the monument finished in two years.

Earl Cadogan visited the sculptor during May 1867; he liked the discarded equestrian statue of Wellington so much that he wanted to bring the question of Dean Milman's refusal to have it in the cathedral to the attention of the House of Lords, but Stevens, who had not given up hope that the decision might still be reversed, persuaded Cadogan that this move might be unwise at that moment.[1]

Stevens did not apply for the instalment of £1,400 due to him in August, and it was not until the beginning of February 1868 that Penrose wrote to the First Commissioner to let him know that considerable progress had been made on the monument, and that Stevens now had fifteen workmen employed by him. Consequently Penrose had no hesitation in reporting that the money was now due.[2]

The months passed away, 1868[3] went by

[1] Penrose papers, R.I.B.A. Letter from Stevens to Penrose, 10th May 1867.

[2] In December 1867, however, Stevens was writing that 'I remained at home to fall ill and have been more or less ill ever since till now. I paid off my doctor on Saturday and am, excepting for a little lameness, well.' (K. R. Towndrow, *op. cit.*, p. 210.)

[3] During 1868 Stevens found time to decorate the hall and staircase of Melchet Court for Lady Ashburton.

and at the end of the year Penrose told the government that Stevens needed no more money at the moment, but that he was preparing to send some of the monument itself to the cathedral. This meant that the time had come to consider the preparation of the chapel itself. If the intention were to remove only the desks there, the cost would be about £10, but this figure would become hundreds of pounds if a new pavement in marble were considered.

On 11th January 1869, Stevens let Penrose know that work would probably begin in about three months' time in setting up the monument, and that he soon hoped to start casting the bronze portions. Provided he had some money to pay the workmen Stevens

thought that two-thirds of the monument would be in place by the end of 1869.[1]

Penrose consequently went ahead and asked the firm of Cubitt's to estimate for an iron framing to spread the load of the monument over the vault beneath. On 8th March Penrose sent Cubitt's estimate of £50 to the Office of Works, which was for the new work, with an additional £10 for the removal of the old fittings;[2] as the necessary sanction was obtained, the work was finished by the end of June. The following week Penrose reported that he did not know yet what payments Stevens might

[1] Penrose papers, R.I.B.A.
[2] *Ibid.*, 8th March, 13th March 1869.

be expecting, but there were, however, one or two points which he would like cleared up:

'Nothing has been settled as to what is to be done to the walls, pavement, ceiling, &c. of the chapel; and if I may be allowed to advert to it, up to this time no arrangement has been made, or in any way suggested as to any remuneration on account of the commission with which I have been honoured as to a general superintendence of the work, and more particularly of that part of it which is in Mr. Stevens's hands, and which it may be easily understood has been rather an arduous task. It occurs to me, however, subject to your decision that the consideration of this as well as of that relating to the completion of the chapel, may with great propriety be deferred until Mr. Stevens's work is considerably more advanced.

I saw Mr. Stevens on Saturday at Haverstock Hill, and understood from him that you were expected the same day. Mr. Stevens assured me that he intended very shortly to commence building the monument, and I am glad to be able to report the arrival at the cathedral of some of the marbles. Several of the columns and portions of the step have already been received.'

Five days after this Stevens wrote to Penrose that when the steps were in place two or three days later, he would be coming to the cathedral when, he hoped, Penrose would be able to spare a little time to help him to set out the work.

By July, the sculptor wanted some more money, and applied to the Office of Works.[1] They sat on this request for a few weeks, and then asked Penrose how much he thought Stevens should be given. Penrose was satisfied that Stevens was now making good progress, but as he was in need of money for buying bronze he should be given no less than £2,200.

This would leave only £1,543 with which to complete the monument at its original figure.

On 18th November Lord John Manners[2] asked Penrose for a progress report, and then sent James Fergusson[3] to St. Paul's Cathedral to make a site report of his own.

By now, yet another year had gone by, and the Office of Works was now preparing its estimates for the year 1870–71. So once again they asked Penrose if he thought Stevens would honour his agreement and finish the monument during the year for the agreed sum of £14,000. Noting that Penrose had brought up the subject of his own commission George Russell asked him to send an account of the gross liabilities which the Treasury would have over and above the agreed £14,000. Penrose sent the following reply to the First Commissioner, who was now Acton Smee Ayrton,[4] on 20th December 1869, and then sat back, no doubt a worried man, to wait for the reply that was bound to come:

'Firstly, I am of the opinion that it is impossible to hope that Mr. Stevens will complete his monument during the year ending March 31st 1871. There is every reason to expect that he will make great progress, and that the monument will assume an extremely effective appearance by that time, but the magnitude of the work and its elaborate character, to which should be added the scrupulous care with which every part, whether constructive or artistic, is being finished, can hardly fail of protracting its completion considerably beyond that date.

At the same time, I do not hesitate to say

[1] Penrose papers, R.I.B.A., 12th July 1869.

[2] It was in this year, 1869, that Manners had appointed Stevens to the committee which had been set up to report to the Office of Works on the condition of Henry VII's tomb in Westminster Abbey.

[3] James Fergusson, F.R.S. (1808–86), writer upon architecture, Inspector of public building and monuments. His design for the monument to Prince Albert is reproduced in *Designs for English Sculpture 1680–1860* by John Physick, 1969.

[4] Acton Smee Ayrton (1816–86), politician, First Commissioner of Works between 1869 and 1873.

PLATE 56. *Detail of the full-size model — the Garter and supporters. This feature was modified in the actual monument. Victoria and Albert Museum, Department of Architecture and Sculpture, No. 407–1889.*

that the payment of £430 to Mr. Stevens between this date and 31st March next (1870) will be warranted both by the value of what has already been executed, or is in progress, and by its policy in promoting the steady promotion of the work.

And furthermore I consider that for the same reasons the balance of (I believe) £994 which will remain to Mr. Stevens out of the stipulated sum of £14,000 should be included in the estimates of 1870–71.

In Mr. Russell's letter I was also kindly invited to lay the question of my claim for remuneration before you.

I believe that professional usage warrants my claiming a commission of $2\frac{1}{2}$ per cent. on the value of these works as executed, on the designs of all of which, I may observe, I was consulted by the First Commissioner of Her Majesty's Works for the time being, and was employed in arranging the terms of payment with the artists, in inspecting their performance, and in certifying the amounts to be paid to them. The sums already paid amount to £17,366, viz.,

	£
To Calder Marshall, R.A.	2,420
To W. F. Woodington, R.A.	2,420
To Messrs. Cubitt & Co.	60
To Alfred Stevens, to this date	12,466
	17,366

The commission on the above, £434 3s.

As to the question of expenditure on collateral works, I am not aware of anything likely to be called for until the final or proximate completion of the monument, when the ceiling and walls of the chapel must be cleaned even if there be no other expenditure for decoration, and a marble pavement for the chapel (now that the wooden floor of the late Consistory Court is removed) is absolutely necessary. The cost of these works must obviously depend upon their design. I suppose, however, that if the expenditure be kept down to its lowest possible limits, £550 would suffice for these purposes.

The gross amount asked for then appears to be as follows:

	£	s.
Marshall and Woodington's work	4,840	0
Messrs. Cubitts, foundations, &c.	60	0
Mr. Stevens's undertaking	14,000	0
Architect's commission, as above	472	10
Cathedral expenditure, i.e. minimum sum required as above	550	0
	19,922	10'

Events were now moving remorselessly towards tragedy. Lord John Manners had been replaced at the Office of Works by the most unsympathetic Acton Smee Ayrton, and the temperature of Whitehall towards Stevens was cool. Ayrton acknowledged Penrose's letter, and then asked him how much money Stevens would want during the next financial year, bearing in mind that Stevens was under contract for £14,000. Penrose undoubtedly saw the warning light begin to flash, for he sent his reply to Russell on 29th December, saying that it seemed that he ought to send

Ayrton a detailed statement of the whole matter:

'In 1858, during the session of Parliament, Lord John Manners, then First Commissioner, inspected 10 designs of those sent in for the Wellington Monument, which the judges had selected for preference, and formed his own opinion upon them, viz., that although Mr. Marshall's and Mr. Woodington's designs had been selected for premium, Mr. Stevens's design was the best for the purpose of the proposed monument.

It was accordingly decided by the First Commissioner that Mr. Stevens should execute the monument, but that some works in connexion with it should be done by Messrs. Marshall and Woodington.

These arrangements were mentioned in Parliament, and after a debate of some length, agreed to, on the understanding that Mr. Stevens should place his model of the portrait figure in its place in St. Paul's.

It should be mentioned that simultaneously with the arrangements last referred to it had been decided, in consequence of a representation from the late Dean of St. Paul's, that the monument, instead of being placed under one of the arches of the nave of the cathedral, which had been the site proposed to the competitors, should occupy the chapel which had formerly been used for the Bishop's Consistory Court, and this gave the opportunity for placing Messrs. Marshall and Woodington's contributions on the walls of the chapel.

The question now arose how to provide for the cost of these associated works as well as for the proper decoration of the chapel out

PLATES 57, 58. *Valour and Cowardice. Full-size plaster group. Victoria and Albert Museum, Department of Architecture and Sculpture, No. 321b–1878.*

of the £20,000 voted by Parliament for the monument, and which sum had been proposed to the artists who embarked in the competition.

A paper was drawn up and sent to Mr. Stevens from the Office of Works, 9th September 1858, offering him £11,000 for his monument, thus reserving £9,000 for the collateral works.

Mr. Stevens declined any share in this arrangement, but would undertake to do his part for £15,000, which he was subsequently induced to abate for £14,000.

At the same time it seems perfectly clear both from his statements at the time (which also may be confirmed by reference to his letters) and by his subsequent prosecution of the work, that although the terms of his commission left him at liberty to reduce the cost of his monument to meet the abatement from the form for which it was designed, he himself never thought of making any such reduction, and he affirms that he did not think himself at liberty to make it, with the single exception, at least, of the equestrian figure on the top, which although in his opinion of great importance to the design, he felt himself obliged to give up. So that whether by a self-imposed task, or by a mistake in interpreting rightly the orders given him, he has carried on the work with the prospect of a heavy loss before him.

In addition to this it was part of his instructions to prepare a complete model of the whole monument, and to place it in the Consistory Court.

The condition as to the complete model has been sufficiently carried out, but that of his putting it up in St. Paul's (except as to the model of the effigy) has been waived.

This preparation of a complete model of so large an architectural work is quite unusual, and has been very costly, and I believe the cost of it almost entirely escaped from Mr. Stevens's calculations at the outset. He now estimates that it has cost him £2,000 more than

if the work had been carried out as it would have been in ordinary cases, chiefly from working-drawings, and with full-sized models of the sculptural parts only.

This struggle with insufficient funds for carrying out what Mr. Stevens considered to be his duty, has been at the bottom of all the delay which took place in the preparation of the model, namely, during the time which elapsed from November 1858, when the contract sum of £14,000 was agreed to, and

March 1867, when the model was considered as finished, and Mr. Stevens was authorised to proceed with the monument.

The same difficulties, although they are not yet much in action (as Mr. Stevens has been supplied with sufficient funds to enable him to make present progress) will inevitably recur long before the monument is finished.

It was about two or three months ago that I came to feel certain of this contingency and have had many anxious conversations with Mr. Stevens on the subject, and I believe I am able to indicate the course he proposes to pursue, namely, to make all the progress he can with the money he has in hand, and with as much as may be supplied to him out of the balance of the £14,000 next year, and then to leave this work for the purpose of prosecuting private commissions until such time as he is able to earn sufficient money to resume it.

His pride in his work is such that he may be trusted to do this if his health should last, but it certainly places the matter on a precarious issue, and which ought to be taken into consideration before it is too late.

On one point I would beg to assure the First Commissioner that I am prepared to venture my professional reputation, namely, that from what I have seen of the work in progress, and what I know of Mr. Stevens, I am certain that however far from complete the monument may be when the stipulated sum of £14,000 has been expended, it will be fully worth the money, even quantity for quantity, as compared with the price of other monuments, and further it will be so remarkable for its beauty and finish that there will seem to be a greater propriety in assisting Mr. Stevens to prosecute the work uninterruptedly than in holding him strictly to the letter of his contract . . .'

This report and defence by Penrose was not calculated to turn aside Ayrton's animosity. The suggestions that the monument was not going to be finished soon, and that it was going

to cost a lot more yet, added to the hint that Stevens was prepared to put it to one side and look for other work must have caused an explosion in Whitehall on 30th December 1869, for Russell replied at once to Penrose that Ayrton had read his report with great concern, as Penrose had suggested for the first time that Stevens was not going to be able to fulfil his contract. Penrose was asked to state when he thought the monument would be finished, and how much money it was expected to swallow during the next financial year. Russell ended his letter by adding that the First Commissioner declined to relieve Penrose of his responsibility which he would be expected to fulfil should Stevens 'ultimately fail in his performance'.

Penrose answered on New Year's Eve; he stated that he had not suggested that Stevens would not fulfil his contract, but that there might be delay, although Stevens recognised his obligation to complete the monument for the £14,000. He was not in a position to estimate the date of completion. Referring to the last paragraph of Russell's letter, Penrose assured Ayrton that he would not shirk his responsibility, 'but that I am not aware of any beyond that attaching to an architect in the

PLATES 59, 60. *Truth and Falsehood. Full-size plaster group. Victoria and Albert Museum, Department of Architecture and Sculpture, No. 321a–1878.*

super-intendence of a building erected from a design of which he is not himself the author'.

Matters rested for a month, with the protagonists wondering what was going to happen next. It was Penrose who found out first, when Earl Cadogan wrote to him asking how the monument was coming along. When he had visited Stevens eighteen months before, he had thought that it was in a fairly advanced state, so surely the work was nearing completion now. However, he was going to raise the matter in the House of Lords, and hoped that he would find someone who would do the same in the House of Commons.[1] Cadogan wrote again in March to say that he hoped that he would ask the question before Easter.[2] 'Someone has to be blamed,' he said, and the fact that Dean Milman had not allowed the equestrian figure, was not relevant to the delay. However, he hoped that Penrose would co-operate, and answer the questions he was going to ask. Two days later Cadogan wrote again.[3] He had no objection to Penrose writing to Ayrton, but expressed the view that the same delaying tactics would be employed as on the previous occasion when he had failed in his attempt to have the matter raised in Parliament. He then asked for the past history of the monument; if Penrose were not willing to supply this information, then he put it to him 'whether it will not tend to create an impression on the part of the public that the Dean and Chapter are more or less involved in the blame that no doubt accrues exclusively to the successive Chief Commissioners, and I am compelled, in making my statement, to say that I am treating from memory, in consequence of the refusal of yourself, acting on behalf partly of the Chief Commissioner, but principally on that of the cathedral authorities, to supply me with information that certainly cannot be looked upon as confidential'.

Assailed by both Ayrton and now Cadogan,

[1] R.I.B.A., Penrose papers, 31st January 1870.
[2] *Ibid.*, 22nd March 1870.   [3] *Ibid.*, 22nd March 1870.

Penrose answered the latter; what he said is not recorded, but it drew from Cadogan the following: 'I am sorry you gave yourself the trouble to enter into a lengthened explanation as to respect to Marochetti whose name was never even mentioned by me in connection with any enquiries I was anxious to make. I cannot help thinking with reference to the point, that you must have understood throughout, the object I had in view in again stirring the subject, and that you thought you discerned an . . . attack on the decision of the judges, and a desire to open the case, in one or two of the queries I put to you. I think that you would hardly have found so much difficulty as you seem to have done in answering them.'[1]

Cadogan asked his question in the Lords, and the Marquess of Lansdowne promised to publish all the correspondence between Stevens and the Office of Works. Now that Cadogan had reminded it, *The Art Journal* again breathed fire and began to clamour for the blood of both Penrose and Stevens.

In the meantime Ayrton wrote a Minute in which he recorded that he had visited Stevens's studio, and St. Paul's Cathedral. He was surprised to find the state of the monument entirely at variance with that which he had been led to expect from the payments which had been made on Penrose's advice, and asked the Director of Works, and the Surveyor of Works to investigate immediately and to report to him on how much time and money was going to be required to complete the whole of the canopy and the recumbent effigy of Wellington, and the groups of sculpture?

The required report was to include the cost of all wages and material and other outgoings, but was to exclude payments to Stevens, though they should ask how much government money was still in Stevens's possession. Letters should be written to both Stevens and Penrose giving

[1] R.I.B.A., Penrose papers, 31st March 1870.

PLATE 61. *No. 1: Present state of the monument. The dark parts are fixed. The rest of the Marble work shown above is ready to be taken to St. Paul's, 27th April 1870. B.B.B.B. Parts not worked. From* Correspondence relative to the Wellington Monument, *Her Majesty's Stationery Office, 1870, Victoria and Albert Museum Library, MacColl Collection.*

such details of this investigation as may be thought necessary. The letter to Penrose was sent on 14th April 1870, in which he was asked to be present at Stevens's studio at 11 o'clock on the morning of 26th April. Stevens was not told until 21st April that the Director of Works, the Surveyor of Works, and Penrose would be meeting at his studio, and he was requested to give them such information as they might require.[1]

The meeting took place as arranged, and on 31st May Douglas Galton, C.B.,[2] and Henry A. Hunt presented their report on the state of the Wellington Monument to Ayrton. It gave a list of the original prize-winners, and the fact that Calder Marshall and Woodington had made reliefs for the Wellington Chapel, which had been completed and paid for in 1863.

The report went on:

'In 1858 Mr. Stevens undertook to prepare a full-sized model of the monument and to erect it in St. Paul's Cathedral. He also undertook to complete the monument, including the cost of the model, for the sum of £14,000.

Instead of erecting the model in St. Paul's Cathedral, it was built in Mr. Stevens's studio at Hampstead, which had to be enlarged for the purpose.

Mr. Penrose the Cathedral architect, was requested by the First Commissioner to superintend Mr. Stevens's work, and to certify from time to time the amount of money to be paid to him on account.

From 1858 to 1869 payments have been made accordingly to Mr. Stevens, amounting in aggregate to £13,006.

The work performed by Mr. Stevens during that period is as follows: The full-sized model of the general design has been completed and is now in Mr. Stevens's studio.

The architectural portion of the monument which is in marble, is in part prepared and fixed in the Cathedral, but to complete this portion of the whole design it is estimated that

a further expenditure of £2,500 will be required.

The purely sculptor's work—consisting of the sarcophagus, the recumbent figure, the subordinate groups, trophies, and the crowning feature on top, all of which are intended to be of bronze metal is not yet commenced, excepting only some of the required modelling. The estimated expenditure, for the bronze castings and for fixing them is £10,000.

PLATE 62. *No. 2: Monument without the bronzes. (A) Slab not purchased. From* Correspondence relative to the Wellington Monument, *Her Majesty's Stationery Office, 1870, Victoria and Albert Museum Library, MacColl Collection.*

[1] For some reason Ayrton minuted the Assistant Secretary and told him to find out whether the Office of Works had ever agreed to any deviation in the monument from the full-size model; he was told that there had not been any such agreement (P.R.O., Works 6).

[2] Sir Douglas Galton, K.C.B. (1822–99), Director of Public Works and Buildings from 1869 to 1875.

Much, however, remains to be done in preparing the models and moulds for casting, which must be the work of a sculptor, and therefore provision must be made for the personal services of any sculptor who may be employed to complete the work, and we think therefore that £2,500 should be provided for that purpose.

It will be necessary to lay a marble floor in the chapel and to do some other works there, which are estimated to cost £600.

In the face of the First Commissioner's letter of the 30th December 1869, we abstain from entering into the question of Mr. Penrose's claim for remuneration.

The summary of the expenditure up to the present time is:

	£
Mr. Stevens	13,006
Mr. Marshall	2,420
Mr. Woodington	2,420
Messrs. Cubitt, for floor	60
	17,906

The estimated future expenditure is as follows, exclusive of Mr. Penrose's claim:

	£
For the completion of the marble floor	2,500
For the bronze casting and fixing	10,000
For completing the models and moulds for casting	2,500
For marble floor, &c. in chapel	600
	15,600
Expenditure already made	17,906
	33,506

We append sketches (Plates 61–63) which have been prepared by Mr. Buckler, an Assistant Surveyor in the Department, showing the prize-model of 1856, the full-size model which was erected, and the present condition of the monument in St. Paul's. 31st May 1870.'

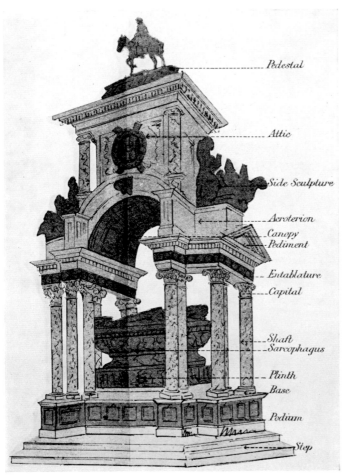

Pedestal

Attic

Side Sculpture

Acroterion
Canopy
Pediment

Entablature
Capital

Shaft
Sarcophagus

Plinth
Base

Podium

Step

PLATE 63. *No. 3. Monument with the bronzes.* *From* Correspondence relative to the Wellington Monument, *Her Majesty's Stationery Office, Victoria and Albert Museum Library, MacColl Collection.*

VI

Government Action—1870

Ayrton sat on this report until 20th July on which day George Russell wrote to both Penrose and Stevens. Penrose was told that Ayrton would make the arrangements to see to the completion of the monument, and that it was necessary to put an end to Penrose's services as the consulting and certifying architect. Moreover, there was to be an enquiry into the nature of Penrose's liabilities arising from the certificates which he had signed.[1]

Stevens was told more or less the same; Ayrton could not foresee the completion of the monument in any reasonable time, and in view of Stevens's failure regarding his contract, Ayrton would have to make other arrangements. As Stevens had been paid nearly all the £14,000, in order to protect the public's interest, Stevens must hand over to the Crown the model, all unfinished work and material. Mr. Buckler would go to Stevens's studio to make an inventory, and to take charge of the monument. If Stevens played fair, Ayrton would recommend to the Treasury to take a lenient view of the serious liabilities which he had incurred. Before Stevens received this letter, ironically however, he had written on the same day as Ayrton, asking for yet more money.

Penrose told Russell that he was glad Ayrton was making 'arrangements to ensure the proper completion' of the monument, but Stevens did not admit that he had failed his agreement, and wrote, 'I must therefore be allowed to complete with my own hands my design. This I shall be prepared to do "within a reasonable period", and if required, for the sum originally agreed upon.' To this he was to get no reply at once, except for another request to deliver the monument at noon on 27th July.

On that day, 27th July, back at the Office of Works, Ayrton instructed his Solicitor to 'take immediate proceedings against Mr. Stevens and if practicable seize all the property referred to in Mr. Buckler's list immediately'.[2] But Horace Frere of the Solicitor's Department prudently sought counsel's advice, which he sent to Ayrton on the following day:

'After perusing all the papers in this case, I am of the opinion that there is great difficulty in dealing with Mr. Stevens now in the manner which the First Commissioner would seem to suggest. The authorities of the Board of Works have no power by law to enter upon Mr. Stevens' premises and to seize the property there which they may consider part of the materials for executing the monument. Assuming that the First Commissioner is determined to take the work out of Mr. Stevens' hands and to bring the matter to a termination, the only steps which could be taken with a reasonable prospect of success would be, first to secure possession of the materials now deposited at St. Paul's and next to request him to transfer all the materials in his studio which are fit for annexing to the work already done and to give up possession of all the other

---

[1] Parliament ordered that all correspondence between the First Commissioner, Penrose and Stevens must be published as a Blue Book; see *Correspondence relative to the Wellington Monument, St. Paul's Cathedral*, H.M.S.O., 1870. On 21st February 1871 the *Further Correspondence relative to the Wellington Monument between Mr. Penrose or Mr. Stevens, with any Department of Her Majesty's Government up to the present time* was published.

[2] Public Record Office, Works 6.

materials which he has in his possession intended for the completion of the Monument. It may be that though he refuses to give up the keys of his premises and so entirely stop his business, he may not refuse so reasonable [*sic*] a request as to the surrender of all the materials which really belong to the Crown. Supposing that he declines to adopt this course the question arises what proceedings at law may be taken by the First Commissioner? I think that though the original arrangement did not expressly state a period within which the monument was to be completed, yet the law would imply that it was to be completed within a reasonable time and that a Jury would say that such reasonable time had long since elapsed though Mr. Penrose on whose certificates the advances were made seems to think that he has a claim for further indulgence.'[1]

If Ayrton wanted proceedings brought against Stevens, then this would have to be through the Attorney-General for breach of the implied condition to execute the monument within a reasonable time; but, thought counsel, such an action would not be heard quickly, probably not until the next Michaelmas term.

Ayrton, however, wanted to strike while the iron was still hot, and the week afterwards, on 2nd August 1870, Horace Frere, on behalf of P. H. Lawrence, the Solicitor to Her Majesty's Works, told Stevens that he had been 'instructed . . . to take the necessary measures to enforce the rights of the Crown in reference to the non-fulfilment of your contract for the erection and completion of the Wellington Monument, and to your declining to deliver up to the Commissioners the model and all the unfinished work and materials belonging to or connected with the Monument, as required by the Board's letters to you of the 20th and 25th ult.

[1] Public Record Office, Works 6.

'In reference to your communication of the 25th ult., in which you observe that you must be allowed to complete with your own hands your design, and that you are prepared to do so within a reasonable time, if required, for the sum originally agreed upon, I would call your attention to the Board's letter of the 20th ult., by which the First Commissioner, for the reasons therein stated, absolutely determined your contract, from which it follows that you cannot be allowed to proceed further with the work, and it must therefore be withdrawn from your hands.

'Under these circumstances, and before taking such proceedings as the Law Officers of the Crown may deem advisable, I have to request that you will inform me distinctly, and without delay, whether you are prepared or not to deliver up to the Commissioners, or to transfer to St. Paul's, the model and all the materials in your studio, or in your possession, which are fit for annexing to the work there already done, and to give up possession to the Commissioners of all other materials, which you have in your possession intended for the completion of the Monument in question.

'In the meantime I have to request that you will not part with the custody of the model or any portion of the works and materials to any other person than such officer as may be authorised by the Commissioners to receive the same on their behalf.

'I have also to request your immediate reply to this communication.'

You will get a full answer when I have consulted my friends, was the brief reply which Stevens sent on 4th August. He was not prepared to abandon the monument without a struggle, and during the next two days prepared a letter which he sent to the Prime Minister, Gladstone, on 6th August:

'May I venture to ask your kind consideration of my case, as sculptor of the Wellington Monument, of which work, now in an advanced state, the First Commissioner of Her Majesty's Works has signified his determination of depriving me. My excuse in thus trespassing upon your time is this:—

1stly. That, as I felt a great injustice is contemplated, I have the right to appeal from the Department to the highest authority.

2ndly   That whilst the proposed course inevitably prejudices to the last degree the result as a work of art, it fails of obtaining any advantage to the public purse.

I will endeavour to put the case as shortly as I can, premising that, should any confirmation of what is here advanced be asked for, I shall be glad to supply it. I had designed a Monument for the value of which was proposed to the competitors, viz. £20,000, I was induced by Lord John Manners, when he offered me the commission, to do it for £14,000, with the condition that I should also prepare a full-size model of the whole.

I admit that I was at that time sanguine enough to believe that by strenuous and self-denying exertion I should be able to produce continuously both the model and the Monument unreduced in size and richness, for I felt myself, as an artist, bound to do this, although for so greatly reduced a sum.

I readily admit that, although there was no time contract, no time being fixed for the completion of the Monument, much more time has been consumed on the work than I myself expected, or any one else had a right to expect. All my own calculations I am free to confess, both of time and cost, were quite upset, and I was only able for a long time to continue the work at all by undertaking other practice; and the result has been that, as stated below, I have paid more money upon wages and

G

materials than I have received from the Government.

At the commencement the sum of £1,600 was made available to me for the purpose of the model. On this model I did not stint my personal exertion nor rigid economy; but the work proved—owing to its vast scale—far beyond my former experience in monuments—too much for me, and, after struggling in vain with its difficulty, my means became so much exhausted that I was obliged to discontinue the work for two years, and was then obliged to apply for a much larger sum to be expended upon the model, viz., that proportion, one-third, which a sculptor is by custom entitled to at the commencement of the work.

The model was then completed, but £4,666 were entirely absorbed in its production, an outlay, in a great measure, unnecessary, except for the conditions on which the work was given me, as half the cost would have sufficed for the necessities of the Government. I was authorised to proceed with the permanent work in the spring of 1867, with £9,334 available under the agreement. Since then the work has been going on continuously and fully seven-eighths of the marble work are done, and the marble work is more than two-thirds of the whole. Thus, more than seven-twelfths of the whole Monument was completed.

The First Commissioner has stated, in the letter in which I am ordered to give up the work, that "what is done, cannot be regarded as equal to half the entire undertaking" a statement entirely ex parte and unfair. This letter has now been published without waiting for the reply which I have since sent and which ought in simple justice to have been appended to it. Previous to Christmas last, questions were asked me by Mr. Penrose, who was appointed from the first to overlook the work, for the information of the late First Commissioner, as to how I proposed to proceed with the work.

I then stated, as I state now, that I am ready

to act up to my engagements, but I never entered into a contract as to time; and if I am expected to complete this costly Monument for the inadequate sum of £14,000, I must have time to complete the work.

I have already put into the work not only every penny that I have received from the Office of Works, but at least £2,000 of my own money. Since then enquiries have been made, both of me and Mr. Penrose, on behalf of the present First Commissioner, asking for estimates of the value of the work yet remaining to be done, and particularly we were recommended to send in safe estimates with a good margin, and with apparently the most kindly expressions of sympathy with me and my work.

On this understanding Mr. Penrose obtained an estimate of the value of the marble works remaining then unfinished, £1,800, and I obtained a tender from a bronze caster £3,000 which, to satisfy the recommendations above alluded to, was sent in at £6,500.

For these sums, together making £8,300, I should have been most willing to go on continuously with the work, and to give my undivided attention to it, and to finish it in 24 months.

Mr. Galton and Mr. Hunt who were also instructed by the First Commissioner to make estimates for his guidance, nearly doubled these figures (already, in my opinion, quite sufficient), and I will admit that such a report may well have staggered the First Commissioner.

I hope, Sir, I have said enough to induce you either to intercede with Mr. Ayrton for me, that he may do me more justice, or to refer the whole matter to some one person of high position and attainments; or at any rate, as nothing, by his own statement in Parliament, could be done till next Session, to leave the matter till then, not more prejudiced than it has thus far become, when it may be properly brought before Parliament. In the meantime

I should not be idle, but propose to be getting the work as forward as my private means will allow.

May I now conclude with an argument which is independent of the plea which I trust has not been addressed altogether in vain to your sense of justice. If a new arrangement should be made, and the work taken out of my hands (I presume that the First Commissioner has ascertained that he can do so legally, and reserving all my legal rights if I am driven to defend them), and supposing that a sculptor of talent and character could be found to accept such a commission, it must cost much more than if I finish the work myself.

From what has been published, Mr. Galton and Mr. Hunt appear to have reported that the cost of finishing the Monument will be, under such circumstances, £15,000, and half a year's delay would be necessary before it could be resumed, whereas I am prepared to proceed from the present time, and to finish the Monument, independent of the crowning figure, which has never been settled, for £4,500, by midsummer 1872, or my complete design for an additional £1,000, and a proportionate extension of time.

I was quite unprepared for this matter being brought before Parliament, and therefore to the public, in the manner it has been brought, at the very close of the Session, without even giving me an opportunity of bringing forward my own case. I feel this all the more from a leading article in "The Times" of today (6th August), drawn up from the one-sided and insufficient materials of the Blue Book, which presents a most unfair view of the transaction, and in which it is repeatedly stated that public money has been wasted, an assertion which I most emphatically deny, except indeed as respects the unnecessary cost of the full-sized model as before noticed.

I have also great reason to complain of the bad representation of my design which has appeared in the Blue Book, which cannot fail to prejudice public opinion against it.' (Plates 61–63.)

Penrose wrote to the Hon. W. Cowper-Temple, M.P., a former First Commissioner, to say that Stevens had been advised to enter into no new contract, but simply to ask if he could carry on with his work 'anywhere and under any conditions except such as would injure his design'.[1] However, there would not have been anything that Cowper-Temple could have done to help Stevens.

The Office of Works, not knowing at this time of Stevens's letter to the Prime Minister, was not satisfied with Stevens's brief reply to them of 4th August, in which it will be remembered he had said that he was consulting his friends. On 10th August 1870, Horace Frere wrote asking for an immediate reply to the letter of 2nd August. As by the 26th of that month Stevens had still not written, Frere told him that in view of this 'it has now become necessary to move in this matter, and I have to ask you to refer me to your Solicitor, who may be authorised to act on your behalf. I must request an immediate reply to this communication to save you personal annoyance and inconvenience.'

As on previous occasions when Stevens was faced with a definite threat of action against him, he at last stirred himself. The day following Frere's letter, that is on 27th August, Stevens sent this letter to the First Commissioner:

'In reply to Mr. Lawrence's letter to me of August 2nd, and to the two letters signed by Mr. Russell which preceded it, I am prepared with the following answers:—

In reply to the first-mentioned letter, I beg to state, in compliance with the requisition, that I should not part with any of the works prepared for the Monument except by sending them to St. Paul's, etc; that since the date referred to I have continued sending down to St. Paul's all the finished marble works. Three loads have already been sent since then, and I am preparing more to follow immediately. Additional work has also been fixed on the Monument; the whole of the marble work (with the exception of one slab) has now either been fixed, finished, or got out.

I am also engaged in cleaning up my finished models so as to be ready for casting, and in this operation I must observe that an immense additional amount of labour has been thrown upon me by the necessity I was under of painting the models bronze colour, for the exhibition of the design in 1866, which has now to be scraped off.

At the rate I am now proceeding, at least one-third of the models will be ready by the end of October, which I shall be prepared to give up to some authorised person or to send to St. Paul's.

At the same rate I shall be able to furnish another fifth part of the whole by the end of January 1871.

In Mr. Russell's letter of the 20th ultimo, I am required to give every facility to the service in question.

In the desire to act to the fullest of my power in conformity with this direction, I beg to submit the following proposition:—

Let someone be appointed by the Office of Works to pay for all materials and labour, and all expenses of whatever kind other than my own personal work.

I will devote my own undivided exertion to finishing the Monument *according to the present design*.

By this I mean to include the preparation of the models, the superintendence of the casting, the final chasing of the work after the founder, and the superintendence of the fixing, both the marble and the bronze work, until the Monument is finished.

To these offers, and with a view to facilitating the completion of the Monument, I

[1] R.I.B.A., Penrose papers, 11th August 1870.

append an estimate of the cost and duration of the work, if carried on in the manner above stated. On this point it will scarcely be questioned that I am in a position to speak with some special knowledge of the subject.

I consider that 15 months from the time of full recommencement of the works will be amply sufficient for the completion, and that the cost will not exceed £5,000.

I base this calculation on the following facts:—

As to Time—Considering the present state of forwardness of the marble work, four or five months will finish the whole of it; and as to the bronze work I do not speak without considerable personal experience of this material, and my opinion can be easily verified by reference to practical bronze founders.

As to the Cost—So much additional progress has been made with the marble work since April last, when £1,800 was sent in as an outside estimate, that it cannot now exceed £1,000.

For the bronze work a tender was offered me by a bronze founder to execute the whole of the bronzes shown in my design for £3,000, including the metal, but exclusive of the fixing; and as this estimate included the equestrian figure, which I have never been bound to supply, I consider it ample for the thorough execution of all the bronze work contemplated in my contract.

In this letter I have addressed myself solely to answer the letters above cited, and do not enter at all upon any discussion of the real merits of the case.'

This plea to be allowed to carry on with his work brought absolutely no encouragement from the government. By now Gladstone (who had been one of the original judges in the 1857 competition), ignoring Stevens, had unloaded the latter's letter on to the First Commissioner. Ayrton minuted Douglas Galton to 'go carefully through the accompanying letter

from Mr. Stevens, and report on the . . . allegations in it . . .'[1]

Lawrence of the Office of Works replied both to the letter to Gladstone and to that of 27th August to Ayrton. Lawrence on 23rd September answered none of Stevens's proposals, but instead stated that the government had been advised that it was entitled to possession of all works and materials. If this advice were correct, then they would not enter into the question of the completion of the Monument until they had taken charge of it. 'I am therefore instructed', he continued, 'to ask categorically for an answer to my letter of the 2nd August, whether you are willing to deliver immediate possession of the model and materials therein mentioned, as in the event of your claiming the right to hold those against the expressed wish of the First Commissioner, it is his desire to try that question by an appeal to a legal tribunal, and I am instructed to take steps to that effect, and shall accordingly be obliged by a reference to your Solicitor as requested in my letter of the 26th August.

'Should you, however, think fit, as I hope you may, to comply with the request of the First Commissioner, I am instructed to say that after delivery of the model and materials to an officer of this Department, he will be prepared to consider any communication you may desire to make to him with reference either to the completion of the Monument or the adjustment of any claim or accounts between the Board and yourself, which may have arisen out of your contract.

'As the time which has elapsed since the 2nd August is considerable, I trust that you will favour me with an early reply to this communication.'

Acton Ayrton then was obviously adamant in his intention to relieve Stevens completely of all to do with the monument, and one might have expected Stevens to help his own case

---

[1] Public Record Office, Works 6.

by complying. But, as had happened so often before, Stevens chose to take no notice of the Board's letters. He was asked again on 1st October for a reply, and finally on 24th October, in which letter Lawrence added that as Stevens had not thought fit to reply to the previous letters, the First Commissioner had ordered legal proceedings to be instituted against him. Consequently, unless Stevens deigned to answer before 28th October, he would hear from the Attorney-General. If, also, he would only bother to send his solicitor's address then he would not have the annoyance of 'personal service of protest'.

Once, again, when faced with the threat of a firm stand by the government, Stevens decided to do something about it. On 25th October he said that he was prepared to give up the model and materials in two weeks, by which time his workmen would have finished certain necessary work. Stevens continued by declaring that his own superintendence was of so much importance to the monument that he felt it his duty to keep the work as long as possible. He was relinquishing it now only because he had not the means to defend its retention in a court of law. This was reported to Ayrton by Lawrence, who advised in a Minute, 'I think it would be to the advantage of the Commissioners to accept this offer, as they would not by process of law obtain possession for a considerably longer time.'

The next step was taken by Lawrence, who acknowledged Stevens's concession, and told him that the First Commissioner probably would write to him. Ayrton himself, though, did not bother with Stevens,[1] because the next communication the sculptor received was again from Lawrence stating that George Buckler of the Office of Works would be

making arrangements to take possession of the Monument on 8th November.

Buckler, however, was not quite so swift off the mark, because it was not until 9th November that Stevens was told that the full-size model would be boarded up on 14th November and that he should make certain that the small competition model, the loose parts of the large model, and the marble of the Monument should be moved into the space in the studio which had been marked out for them. While everything was being sealed off, Stevens would be allowed to keep one workman present in the studio. Having got his own way at last, Ayrton moved quickly. Everything related to the Monument was sealed in the studio at Haverstock Hill, and the key was taken away to Whitehall; until some sort of decision was reached Stevens was to receive £2 a month as rent.

Ayrton then wrote to Stevens telling him to stop working at St. Paul's, as he had not been so authorised since his contract was terminated on 20th July. Stevens replied that all his men had been doing was to fix some marble slabs which had been rather insecure. A day or two later Stevens was told that the time had arrived for him to

'address a memorial to the Lords Commissioners of Her Majesty's Treasury through the First Commissioner, respecting the claim of the Crown against you for the moneys you have received beyond what was due to you under your contract. The First Commissioner, however, thinks it right to call your attention to the serious errors which appear to exist in the letter addressed by you to the First Lord of the Treasury on the 16th August last, as any erroneous representations in your application to their Lordships could only have the effect of defeating its object.

In your letter above mentioned you represent yourself as having been induced by Lord John Manners, when First Commissioner,

---

[1] Ayrton would have been quite out of sympathy with this (to him) strange sculptor, who dressed like (and was often mistaken for) a Roman Catholic priest (Frontispiece), who had peacocks strutting about his studio, and who sometimes kept a small dog in the breast pocket of his coat. (Sir Walter Armstrong, *op. cit.*, pp. 40, 43.)

to undertake a work designed at a cost of £20,000 for £14,000, and as entitled to one-third of that sum on the completion of the model, according to the usual mode of paying sculptors for their works, and as having been unfairly treated.

The First Commissioner is unable to find the slightest proof in the records of this office of these statements. The letter to you from this office on 9th September 1858 shows that you were to prepare a model of a monument to cost £11,000, and that payments proportionate to the progress of the work were to be made to you on the authority of Mr. Penrose. The letter from Mr. Penrose to this office of the 25th November 1858 shows that you fully considered the cost with him, and that you framed the charge, with his approval, at £3,000 for the model, and £11,000 for the monument.

The letter of Mr. Penrose of the 28th November 1860 clearly shows that you and he understood that the model was not to be the finished model of the sculpture, but only a general model to show the suitableness of the design for the situation and its general character, and that it should have been finished and put up in St. Paul's in June 1861, according to your guarantee, on the faith of which you received £1,600.

The original design of making the Duke of Wellington ride on the top of the canopy over his own recumbent figure having been abandoned, you were to substitute a suitable group of sculpture, which ought as an equivalent to have been a most important work of art. This crowning work you have never even designed, nor did you erect the model in St. Paul's by June 1861. It was only in March 1867 that the model was so far advanced, though still imperfect, as to admit of its inspection in your studio; and the removal to St. Paul's, the purpose for which it was originally designed, was abandoned in your favour.

But there is a wide difference between the state of your model and the finished model of a sculpture from which the sculpture in marble, or the founding in bronze is undertaken; and in fact when your contract was determined there was not, nor is there now, a single figure modelled ready for the casting; all the work involving the higher art of the sculptor remain to be done. You could not, therefore, be entitled to an advance of the one-third usually paid on the approval of the model.

The work which it is apparent on inspection you have really done consists of the marble work now erected in St. Paul's, and the pieces deposited there and in the inclosure at your studio in the possession of this office. The value of this can be readily ascertained, if necessary, and with the value of the bronze given up by you, and the cost of the model, which is much less in value than the original allowance for it of £3,000, is all that can be set off against the claim of the Crown for the sum of £13,006 which you have received.

It is possible, however, that from your want of experience in the execution of great works like that with which you were entrusted you may unintentionally have expended the public money in a manner equally unprofitably to yourself and the public; that you have not gained what the public have unfortunately lost, and that you are not now in a position to make good this loss. Should you be able to establish this to their Lordships' satisfaction they may be induced to regard the result as the consequence of the experiment which was made in selecting you for the execution of the work and deal with your application accordingly.

In your letter you have also imputed to the officers of this Department a disposition to treat you unfairly in the investigation they were directed to make; but the First Commissioner has carefully inquired into the circumstances and is satisfied that they acted towards you with great moderation, and that their report is a fair and impartial statement of facts; but, as the public interest would not admit of your 're-employment on a work on which you have repeatedly failed, it is necessary to explain to you the course which it may be expedient to adopt for the purpose of ensuring the completion by some sculptor of established eminence.

The First Commissioner, on receiving your application to the Lords of the Treasury, will be happy to forward it, and, so far as the facts will admit, will be prepared to recommend it to the favourable consideration of their Lordships, in accordance with this assurance; but, in any event, it will be necessary to have regard to the liability of Mr. Penrose for any loss which the public may sustain in consequence of the payments to you having been made in his certificates that they were in accordance with your contract.'

The Treasury, which had endorsed Ayrton's action in terminating Stevens's contract, did not agree with his view that other artists should be invited at once to submit tenders for the completion of the monument, but thought it 'would be preferable in the first instance to obtain advice of some competent authority, whose professional position would give weight to his opinion, as to the course to be adopted for turning to the best advantage the materials which, so far, had been supplied'.

On 16th July 1870 Ayrton told the Treasury that he was looking for a person so suitably qualified, but carried on with his own plan so that in November the Treasury was surprised to receive the draft of a circular which Ayrton proposed to send to sculptors inviting them to send in designs and estimates for the completion of the monument, part of which read:

'You will understand that you are left entirely to the dictates of your genius in making the drawing. It is right I should add that I have forwarded the Circular to several other sculptors and that H.M.'s Government will select the work they think the best, but those not selected will be received in confidence and returned to the sculptors as their own property—without any copy being retained, leaving it to the Sculptors to give to them any publicity they may desire . . .'

A Mr. Thomas Sharp,[1] and a Mr. F. J. Williamson[2] hearing rumours of the Commissioner's proposals, wrote to him, each suggesting that he was very competent to complete the monument for the government. George Russell wrote to the Dean and Chapter to inform them that the Wellington Monument had been put under the charge of the Office of Works and asked 'that such steps as may be necessary for its security during construction may be allowed by the Dean and Chapter to be taken'. The Dean and Chapter were glad to co-operate, but wanted to know the name of the architect (sic) who had been chosen to complete the work and were somewhat worried about any possible changes to the design which had been chosen by Dean Milman on their behalf.[3]

Ayrton was told on 17th December that the Lords of the Treasury regretted that he had not complied with their request, and that they remained of the opinion that Ayrton must still find the competent person to advise him, and in whom the public would have confidence. The Treasury felt that as, in any case, one competition had ended in failure, Ayrton should not repeat this mistake by inviting another competition in which the government, for which it was 'ill-qualified', would have to act as judge. On 20th December Ayrton replied that it would, no doubt, be practicable to request only one sculptor to submit a sketch for

[1] Thomas Sharp (b. 1805), studied at the Royal Academy Schools in 1831, exhibiting between 1830 and 1869 (see Rupert Gunnis, op. cit., p. 348).
[2] Francis John Williamson (1833–1920) also studied at the Royal Academy Schools, and then under J. H. Foley, exhibiting from 1853 to 1897. He carved the recumbent effigy of Dean Milman (d. 1876), in St. Paul's Cathedral.
[3] Chapter Minutes, St. Paul's Cathedral, 23rd November 1870.

approval, and if it were not approved, to invite another, and so on; 'but knowing as I do that there are very conflicting opinions on the subject, it appears to me necessary to compare them by the proposed standard of drawings on the same scale, with an estimate of cost, without which I am unable to judge whom it would be desirable to employ, and I regret, therefore, that in the present state of the question I am unable to recommend any sculptor to your Lordships for employment. This, however, will not prevent your Lordships nominating a sculptor if your Lordships prefer that course.'

The opinionated Ayrton then added that he ventured to think that 'the failure which has already been experienced in the execution of this work did not arise from competition, but from the First Commissioner not being guided by the results . . . in the selection of a competent sculptor'.

It was obvious that Ayrton wished to pursue his own path, and not that which had been selected by the Treasury, and it may well be that the First Commissioner was as disliked by his colleagues as by many other people,[1] because the Treasury took the very unusual step of publishing its Minute which had been sent to Ayrton, and then went on:

'As it appears from this correspondence that the First Commissioner was averse from adopting the course suggested by the Treasury as preliminary to any final arrangement, viz., to take counsel with some one person of authority competent to give judicious professional advice, the Chancellor of the Exchequer undertook to give effect to the view of their Lordships, and placed himself in communica-

tion with Mr. James Fergusson, whose special qualifications for advising in a matter of this sort are well known, and who, from his recent connexion with the Office of Works, was already acquainted with the details of the case.

After full consultation with Mr. Fergusson, and after other independent inquiry, the Chancellor of the Exchequer satisfied himself:

1. That no artist of any celebrity would undertake to finish a work designed, and so far executed, by another hand.

2. That even if such a person were to be found, it was not to be expected that he could carry on the work with the same harmony and perfection as its original designer.

3. That on the whole, therefore, although the experience of the past undoubtedly at first sight pointed to a different conclusion, the best arrangement would seem to be that the Monument, which is admitted to be a work of great merit, should be finished by Mr. Stevens.

4. That such an arrangement must be contingent upon some satisfactory guarantee being obtained for the due completion of the Monument for a stated sum, and within a stated time.

5. That the guarantee must be in a form of a contract entered into with some independent person willing and able to accept a direct responsibility for the completion of the monument by Mr. Stevens, according to the terms to be agreed upon.

The Chancellor of the Exchequer states that Mr. Fergusson, acting under his instructions, has succeeded in effecting an arrangement upon this basis, the details of which are explained in a letter addressed to him by that gentleman, and in the accompanying draft contract, both of which he now lays before the Board.

It is proposed that Mr. L. W. Collmann,[2]

[1] Walter Armstrong in *Alfred Stevens*, p. 36, was of the opinion that Ayrton had been appointed Commissioner of Works by Gladstone more to 'silence an inconvenient critic than because of any fitness for the post. He notoriously despised art and all its manifestations, and believed himself to be possessed of a new and effectual method of managing its sometimes stubborn professors.'

[2] Leonard William Collman, an architect, who had once been a pupil of Sydney Smirke, R.A.

as to whose competency the Chancellor of the Exchequer has satisfied himself, shall contract with the government for the due completion of the Monument by Mr. Stevens within a period of $2\frac{1}{2}$ years, for a total sum not to exceed £9,000, including contingencies, of which £1,000 will be paid on the execution of the agreement, and the remainder by instalments upon certificates, signed by two persons, whom the Chancellor of the Exchequer proposes shall be Mr. Fergusson and Captain Galton, that the progress of the work justified the payments.

The Chancellor of the Exchequer has no hesitation in recommending the adoption of this arrangement as the best that the circumstances will admit of.

The total estimate for the Monument, including the bas-reliefs and the decoration of the chapel, will thus be raised from £20,000 to £28,000, but it is evident that in undertaking to execute his portion of the work for £14,000, Mr. Stevens considerably underestimated the expense which he must incur, and it is to this error and the embarrassment thereby caused to him that the delay which has taken place must in a great measure be attributed.

There seems little reason to doubt that, when completed, the work will be neither extravagant as regards its cost, nor unworthy of the object for which it is designed.

My Lords approve and desire that the papers may be transmitted to the Solicitor, with directions to examine and settle the draft, which should be executed by the Treasury as the contracting department on behalf of the Government.

Transmit copy of this Minute to the First Commissioner of Works. State that my Lords propose that the contract shall be executed by the Treasury on behalf of the government. In accordance with the proposal in their Minute, my Lords desire to entrust Mr. Fergusson and Captain Galton the duty of certifying as to the progress of the work from time to time, as a

condition precedent to the payment of the instalments, and they will feel obliged to the First Commissioner if he will allow Captain Galton to undertake that duty.

Add that, as all the preliminaries of the arrangement have been concluded, it is desirable that the model and the material for the Monument should at once be restored to the custody of Mr. Stevens, in order that he may resume work without delay, and my Lords request the First Commissioner to give the necessary instructions for that purpose.'[1]

On the 23rd March previously, James Fergusson had written to Robert Lowe,[2] the Chancellor of the Exchequer:

'Immediately after the interview I had with you, I put myself into communication with Mr. L. W. Collmann, of George Street, Portman Square, as he was the only person I knew at all likely to be able to assist in the matter. I have known Mr. Collmann for more than 20 years, and at intervals during that period he has carried out several considerable contracts for me, or under my superintendence, and in every instance entirely to my satisfaction. No pecuniary difficulty or disputed item ever occurred in his accounts. My principal motive, however, in applying to him in this instance was that I knew him to be a personal friend of Mr. Stevens, the sculptor employed to execute the Wellington Monument, and as more likely to work harmoniously with him than any other person I was acquainted with.

After various negotiations, an agreement has been settled between Mr. Collmann and Mr. Stevens, by which the whole artistic control of the works necessary for the completion of

[1] On 27th April, Ayrton told the Treasury that he considered the minute prejudicial to himself, but after some discussion it was published substantially as drafted. (Public Record Office, Works 6.)

[2] Robert Lowe (1811–92), politician, 1st Viscount Sherbrooke, Chancellor of the Exchequer between 1868 and 1873.

the Monument is to remain with the latter, while Mr. Collmann undertakes the direction of the business part of the arrangement, and the whole pecuniary liability. Contracts have also been provisionally entered into by Mr. Collmann with a bronze-founder, and with the other parties whose services may be required. Everything is now so far settled that Mr. Collmann is now prepared to enter into a contract with Government to complete the Monument in two years and one-half from the time of the signing of the contract, and for the sum of £8,500; £500 additional being reserved for extras at present not foreseen, and on the understanding that it will not be asked for if not wanted.

The sum is made up of the following items:—

To be paid to Mr. Stevens in repayment of a loan he contracted to complete the marble work after the Government had refused him further advances	£1,000
To be paid Mr. Stevens by instalments during the continuance of the work for his establishment in preparing the models, etc. a total sum of	£1,500
For completing the marble work	£1,000
For the bronze work	£5,000
Contingencies, as above	£ 500
	£9,000

I have gone carefully through these estimates, and have satisfied myself that the Monument cannot be completed in a satisfactory manner according to Mr. Stevens's design for a less amount, and am fortified in this opinion by the Report to Her Majesty's Board of Works given in by two such competent authorities as Captain Galton and Mr. Hunt, who estimate these services at £15,000. I am also of the opinion that the work cannot be completed in less time; and am convinced that if Mr. Collmann undertakes it, he has the means, and will do all that can be done by any one, to carry the undertaking to a satisfactory conclusion.

Under these circumstances, I beg leave to forward to you herewith the draft of a contract embodying the above conditions, *inter alia*, and which if approved of, Mr. Collmann is prepared to enter into with the proper authorities on the part of Her Majesty's Government.

Should this course not be adopted, the only alternative appears to me would be to take the work at once out of Mr. Stevens's hands, and employ some other party to complete the Monument. This does not appear to me feasible, because I am convinced that no sculptor of any standing in his profession would undertake to finish a work already carried so far by another. Even supposing, however, that a sculptor of equal ability with Mr. Stevens were found willing to do it, he certainly would not—most probably could not—complete his design. A new design and new models would have to be made, causing infinite delay and great risk of incongruity between the two parts of the Monument; and I also feel convinced that if the same extent for bronze work is to be employed, and of the same elaborateness, it could not be done for less money, or in less time.

Taking all the circumstances of the case into consideration, I have no hesitation in recommending Her Majesty's Government to enter into the proposed agreement with Mr. Collmann with any such modification as further discussion of its clauses may suggest as desirable for the proper carrying out of its intentions.'

VII

The Monument 1871–1878

The contract between Collmann and the Treasury was signed on 26th June 1871, in which Collmann agreed to complete Stevens's design, less the horse and rider,[1] for £8,500, within two and a half years from the date of the agreement.

The key of the studio at Haverstock Hill had been given to Collmann on 31st May 1871, who signed a receipt for the Office of Works,[2] and shortly afterwards Stevens was at last allowed to return to work under the watchful eye of his friend, who in his turn was responsible to Douglas Galton and James Fergusson. Stevens's biographer, Sir Walter Armstrong, asserts that the sculptor took some slight revenge on Ayrton by giving the First Commissioner's features to the face of Falsehood in the group 'Truth plucking out the tongue of Falsehood'.

According to Hugh Stannus in his *Alfred Stevens*, the sculptor's first intention had been to cast the bronze parts of the monument himself and in December 1869 he had bought five tons of copper for the purpose. Stevens abandoned this idea, however, when he discovered how much money he would have to spend on the equipping of his own foundry.

Henry Young, a man in his early twenties, came to the rescue. He was the chief moulder at a foundry in Manor Street, Chelsea, who applied to cast the monument's figures; and

in 1871 contracted with Collmann for all the bronze work. On the strength of this contract he set up his own business in Eccleston Street, Pimlico, engaging several craftsmen to assist him. Alfred Stevens promised that he would provide the models quickly, but did not keep to his timetable and eventually was nearly two years behind schedule;[3] this caused Young to lose a not inconsiderable sum of money, as he was forced unprofitably to retain his workmen during the long period of waiting.

On 21st August 1873, Colonel Henderson, of the Police, at Scotland Yard, received a letter from a Mr. R. A. Whitelocke:

'H. Young was a Moulder in the employ of Messrs. Holroyd in their Foundry in Manor Street, Chelsea, now known as Masefields.

About two or three years ago, being promised support, he set up as a Founder himself, in Eccleston Street, Pimlico.

He was, and is, employed to cast the Wellington Memorial, to be fitted up or erected in St. Paul's Cathedral Church, a portion of which has been cast, much remaining to be done.

Government supplied him with Copper in Ingots (said to be seven tons) to form the Bronze for the casting.

This Copper has been used for other purposes, one job alone taking two tons of it.

The castings completed have been made from a metal so inferior that it will not stand, being bits of old brass candlesticks and all the

---

[1] Stevens was still hoping, even at this time, to be allowed to execute the equestrian group. In a letter, probably to Penrose, 29th December 1870, he hoped that 'the Dean will insist upon the monument being finished according to the original design. This I am satisfied he has power to do, and thus would put a stop to Mr. Ayrton whose scheme is as you know to cut off the composition at the arch.' (R.I.B.A., Penrose papers.)

[2] In the Public Record Office, Works 6.

[3] Stevens was still worried about his health. In a letter to Alfred Pegler, of early 1872, he said that he 'felt it would have come to a breakdown'. Reports in the newspapers during 1873 throwing doubts on his sanity caused him to ask Pegler to deny them whenever he could. (K. R. Towndrow, *op. cit.*, pp. 239, 240.)

rakings and scrapings which could be obtained from Marine Store Dealers.

What the future castings will be made of is a puzzle.

The Copper as supplied by the Government has been a Godsend to him; set him up, as it were, and enabled him to take work which otherwise he could not have done.

An examination of the Castings made would show the quality of the material, it being more an inferior brass than bronze.

Not a bit of any casting was weighed (as is usual), when going out of the Foundry, so that the men say any weight will be charged by their Master, who imagines that the work, once put up, will not be taken down again merely for the purpose of weighing.'[1]

Scotland Yard had to act on this allegation of fraud and a Sergeant Lansdown was sent to make enquiries about Whitelocke. He reported that Whitelocke was an auditor and accountant employed by Messrs. Cheston & Son, Solicitors, at 1, Great Winchester Street Buildings in the City, and lived at 8 Wellington Square, Chelsea, being 'well known in that neighbourhood as a respectable gentleman'. The sergeant's enquiries about Young showed that he employed 30 workmen.

The letter, and the report by Sergeant Lansdown, were sent to the Treasury by William C. Harris, Assistant Commissioner, on 1st September 1873, and the Treasury at once made their contents known to the First Commissioner of Works and Leonard Collmann.

Collmann replied to the Treasury on 16th September saying how surprised he was to learn of Whitelocke's charges which to him seemed to be:

'1. Stealing Government Copper.
2. (The Castings not having been weighed) The intention to charge for a greater weight than is supplied is imputed.

3. That the metal is not Bronze at all and that it is an inferior Brass.'

Collmann stated, (1) that by his contract with Young, the founder was not bound to use the same metal which Collmann had received from the Government and delivered to Young. (2) They did not contract to make the castings of a certain weight. Therefore he, Collmann, could not complain unless the metal was thinner than it should have been. (3) He was satisfied on the quality, but if the Treasury wanted the metal checked he would either forward pieces cut from the figures, or be in attendance whilst Treasury officials took their own samples.

Collmann met Whitelocke and three workmen who had said that they were prepared to prove the charges. When he asked them to sign Whitelocke's statement they refused to do so, but 'they would however be willing to give evidence at the trial and "would like to see Young punished"'. Further enquiries by Collmann showed that Whitelocke was the secretary to a working men's club where he had heard the workmen talking among themselves: two of the three men had been discharged by Young for habitual drunkenness; the third man was employed by Young's former employers, Messrs. Masefield & Co. at the Manor Street Foundry, and had applied to Young for employment and been refused. Young himself considered the whole affair to be a conspiracy.

But the damage was done. Eighteen samples of the bronze were sent to Professor Abel, the War Office's expert at Woolwich, whose report was back with the First Commissioner of Works early in 1874. It was sent to John Percy[2] at the House of Commons for his comments, which on 14th April were:

'In only one of the analyses does the metal approximate in composition to bronze. I

[1] Public Record Office, Works 6.

[2] Presumably John Percy, F.R.S. (b. 1817), appointed in 1851 Lecturer on Metallurgy in the Government School of Mines.

should designate all the specimens . . . as brass containing a low percentage of zinc . . .

I was engaged by the Office of Works about 20 years ago in the examination of one of the bas-reliefs on the Nelson Monument, namely, that on the South Side representing the "Death of Nelson". The founders were charged with fraud before Lord Campbell at the Guildhall and convicted . . .'[1]

Percy's opinion was that there had been loose-ness in the specification for the Wellington monument, and that Young ought to have been made to use an alloy of a given specifi-cation.

Argument went on for some weeks and Galton was asked to find out what metal had been used on the Column in the Place Ven-dôme in Paris. 'I know all sorts of rubbishy metals have been used by sculptors, but that is no reason why the practice should be sanctioned by a Government in the execution of a national monument. I don't think sculp-tors, or decorators (like Collmann) generally, know much about alloys. Poor Mr. Collmann! Let him get a bit of bronze and try whether he can't file it', wrote Percy on 30th April. The Treasury and the Office of Works must have been appeased in the end, as there does not seem to be a record of any action against Young the founder.

In the meantime Stevens was causing some anxiety to his two official overseers. They were taking their task seriously, and when Collmann on 25th June 1872, asked for some money to pay Stevens, with the horrible example of Penrose to remind them, Galton and Fergusson debated whether they should visit the studio to check that Stevens had actually done the work which Collmann had certified. Some months later both were very annoyed with the sculptor, and Fergusson on 28th March 1873 sent Galton the draft of a

letter he wished to be sent to Stevens. Galton refused, however, to sign it. 'I am very sorry . . .', answered Fergusson, 'matters are getting serious and unless we take some steps we are, I think, incurring a very serious responsibility.

'As I understand that your objection is only to our opening communication *direct* with Mr. Stevens, do you see any objection to our sending a letter in the form of the accompany-ing draft to Mr. Stevens?'

Galton answered suggesting strong action, what it was does not now seem to be recorded, but, whatever it may have been, it did not meet with Fergusson's approval. 'Till I am convinced', he wrote, 'that . . . all other means of arranging the trouble with Stevens have failed, I am not prepared to recommend gov-ernment to adopt the very summary measures your note suggests.

'I have very little doubt that Mr. Collmann would be only too glad to be relieved of his contract. But what next?'[2]

There are not any notes which definitely help in finding out what this trouble with Stevens was, but a month later he refused to let Galton and Fergusson see his modelling. Fergusson became annoyed over this on 27th July, 'Unless Stevens says he will show us the models if we come up I am not going to waste my time in order to look foolish as we were the last time we made the attempt.'

From about this time Stevens's health started to fail him,[3] and he was ill much more frequently. This meant that often he was unable to work, and soon he began to find him-self short of money again. In May 1874,[4] he wrote to his friend Alfred Pegler and told him

---

[1] Public Record Office, Works 6. The relief (1850) is the work of J. E. Carew (1785?–1868). See page 20.

[2] Public Record Office, Works 6.

[3] Stevens suffered a paralytic stroke in 1872. (K. Town-drow, *op. cit.*, p. 232.)

[4] 'I am sick and weary. I feel I have little to live for.' 'I am still getting stronger—all uncomfortable symptoms have gone—the only thing which prevents my being per-fectly well is worry.' (K. R. Towndrow, *op. cit.*, pp. 250, 252.)

that as he was not producing anything for the monument, under the existing arrangement the government was not bound to pay him any money. Pegler took pity on Stevens, and started to send him £10 a week.

During the middle of 1874 the effigy of the Duke of Wellington was sent to Henry Young to be cast. While it was there, an almost unknown sculptor, Charles Bacon,[1] living at 121, Sloane Street, wrote to Lord Henry Lennox, then First Commissioner,[2] to give his view that the effigy 'would disgrace a country stone mason or an academy student of three months standing'.[3] Galton had seen Stevens's model at his studio during June, and then recorded that Stevens intended to finish the bronzes after they were cast, but in view of Bacon's letter he went to the foundry, where Henry Young told him that he had no cause to complain about the models and thought the castings would be perfectly suitable for their position in the Cathedral. However, Galton hoped that Fergusson would also go to the foundry in Pimlico in case anything was going wrong.

On 19th October Stevens was, yet again, short of money, 'Please say that you will send me some,' he implored Fergusson, 'I shall then show your letter to the Bank Manager, at present I believe he thinks I am something of a swindler—The amount of the debt and interest is about £600.' However, he got nothing out of Fergusson who, in a very cool letter, told Stevens that he should know the arrangement perfectly well, Fergusson was not going to send him money on account under any circumstances.

Early in 1875 Stevens was ill again, and still writing to Pegler about his money difficulties. By the 30th April[4] he had resumed work after having been confined to his room for two weeks, but suddenly, during the morning of the following day, 1st May 1875, he died.[5]

Even after his death *The Art Journal* was ungracious: 'We confess', said Stevens's obituary notice, 'we know nothing of Mr. Stevens's works, simply because they have never come before us—so far as we recollect—except his design for the Wellington Monument sent in to the exhibition . . . and this was far from having our approval.'

Having got over the first shock Collmann reported to Lord Henry Lennox on 4th May about 'the exact state of all models required for the completion of the [Monument] which have been left unfinished owing to the sad death of my poor friend the late Mr Alfred Stevens.'

The group, 'Truth and Falsehood' was cast in plaster and would be ready to be sent to Young's foundry in a week. The soffit of the Arch over the recumbent effigy incorporated a small sculptured panel which had still to be cast in plaster; and the four cherub-heads supporting the bier were already cast in plaster. This small amount of work were the only models remaining incomplete in 'the slightest degree'.

Collmann listed Stevens's pupils: Henry Hoyles, William Ellis, Reuben Townroe, James Gambel (*sic*), Hugh Stannus.[6] One of

---

[1] Charles Bacon (1821–85?). In 1874 Bacon was chosen to execute a statue of Prince Albert which was being given to the City of London. It stands at Holborn Circus. *The Art Journal* did not comment on the work, except that it could not 'too narrowly examine a gift horse'. (Rupert Gunnis, *op. cit.*, p. 24.)

[2] Lord Henry Lennox (1821–86), third son of the 5th Duke of Lennox.

[3] Public Record Office, Works 6.

[4] 'I have been for some days too ill to do anything' (22nd April), and on 30th April Stevens told Pegler that he was very well. (K. R. Towndrow, *op. cit.*, pp. 255, 256.)

[5] A medical report was of the opinion that Stevens had suffered from 'general debility, dilatation of the heart for two years, cardiac dyspepsia, and three attacks of angina'. (K. R. Towndrow, *op. cit.*, p. 232.)

[6] Henry Hoyles of Sheffield, pupil and assistant; William Ellis (1824–82); Reuben Townroe (1835–1911); James Gamble (exhibited 1875–92); and Hugh Hutton Stannus (1840–1908). While working for Henry Hoole of Sheffield, c. 1850, Stevens took several local students as assistants, of whom probably the best known is Godfrey Sykes.

these men, he suggested, should be chosen to complete the work outstanding. His own choice was Hugh Stannus 'my chief assistant in artistic matters, having been recommended very highly to me some years ago by Mr. Stevens . . .' The First Commissioner and the Office of Works decided that in spite of Stevens's death, Collmann's contract with the government was still valid, and so they suggested to Collmann, on 12th May, that he authorise Stannus to see to the completion of the monument as Stevens's successor; work thus went on. In January 1876 Henry Young asked the First Commissioner's permission to exhibit the bronze 'Valour and Cowardice' and the recumbent Duke of Wellington at the Royal Academy. Permission was given as it was thought that the public would be able to see that work was still going on, and the two groups were Nos. 1427 and 1522 at the Summer Exhibition as by 'the late Alfred Stevens, sculptor'—the only works of his to be shown at the Academy exhibitions.

In July 1876 the government suddenly discovered on totalling payments to Collmann that he had received £1,000 too much. An inquest was held and eventually it was agreed to add the money as additional to the Estimates, but the blame was laid at the feet of Galton and Fergusson 'who are presumed to be keeping a watchful eye over the expenditure', which should have meant that they should also have seen that this expenditure was kept within the contracted sum of £8,500.

A Samuel Montrie was employed on 12th August 1876 to complete the carving of the enriched hollow moulding in marble on top of the pedestal. He signed a contract with Collmann, witnessed by Stannus, to do the work to the satisfaction of Stannus for £55 10s. within three months.

There was still no mention of the equestrian figure, so several interested people started a petition in 1876 which was left at the Arts Club for signature. Though probably pre-

PLATE 64. *The Wellington Monument in the south-west chapel of St. Paul's Cathedral, before it was moved into the nave.* c. *1880. Photograph:* National Monuments Record.

sented to the government, nothing came of it.

At last, on 1st August 1877, Collmann was able to write to Fergusson and Galton announcing the completion of the monument. The Consistory Court Chapel was renamed the Wellington Chapel. F. C. Penrose, still Architect to St. Paul's, wrote on behalf of the

Dean and Chapter on 15th April 1878,[1] asking for the government to allow the public to see the monument for the first time at Easter. With a complete about-face *The Art Journal* recorded that the monument was so cramped in its chapel that 'those features which make its individuality glorious above all other British monuments [were] as good as lost to the public'. It was also very near a large south window, the glare from which made it difficult to be seen properly (Plate 64).

The final small skirmish at this stage of the monument's history came when Collmann

applied for payment of some very small out-of-pocket expenses. Argument and haggling continued for about 6 months until at last, on 28th March 1878, the government conceded the victory to Collmann and paid up.

The cost of the monument was totalled on 19th December 1878:

	£	s.	d.
Preliminary expenses—Premiums for Designs and Models. Cost of the Exhibition in Westminster Hall. Advertisements, Lithography, &c.	3,309	9	7
Fitting and decorating the Chapel	561	10	4
Reliefs for the panels in the Chapel	4,840	0	0
Cost of the Monument and the model	22,121	0	0
Architect's Commission	455	3	0
Sundries	21	13	4
	£31,308	16	3

---

[1] A. B. Mitford, Permanent Secretary to the Office of Works, wrote on behalf of the First Commissioner to ask if the Dean and Chapter would take custody of the Monument on 16th April 1878.

VIII

The Monument and Lord Leighton

It soon became apparent that the monument in the south-west chapel, hedged in by a screen, was inconveniently sited. The chapel had formerly been used as the Court of the Bishop of London, and it was suggested that in 1858 the Cathedral authorities had consulted neither the bishop nor the judge of the Consistory Court,[1] when the decision was taken to place the monument in that chapel.

When T. H. Tristram[2] was appointed Chancellor of London in 1872 he found himself, therefore, without a Court. So he wrote to the Dean[3] claiming the right of a Court within St. Paul's Cathedral, as every bishop was entitled to have his Consistory within his cathedral church. The Dean then proposed that when the monument was completed, the Court should be held in its former chapel, and that special movable furnishings would be provided. The Dean regretted, however, that he could at that moment see no prospect of the monument being finished. Shortly after the monument's eventual completion in 1878, the Court moved back into the chapel, and very awkward things were found to be. The vast monument all but filled the space so that, when the Court was sitting, Dr. Tristram had to face the monument only a few feet from counsel who were standing with their backs against it. Other officials and the public had to station themselves wherever they could find sufficient room.

Rumblings against the site, and the awkwardness involved, were heard during 1883,

and at the end of 1884, an unsigned report, dated 30th December, was made by the Office of Works:[4]

'There are two matters complained of: the Site occupied by the Monument, and the omission of the Equestrian effigy.

The Site. Having been asked by Sir Benjamin Hall to suggest a site, the Dean and Chapter consented that it should be placed between the Pillars under the first arch from the junction of the Nave with the Dome.

This site was shown on the lithographed plan which was supplied to competing sculptors for their guidance. There can be but little doubt, therefore, that Mr. Stevens, and all the sculptors, prepared their designs with a view to the Monument occupying the Site first chosen.

The fact of the site having been changed is abundantly clear from the present position of the Monument. The reason appears to have been that since the first selection of a Site, the Chapel used for the Consistory Court became vacant, and that the Dean and Chapter considered it more useful for the Monument than the site at first chosen, in which opinion Lord John Manners, the First Comr. of Works, fully concurred.

As to whether Mr. Stevens' design was suited to the new Site both Lord Mount-Temple (then Mr. Cowper) and Sir Benjn. Hall expressed doubts. Lord John Manners is of the opinion that all that is required is to remove the screen enclosing the Chapel, so that the Monument may be seen from the Nave. In

---

[1] Stephen Lushington, P.C., M.P. (1782–1873).

[2] Thomas H. Tristram (1825–1912), Chancellor of the Dioceses of London, Hereford, Ripon and Wakefield.

[3] Richard William Church (1815–90), Dean 1871–90.

[4] Public Record Office, Works 6.

this view, Mr. James Fergusson is stated to concur.

The Equestrian Effigy. There is no doubt that this was omitted by desire of the late Dean. The Rev. W. H. Milman states, however, that the Dean would doubtless have preferred seeing the equestrian statue of the Duke crowning the work, if no more appropriate single figure or group could be designed, rather than it should continue in its unsatisfactory incompleteness.

Mr. James Fergusson has suggested that the model of the equestrian statue which is now in the crypt of the cathedral should be completed and placed in the position for which it was designed. If it were a success, it could be cast in bronze for £1000 or £1500; and if it were not pleasing an urn or other funereal trophy might be substituted. Anything would be better than leaving the monument as it is at present.'

Sir Frederic Leighton, P.R.A., had been pursuing this ideal for some time, together with a suggestion that the whole monument should be removed to its original position in the nave. In August 1888 he wrote to Henry Wells, R.A.:[1]

'The list for the Memorial Committee is practically complete, and though it is not in every particular the list which you or I might have drawn up, it is a good one, and as I told you I think in a previous note, I have not liked to interfere too much, as Agnew[2] has so zealously taken the work on himself. I meant to send you the list but have cleverly come away from home . . . without it. I have of course asked Agnew to add his own name; for the Academy I have proposed the four Trustees—not as Trustees, but because they offer a ready-made group in a body where

none is afore or after—Sir J. Gilbert, Linton and Coutts Lindsay[3] will complete the artistic group for the present. The next step, as I have suggested to Agnew, is to get at the Dean of St. Paul's—this I have offered to do. A chairman will have to be appointed; I should suggest, or rather have suggested, the D. of Cleveland[4]—if he joins; I believe his answer has not yet come in. And there must be a banker: then a letter should appear in the *Times* inviting adhesions and subscriptions, to be published from time to time: is all this in harmony with your own view? . . . Bye-the-bye, *S. Kensington* ought to be represented. I will ask Agnew to write to T. Armstrong'.[5]

In 1890 Leighton expressed the hope, at the Royal Academy banquet, that in the not too distant future the Wellington monument might be removed to the position for which it was designed. He said that in its present position in the chapel it was in an extremely confined space, and that it could only be seen against the light of the south window. For two years following this speech Leighton solicited the support of the Dean and Chapter, the First Commissioner of Works, the Duke of Wellington, the Cathedral Architect, and many others. By April 1892, then, he was in a position to start a fund for the removal with a donation of £50, together with £50 from the Dean and Chapter;[6] it was estimated that a total sum of about £1,000 would be required. Coupled with this project was another which Leighton hoped would be the means of completing the equestrian statue; this other fund Leighton opened with a further donation of £50.

---

[1] Henry Tamworth Wells, R.A. (1828–1903). (In *The Life, Letters and Work of Frederick Leighton* by Mrs. Russell Barrington, 1906, Vol. 2, p. 286.)

[2] Sir William Agnew, Bart. (1825–1910).

[3] Sir John Gilbert, R.A. (1817–97); Sir James Dromgole Linton, P.R.I. (1840–1916); Sir Coutts Lindsay, Bart. (1824–1913).

[4] Henry Powlett, 4th Duke of Cleveland, K.G. (1803–1891).

[5] Thomas Armstrong, C.B. (1832–1911), Director of Art in the Department of Science and Art.

[6] Recorded as only £5 in the Chapter Minutes, 18th May 1892.

Within a month the money received or promised had amounted to £785, among subscribers being the Duke of Westminster, the Archbishop of Canterbury, Sir J. Millais, Sir H. Layard, J. Pearson, Norman Shaw, G. F. Watts, Val Prinsep, and E. Poynter.[1] The fund for the equestrian statue had reached £371 by the same date, with donations from most of those named above, and from Somers Clarke, and Percy Wyndham,[2] among others, so that by November 1892[3] Leighton was able to write that although he had set the work going before he had received all the money he required, he had just received a cheque from 'young Lehmann' for £300 which was just the exact amount still needed.[4]

While the work was in progress some doubts were raised about the sculptured groups, and the position of the effigy. A correspondent to *The Times* wrote:

'Will you give me space to point out, before it is too late, that the allegorical compositions . . . are placed in opposition to the designs of Alfred Stevens, as shown in his drawings at the South Kensington Museum? The front view of these groups is turned towards the aisle, and the back view towards the nave. Stevens clearly intended the Duke's figure to lie with its feet to the west.

If it is necessary that the feet should be to

[1] Hugh Grosvenor, 1st Duke of Westminster, K.G. (1825–99); Edward White Benson (1829–96); Sir John Millais, P.R.A. (1829–96); Sir Austen Henry Layard, G.C.B. (1817–94); John Loughborough Pearson, R.A. (1817–97); Richard Norman Shaw, R.A. (1831–1912); G. F. Watts, O.M., R.A. (1817–1904); Valentine Cameron Prinsep, R.A. (1836–1904); Sir Edward Poynter, P.R.A. (1836–1919).

[2] Somers Clarke (1841–1926); Hon. Percy Wyndham (1835–1911).

[3] Letters in the Department of Prints and Drawings, Victoria and Albert Museum (E.1121–1948), indicate that the monument had been dismantled by October. Leighton told Penrose (29th October) that he was glad that 'no accident (of importance) had occurred in the delicate task. I fancy that re-erection is less easy than taking to pieces,' and on 17th December Leighton noted that Penrose was ready to begin rebuilding on the new site.

[4] Mrs. Russell Barrington, *op. cit.*, p. 287.

PLATE 65. *The Wellington monument in the nave, at the end of the 19th century. Victoria and Albert Museum Library, Photograph Collection.*

the east, then that end should be arrived at by turning round the bier under the canopy and not by reversing the entire structure . . .'[5]

Penrose, the Cathedral Architect, wrote to Hugh Stannus to see if he could help, but in the end the groups were replaced as they had been in the chapel.

[5] 2nd August 1893.

The monument, by July 1894, had been placed under the centre arch of the north arcade of the nave (Plate 65), and Leighton wrote to *The Times*[1] asking for contributions towards the second task of completing the group on the summit of the monument; £3,000 would be needed. A rough, unfinished model by Stevens was in existence and 'will, if made accessible, serve as a sufficient guide to the artist who shall be privileged finally to carry out this portion of the cenotaph; that artist should be a man whose genius will carry him worthily through such a task, and whose reverence for the name of Alfred Stevens will insure that close adherence to the leading lines and features of the first design which the public voice could justly demand; such a man, both in his gifts and in his reverence, the Dean and Chapter of St. Paul's have seen in Mr. Alfred Gilbert, R.A.,[2] whose selection for so noble a task will command, I cannot doubt, universal approval.'[3]

[1] 31st July 1893.

[2] Sir Alfred Gilbert, M.V.O., R.A. (1854–1934).

[3] On 16th January 1895, Leighton told Penrose that the question of the horse was in abeyance as there was no more money, and that he had to wait until Parliament reassem-

Leighton, unfortunately for the monument, died a peer of one day, on 25th January 1896,[4] and the proposal lost all its momentum. There was a slight flurry in February 1896, which resulted from correspondence in *The Times* when it was suggested that as Stevens had agreed to the monument being placed in the Consistory Court Chapel, he had therefore abandoned his original intention of an equestrian group. A correspondent to *The Times*, William Woodward, voiced the views of the anti-Stevens faction.[5]

bled before applying for funds, this time, he hoped, with better success. (Letter in the Department of Prints and Drawings, Victoria and Albert Museum, E.1121–1948.)

[4] Sir Frederic Leighton, Bart. (b. 1830), was raised to the peerage on 24th January 1896. He died at 2, Holland Park Road, on the following day, and was buried in St. Paul's Cathedral on 3rd February.

[5] The government exhibited 'a patience and forbearance . . . which reflects the highest credit on the Treasury officials. Mr. Stevens knew perfectly well that (the monument) was to be placed in the Consistory Chapel, and that it was not to be terminated by an equestrian statue. We know that he modelled the monument for that chapel, that he objected to its proposed removal to the north side of the nave, and we may reasonably conclude that the artist was not dissatisfied with the upper storey. If he was, why did he not complete his duty to himself and his employers?' *The Times*, 11th February 1896.

IX

The Equestrian Group

In April 1899 D. MacColl, later Keeper of the Tate Gallery,[1] wrote to Penrose about the model left by Stevens, and from the letters and papers in the MacColl Collection in the Victoria and Albert Museum Library, we can trace the subsequent stormy history of the completion of the monument. Penrose replied through the Clerk of the Works to the Cathedral, E. J. Harding, that the head of the Duke was in the possession of Hugh Stannus, so MacColl wrote to Stannus, only to receive a blunt, and not altogether satisfactory answer:

're Stevens: I beg to acknowledge the due receipt of your favour of 24th. Inst. and to inform you I have, at length succeeded in deciphering more than half of your writing; and as I understand it, you mention something about the Wellington monument at St. Paul's about which you are writing a book. I am very pleased to note that you have an admiration and interest in the work of our great Master and so soon as my more detailed Life and Account of his Work, on which I am at work, is published I will ask you to do me the favour of accepting a copy. I intend that it shall be sold at about 2/6d nett—when ready—as I think there must be many students who would be glad to have such a book.'

There had in 1899 been a revival of interest in the monument arising from a reference to it in an article which MacColl had written for the *Saturday Review*. This led to the Earl of Hardwicke, in the House of Lords, asking what steps were being taken to complete the memorial. Lord Salisbury replied:

'I hope I may be forgiven if in my answer I show that my knowledge of this matter is not complete. The money voted by Parliament to the erection of this monument has been expended, and a full-size plaster cast of an equestrian statue was completed from Mr. Stevens's designs. Somehow or other the model appears to have belonged to Mr. Stevens, and from his executor it was purchased by a pupil of Mr. Stevens, a Mr. Stannus, and he from the Cathedral authorities obtained permission to store it in the crypt [Plate 66]. The intention was that the statue should be in bronze, but, the money having run short, work was arrested in its present stage of development. It is fair to add that not the whole of the statue is in the crypt; the head has been separated—it is very extraordinary how the heads of distinguished persons have become separated from their bodies—and has been retained by Mr. Stannus at his private house [Plate 67].[2] I imagine that it is a question of money whether development shall be carried to its natural conclusion, and for the answer whether the money will be furnished I must refer my noble friend to the proper authority.'

Stannus then wrote to *The Times* (28th April 1899) to say that only the head of Stevens's model was in anything like a finished state, and that it had been much admired by

---

[1] Dugald Sutherland MacColl (1859–1948), art critic of the *Spectator*, *Saturday Review*, etc., editor of the *Architectural Review*, Keeper of the Tate Gallery, 1906–11, Keeper of the Wallace Collection, 1911–24. MacColl's handwriting was very bad, and many of his notes in the MacColl Collection are virtually indecipherable.

[2] In a hat-box.

PLATE 66. '*Where is the Duke of Wellington's head?*' *The statue designed for the Wellington tomb, as it stands in the Crypt of St. Paul's. A flashlight photograph reproduced in* Black and White. *Victoria and Albert Museum Library, MacColl Collection.*

the 2nd Duke of Wellington as being a very fair representation of his father in middle age. The rest of the model, that is the figure of the Duke, and of the horse, was in a very rough state, and would need a great deal of work to be done on it by a sculptor.

The disinterest of the government did not, however, deter MacColl. He, and a number of interested people, made certain that the Dean and Chapter of St. Paul's were willing to consider the proposal. They then made careful and secret enquiry among a selected group of potential subscribers to obtain an estimate of what funds might be available. The answers to these enquiries must have been encouraging as the proposers then formed a committee. The Bishop of Stepney[1] agreed to act as chairman, the treasurer was to be Lord Hardwicke, Harold Hodge,[2] the editor of the *Saturday Review*, became secretary, and other members were MacColl and Herbert Trench.[3] Later they were assisted by John R. Clayton[4] who had been closely linked with Lord Leighton during the previous decade when the monument was removed from the south-western chapel. By having Hodge on the committee they had a means of publicity, of which, of course, they made use later.

The Dean and Chapter were then approached again and gave their consent to the scheme, subject to certain conditions which were to be strictly followed—namely, that the Dean and Chapter should approve of the sculptor chosen, who should prepare a model, and a statement of what he proposed to do to Stevens's figure to prepare it for the founder. There was nothing in these conditions which

[1] Cosmo Gordon Lang (1864–1945), translated to the See of York in 1909, and later became Archbishop of Canterbury.

[2] Harold Hodge (1862–1937), editor of the *Saturday Review*, 1898–1913, member of the Advisory Council of the Central School of Arts and Crafts, etc.

[3] Herbert Trench (1865–1923), poet, Director of the Haymarket Theatre, later Assistant Director of Special Enquiries at the Board of Education.

[4] John R. Clayton (b. 1861), architect.

PLATE 67. *The head of Wellington, by Alfred Stevens, removed from the equestrian group and preserved by Hugh Stannus. Victoria and Albert Museum Library, photograph in the MacColl Collection. The head is now in the Tate Gallery.*

funds he [Leighton] recognised the necessity of completing the model by sympathetic aid, religiously following the author's design, which is more completely set forth in the small-scale model now at South Kensington'.

MacColl[2] replied by saying that Clayton had exaggerated the incompleteness of the model, it was complete in its essentials and perfectly suitable if the height at which it would be placed, and the dim light, were borne in mind. Although there had been much written about the completion of the monument, there had in fact been nothing published which indicated that MacColl and his committee were actively going ahead in collecting money and had found a sculptor. He was, like Alfred Stevens before him, an unknown, John Tweed.[3] The latter wrote to MacColl, unfortunately not dating his letter, but it was probably in 1901:

'I have spoken to Rodin about the Stevens, he is very pleased to hear that you wish me to finish the Wellington. He has a great admiration for Stevens and twenty years ago he sought out the monument, then no person knew of him, he was quite forgotten. He wanted me to go at once to see the Committee so that I might get the job, he says my time spent here, would be helpful. You might let me have a weeks notice at least of your meeting so I can prepare any sketch. Let me know as soon as possible what you wish. Until I can see the horse out from the wall, and see the head of Wellington, I cannot quite say what should be done. Then I'd suggest *a piece-mould* should be made and a cast bronzed and placed in position. You talked of Stannus as architectural adviser, does that mean anything. Before putting up the horse, a model would require to be made for the pedestal, now

did not accord with the views of the members of the committee, so they readily agreed.

MacColl, who seems to have been the dominant member of the committee over the question of the actual sculpture, wanted no interference with Stevens's model. It was his intention to render it in bronze exactly as it had been left by Stevens (Plate 68). John Clayton in January 1901[1] stated that the model was of pronounced roughness throughout; it was only a dummy which bore no traces of Stevens's ability to model. Clayton wrote also that Lord Leighton had told him that it was not possible to use the plaster as it then stood, and that 'in resolving to appeal to the public for

[1] *Saturday Review*, letter, 30th January 1901.

[2] *Saturday Review*, letter, 16th February 1901.
[3] John Tweed (died 1933), sculptor, whose work includes the memorial to Earl Kitchener of Khartoum, set up at the Horse Guards, and the Rifle Brigade War Memorial, Grosvenor Gardens, London.

PLATE 68. *The full-size model of the equestrian group, as seen from the north aisle of the Cathedral. Victoria and Albert Museum Library, photograph in the MacColl Collection.*

would I have to see to that, it would be better I should. Then have I to send cost of scaffolding and casting. This means a great deal of work, so I would require some time before your meeting if it is needed at start. We might go again to see it together. Rodin hopes to be in London in the Spring.'

It appears that Tweed did not realise properly that MacColl wanted him only to prepare a model for the statue reproducing Stevens's design in its entirety, with only few minor

modifications after a cleaning-up of imperfections. This was to lead in a few years time to a complete break between the sculptor and MacColl.

Another storm about the monument broke on the 9th January 1903. M. H. Spielmann[1] wrote a letter to *The Times* in which he drew attention to a rumour which was current that the Wellington monument was to be completed and he hoped that a competent sculptor would be found for the task. *Black and White* on the following day carried an announcement that this rumour was correct and named John Tweed as the sculptor. This at once brought a flood of protest. John Clayton, the same day, said to MacColl, 'Doubtless you have become aware that the secret as to the Wellington Monument and its completion at the hands of Mr. Tweed is at an end . . . During the past week or two I have several times found that there has grown a strong feeling that Mr. Tweed is not the man for the task. I have been ask [*sic*] if I knew anything of his work and if I had ever seen it. I have been constrained to plead ignorance.'

Clayton was only one of a great number in the same position. An Academician, who emphasised that he was not a sculptor, said that he did not object to Tweed as he knew nothing of his work, but presumed that a committee (however appointed) would choose a sympathetic and competent sculptor. Recently, however, some of Tweed's work had appeared in the newspapers. As a result he, and many others, had come to the conclusion that Tweed was a regrettable choice.

The President of the Royal Academy[2] added extra fuel to the blaze on 17th January by publishing the fact that not only was Tweed actually at work, but that he (not knowing of the Bishop of Stepney's 'secret' committee which had forestalled him) had almost per-

[1] Marion Harry Spielmann, F.S.A. (1858–1948), writer on art.
[2] Sir Edward Poynter.

suaded the government to put up the money for the monument's completion:

'The article which announces Mr. Tweed's appointment gives an illustration of Stevens's model for the group as it was left at his death, by which it will be seen that it is in a most incomplete and fragmentary state . . . This is the first information on the subject that has been put before the public, who have been unaware of what has been doing until the affair is an accomplished fact; for we now learn, not only that the sculptor has received the commission, but that he is actually at work on the statue.

It was only a short time before the appearance of the article in question that I learned from a private source that such a committee was in existence, and I at once took steps, by communicating with the Bishop of Stepney, who acted as chairman of the committee, to ascertain the facts. His lordship most obligingly immediately put me in possession of all the circumstances attending the movement, and confirmed what I had already been told, that Mr. Tweed was already at work on the group. It will presently appear why I was specially interested in the matter. There are many reasons why I think it unfortunate that the Dean and Chapter should have adopted without further inquiry the conclusions of this committee, and in the first place because the present Government, if they have not actually decided on finding the money for the completion of Stevens's splendid monument, have so far given the proposal favourable consideration as to allow the First Commissioner of Works to include £2,000 for the purpose in his estimates for the coming financial year. It was the late Lord Leighton's opinion, when not long before his death he brought the matter to the notice of the Government, that it was their proper function to complete that they had undertaken; but a deaf ear was turned to his pleadings, and he consequently made an

effort to raise the necessary money by subscription, but with so little success that the cost of moving the monument to its present position in the Nave of the Cathedral, which he considered a necessary preliminary to its completion, was defrayed largely by himself, and but a small sum was left over towards the main object for which he had been striving. An effort which I made, in 1900, in pursuance of Lord Leighton's idea, to induce the Government to find £2,000 at which the cost of completion was estimated, was equally unsuccessful. Last year, I thought it my duty to renew the attempt, and through, unless I am mistaken, the generous advocacy of Lord Roberts with a sympathetic Prime Minister,[1] and the concurrence of Lord Windsor,[2] newly appointed First Commissioner of Works—also in full sympathy with the purpose—the Government were, as I have shown, prepared to lend a more favourable ear to the suggestion.

Thus it appears that two separate movements have been going on simultaneously for the completion of this great work, and while the action of the committee for collecting money was quite unknown to those who had approached the Government, it is also to be supposed that the committee in question were unaware that the Government had been so approached.

The Bishop of Stepney himself certainly knew nothing of what had been attempted in this direction, and was as much surprised to learn the fact as I was when I heard the astonishing news that the whole matter had been settled between the committee and the Dean and Chapter, the public being in complete ignorance of what was being done.

Now it would appear at first sight that the action of the Dean and Chapter is conclusive and that the commission for the carrying out

[1] Arthur James Balfour, 1st Earl Balfour, K.G. (1848–1930).
[2] Robert Windsor-Clive, Lord Windsor, First Commissioner of Works, 1902–5.

of Stevens's superb design is irrevocably placed. Yet I cannot but think that, though a sum of money has been collected by the committee, and the execution of this important work has been definitely handed over to the committee's nominee, the Government may and ought to have something to say in the matter. The monument to the great duke is a national concern, and it ought not to be left to a small group of individuals to select the artist, whatever the confidence they may have in him, who is entrusted with a work of national importance, and to dispose of the matter as if it were of no public interest. My hope, therefore, is that the present Government will not, because of a scheme which has been sprung upon us as a *fait accompli*, be turned from their purpose of completing the memorial to our national hero which was begun so many years ago in obedience to a national desire, and which in its unfinished state has been so long a standing reproach to the successive Administrations which have abandoned it.'[1]

The committee, and especially MacColl, until the completion of the monument, looked upon *The Times* and the Royal Academy as their enemies, apparently to be done down whenever possible. Four days after Poynter's letter the committee published a statement in *The Times*, explaining how it had been set up after obtaining the approval of the Dean and Chapter for the proposal. They then had purchased Stevens's model from Hugh Stannus, and proposed Tweed 'whose ability had been vouched for by high artistic authority' (this, as it will later be apparent, was probably MacColl himself). Tweed had then produced, with the co-operation of Somers Clarke, Surveyor to the Cathedral, a small model, of which the Dean and Chapter had approved, with the result that Tweed obtained the commission. The statement then emphasised that the statue was not going to be a new one, but

was to follow the model left by Stevens. In conclusion the committee announced that before Tweed's work was sent to the bronze-founder, it would be placed in position on the monument, so that the public could view it side by side with Stevens's models and drawings. They regretted that they did not know of Poynter's actions, but this had been because he had not approached the Dean and Chapter first.[2]

The Times in an editorial comment, voiced what must have been the thoughts of many. It remarked that though the committee explained its actions, it made no attempt whatever to justify the secrecy which it had maintained for nearly three years. If its members had wished to checkmate the Royal Academy and ensure that the work went to no-one but a member of the Rodin School, then they were to be congratulated, for they had stolen a march on the official sculptors and also placed the Dean and Chapter in a position from which they would find it difficult to withdraw. *The Times* criticised also the Bishop of Stepney for not letting Poynter know what action was proposed in a scheme which Poynter's predecessor, Lord Leighton, had started. The newspaper continued, 'Moreover, the question arises whether the Cathedral Authorities have the right, without consulting the Government, to make substantial alterations in a monument that was paid for by the Government. The Wellington monument is literally, and not only nominally, a national possession commissioned and paid for, very inadequately, we admit—by the Government of the day. It is fairly obvious that any large measures with regard to it should only be undertaken after consultation with the Government's successors. The Office of Works has a grievance on that ground. The Royal Academy has a grievance on the ground that Lord Leighton prepared the way for completing the monument by moving

[1] *The Times*, 19th January 1903.

[2] *Ibid.*, 24th January 1903.

it to its present position. More than all, the public has a grievance on the ground that so large a matter ought not to be settled in a corner. It does not appear, however, from the letters of the Bishop of Stepney and his committee that the Dean and Chapter have any present intention of reversing their resolution. They are politely regretful, and nothing more. It remains to be seen whether the Government will not feel it their duty to interfere on the ground that the monument has been their affair from the beginning and ought to be completed at their cost and under their auspices.'[1]

Four days previously, M. H. Spielmann, who appears to have set himself against Mac-Coll and on the side of the Academy, had expressed disquiet that an 'art writer' and his friends could, on the quiet, undertake to complete the monument, and stated that he had learnt that one of his acquaintances had been informed of the scheme and had been bound to secrecy, 'It's a secret and nothing must be told till the proper time.'[2]

Poynter hit back at the committee's statement on the 2nd February. The leading article of *The Times* left little to be said, but there were two points which required explanation. Why should the committee have taken such pains to have kept their scheme so secret, when they might have gained if it had been discussed openly? Why should the Dean and Chapter have accepted so lightly the choice of Tweed, consulting no-one but their own architect? Poynter did not for one moment believe that the Dean and Chapter were party to this so carefully preserved secrecy, but it appeared that it had never occurred to them that the best possible successor to Stevens should have been found. He was of the opinion, from what he could find out about Tweed's work, that he and Stevens were poles apart, although the Dean and Chapter presumably

thought differently. Poynter then went on to refer to the committee's exhibition on the monument of Tweed's work, before it was cast. This he thought would be the precise moment when any criticism ceased to be useful. 'We shall again as when the commission was given, be presented with the *fait accompli*, and if the criticism is unfavourable it will doubtless be with regret that the committee will, in Mr. MacColl's engaging words, find that "this very simple service to a monumental genius" has become "mixed with questions of party".' Poynter said that he knew Lord Leighton's final views on the question of the equestrian statue and they were such as everyone 'save perhaps the *Saturday Review* committee' would agree with. 'Before concluding,' he said, 'I may perhaps . . . correct a misapprehension of my action which occurred in your leading article . . . to the effect that I omitted to inform the Dean and Chapter of what I had heard of the Government's intentions. As a matter of fact, I did communicate with the Dean and Chapter through the Bishop of Stepney immediately I obtained the information that the Government contemplated taking the matter up. This was three or four days before Mr. Spielmann's first letter appeared in your columns; but then it was too late . . . Until then I was completely ignorant of the Government's intention which, no doubt, had only at that time begun to take a concrete form. The Bishop of Stepney expresses his regret also that I did not inform the Dean and Chapter of my having approached the Government. As things turned out, this is certainly to be regretted, but without knowing whether the authorities would take the matter up it would have been premature to talk of it; besides, I had from the first left it in Lord Robert's able and willing hands. To suggest . . . that I kept the matter a secret is merely an attempt to throw dust in the eyes of the public on the part of those who had their own private scheme, and one which

[1] *Ibid.*, 24th January 1903.
[2] *Ibid.*, 20th January 1903.

they would hardly have kept so secret if they had not feared that exposure to the light of day would have meant its doom.'[1]

The reply by D. S. MacColl was published on 6th February. MacColl made a personal attack on Poynter. He accused him of acquiring inferior paintings at high prices for the National Gallery as well as others of dubious quality, for instance, a Fra Angelico which MacColl claimed was a very poor example and a Vermeer which had no claim to the attribution, and he then asked whether Poynter might not better employ his influence with the Treasury in obtaining money for the national collection than in 'throwing what influence is left to him against the effort to get one thing quietly done amid the official stagnation?' MacColl also accused Poynter of condemning Tweed without having seen any of his work and basing his opinion only on photographs which had appeared in the papers, but the original work of Tweed did not really come into question as what the committee desired was not Tweed's statue, nor anyone else's, but a 'faithful carrying out of Stevens's intentions as far as they are plain from the models'.

'I now come', he continued, 'to Sir Edward Poynter's reiterated complaint against the promoters, that they did not take the public into their confidence from the first. They challenged the Government publicly, which Sir Edward afterwards approached privately. But . . . when Sir Edward Poynter says "the public" what he really means is himself as representing the Academy, and he thus provokes a discussion we had no intention of raising. Sir Edward Poynter will hardly pretend that if the Government had granted his appeal he would have submitted the choice of a sculptor to popular plebiscite. He speaks also of the voice of the Government. It is just as improbable that he would have invited the Government to name the artist. He can hardly,

therefore, make it a grievance against the committee that they did neither of these things. His own "secrecy" I may add, far exceeds theirs, for he has not yet disclosed the name of the "best possible man" whom he would have nominated. Since however, Sir Edward Poynter insists on having reasons for the failure of the committee to consult him, I can suggest some very good reasons that might have prevented the committee from taking the Academy into their counsels, if it had occurred to them that they were called upon to take that step. Once more, let me guard against misconception. The question is not whether there are sculptors in the Academy as good as, or better than, Mr. Tweed. That mixed body obviously includes men capable of what he has undertaken, and of harder tasks. The practical question is whether there could be any certainty that a sculptor nominated by the Academy would be willing to subordinate his own ideas to those of Stevens. On this point the previous history of the movement is far from reassuring. Lord Leighton, in his negotiations, had to contend with proposals to substitute an original design for Stevens's . . .'[2]

As a further step in justification of the committee's action, MacColl, who was the editor, published a lengthy article in the *Architectural Review*,[3] in March, which had been publicised beforehand in the daily press. In this, MacColl reproduced several photographs of the equestrian statue 'accurately piece-moulded and reproduced in facsimile', with the addition of the head of the Duke. From these illustrations MacColl hoped that the reader would be in a better position to understand the references to it which had been made in the statement by the committee, and they would see that in

---

[1] *The Times*, 2nd February 1903.

[2] *Ibid.*, 6th February 1903.
[3] 'The Wellington Monument of Alfred Stevens. A Description, with Illustrations of the existing Models and Drawings for the Equestrian Statue.' *Architectural Review*, March 1903, pp. 87–96.

parts the model was defective, 'the near hind hoof is missing, leaving the leg short; the tail is a mere stump; the drapery of the Duke is fractured, the fingers of the right hand broken, and there are some minor defects, as well as accidental roughness in the surface of the plaster. However, the sketch which was on the summit of Stevens's scale model was useful in supplementing this model, as it supplied the missing part of the horse's leg, indicated Stevens's treatment of the tail and especially showed that the Duke was holding his cocked hat in his right hand, above the horse's neck.'

MacColl continued by asserting that this was Stevens's magnificent design which no living person would have the right to touch, so that any question of finishing the statue would be limited to details. Stevens had obviously not given any final touches to the figure generally except for the Duke's head. Therefore it would be better to leave any discussion over details of finish until the model in its present state had been hoisted on to the monument in the Cathedral, so that its effect could be judged.

The committee carried on with its intentions until the beginning of July 1903. Harold Hodge, the secretary, was able to write to *The Times* to announce that 'a bronze-coloured facsimile of Stevens's plaster model of the equestrian figure for the Wellington Monument, with certain missing parts supplied by his sketch-model, has now been placed in position in St. Paul's Cathedral, and will be open to public view by permission of the Dean and Chapter on Monday next, July 13th and for seven days after [Plates 69–71].'[1]

At the moment of placing the statue in position, however, there had been doubts as to which way the Duke should face, east towards the altar, or west towards the main door.[2] MacColl wrote to the person whom he thought would know, Hugh Stannus. Stannus replied,[3] 'Stevens never said verbally anything about attitude of *living* and *dead*. But he had no doubt had it in his mind as showed in the rough sketch which is plate XXX.III in my book.

'If you imagine the sketch is for a position on the South side of the nave: then it is all right—and you are quite justified in placing the living as riding towards the West and the dead as lying towards East—The sketch was *very* hurriedly done—and he quite accepted the ecclesiologist attitudes tacitly, as far as he could.'

This reply was not quite what MacColl wanted as the monument was on the north side of the nave, so, storing up trouble for the future, the committee placed the group facing eastwards, as had been shown by Stevens on his original sketch of 1856.

The authorities of St. Paul's by the end of 1907 were becoming impatient for something for them to see and in the Chapter Minutes for 11th November it was recorded that 'The Dean and Chapter desire to inform the Committee for the Completion of the Wellington Monument that unless the sculptor Mr. Tweed places his model of the monument for the approval of the Dean and Chapter within two months, the Dean and Chapter will be compelled to reconsider their attitude towards the proposed completion'. Three days later Hodge wrote to the Dean to inform him that the Clerk of the Works to the Cathedral had been told that the

---

[1] When the Dean and Chapter had seen this bronzed replica of Stevens's model they came to the conclusion that, as it was, it was too crude and unfinished. They then saw Tweed and agreed that he should prepare another and more finished model for their inspection (Chapter Minutes, St. Paul's Cathedral, 25th July 1903).

[2] The proposal of the committee entrusted with the completion of the Wellington Monument that the Equestrian Statue should be erected in the position given to it in Stevens's designs, that is, facing eastward, was approved. The committee was requested to submit to the Chapter a report of their intentions with regard to its final treatment of the design after public exhibition of the cast is in its place on the monument, not later than Saturday, 25th July (Chapter Minutes, St. Paul's Cathedral, 8th July 1903).

[3] 3rd July 1903.

PLATE 69. *The monument, seen from the south-west, with a cast of Stevens's equestrian group placed in position during 1903. Victoria and Albert Museum Library, photograph in the MacColl Collection. The cast is now in the Tate Gallery.*

PLATE 70. *The monument, seen from the north-east, with a cast of Stevens's equestrian group placed in position during 1903. Victoria and Albert Museum Library, photograph in the MacColl Collection.*

Plate 71. *The monument, seen from the south, with a cast of Stevens's equestrian group placed in position during 1903. Victoria and Albert Museum Library, photograph in the MacColl Collection.*

model would be put in position forthwith (Plates 72, 73).

Sir Edward Poynter visited the monument with the Bishop of Stepney and Thomas Brock, R.A.,[1] but he was not at all happy with the effect; the statue appeared to be too large. He was therefore of the opinion that the model was not the work of Stevens, but an enlargement by an assistant from the quarter-size model, as an experiment for scale. Therefore he suggested to the Bishop of Stepney that the monument should be left incomplete, as Stevens had designed it as only the 'subordinate scaffolding' for the equestrian group, and that he would have been shocked to think that so clumsy a figure as this model was to remain in position. That thorn-in-the-flesh, M. H. Spielmann, was also disappointed.[2] He urged the Dean and Chapter to withdraw their consent for this unfinished work which would be cruel to Stevens's memory, and damaging to the effect of the monument. He concluded his letter by addressing himself to the editor, 'Surely, Sir, when you yourself use such expressions of parts of the work as "awkwardly placed", "decidedly clumsy", "almost a hunch-backed appearance", and "effect of heaviness", you proclaim the incongruity of the finished work and the new, and the truth of your criticism should discourage such a consummation as that which I now make a last effort to avert.'

Some people were happy, though. Alphonse Legros[3] sent a telegram to MacColl saying that he had seen the statue by lantern and considered it superb. The *Daily Chronicle* found that not much interest in the proposal had been evident, apart from the argument in *The Times*, and thought that Tweed obviously had no intention to improve on Stevens, and that

it was better to trust a sculptor who seemed capable of suppressing himself than to have the new work of someone else.

However, apart from occasional rumblings, the committee seemed for the moment to have had its way. At the beginning of 1908 the argument about which way the Duke should be facing erupted again. The first that MacColl heard of its revival seems to have been in a letter from John Tweed.[4] He wrote that he was glad that MacColl's opinion of the Wellington was so far favourable and hoped that they could meet to discuss some details which needed altering. Tweed continued:

'. . . I would rather you could be at St. Paul's on Monday or Tuesday. I was there with Macartney[5] and Canon Scott Holland[6] and they agreed to have a meeting with Stepney one of these evenings if he could attend. Now I think you should be there too, as it is about the position of the horse, I would prefer it as it is, and as we thought right during the last time it was up, they want it facing west. I think you might write Hodge suggesting a meeting of the Committee to settle the question while it is on a turntable and can be easily changed. They mean to place the horse on the fixed stand so that Macartney's new design for the base be properly tried.'

On hearing this from Tweed, MacColl promptly wrote to Harold Hodge to let him know what was afoot and asking him to call a meeting of the committee. He sent the letter to the *Saturday Review*, but this did not reach Hodge for some days as it happened to coincide with a week-end. Hodge's reply was received by MacColl on the 7th January:

'I think Scott Holland's and Macartney's idea of turning the horse round quite preposterous.

---

[1] Sir Thomas Brock, K.C.B., R.A. (1847–1922), sculptor of the Queen Victoria Memorial at Buckingham Palace.

[2] *The Times*, 16th July 1903.

[3] Alphonse Legros (1837–1911), painter and sculptor, Slade Professor of Fine Art, London University, from 1875 to 1892.

[4] 3rd January 1908.

[5] Sir Mervyn Edmund Macartney, F.S.A., F.R.I.B.A. (d. 1932), editor *Architectural Review*, 1906–20.

[6] Henry Scott Holland, Canon of St. Paul's (d. 1918).

Plate 72. *The monument, seen from the south, with John Tweed's preparatory model placed in position during 1908. Victoria and Albert Museum Library, photograph in the MacColl Collection.*

PLATE 73. *The monument, seen from the south-east, with John Tweed's preparatory model placed in position during 1908. Victoria and Albert Museum Library, photograph in the MacColl Collection.*

Even apart from Stevens' own expressed wish, I should be dead against the horse facing west. Everything in a church converges on the Altar.

Scott Holland as an ecclesiastic ought to be ashamed to suggest anything else. Fancy his wanting the Duke and the horse to turn their backs on the High Altar.

Artistically, too, I think the figure would lose. But, of course, Stevens' own view absolutely settles the matter. I have not been able to see Stepney, but I have seen Beckett who strongly takes the same view. I do not think there is any need to hold a committee on the point for, strictly, it is not a matter on which the committee has a right to say. It is, of course, solely within the right of the Dean and Chapter, but by all means put it strongly that, so far as you know, every member of the committee is dead against any change in the horse's direction. I have no doubt Stepney will be too. I feel so strongly on the point that if the Dean and Chapter made it a condition that the horse should be turned, I think I should advise letting the whole thing drop. As the Cathedral people certainly would never find the money for themselves, they would then have to do without the figure, or take it as we want it.'

This reaction by the secretary to the committee, have it as we want it or go without, obviously never became public, because surely Spielmann and possibly Poynter would have made capital out of it. If they were able to persuade the Dean to insist on the Duke and the horse facing westward, Poynter would have been able to put forward his scheme, and Harold Hodge appears to forget that Poynter would probably have obtained money from the government. But all was quiet, even *The Times* apparently taking no more interest in the affair, for a week later Hodge again wrote:[1]

'I have just heard from the Bishop of Stepney that the controversy as to the Orientation(!)

[1] 14th January 1908.

of the horse still rages. Stepney is with me in supporting the Eastward position. Scott Holland is dead West. Stepney suggests that we should have a committee meeting to consider the question and I think we must, but Beckett is unfortunately at Biarritz . . . So far there seems to have been no hostile comment. I doubt if the Times means to refer to it at all, though of course it may be that they are gathering themselves for a determined attack.'

This brought a reply from MacColl,[2] who told Hodge that the evidence was quite clear that the horse should face eastwards; which prompted Hodge to ask if the evidence came from Stevens himself. Hugh Stannus in the meantime had told MacColl his version of Stevens's proposal and it appears to be something quite different:

'I went to the Welln Mont to see the Horse; and I was sorry to see the Horse the wrong way about, and contrary to the intention of Stevens, who arranged for the *living man* to be "riding towards the Setting Sun".[3]

I hope you will, in your influence have this rectified, for, besides being against Stevens'

[2] 13th January 1908.
[3] The original drawing of 1856 shows that Stevens had drawn the horse and rider facing east, and the recumbent Duke lying with his head towards the east. Today the monument is so arranged that the effigy lies with its head at the west.

Stannus in his *Alfred Stevens and his Work*, 1891, Plate IV, reproduces his own drawing showing the complete monument as he hoped it would be in the nave; here the equestrian Duke is riding westwards.

Stannus in the same work (p. 20) writing about a preliminary drawing states, 'it shews an error; the effigy being represented as having its feet towards the West, and the living man as riding towards the East. This was afterwards corrected by Stevens, perhaps bearing in mind Street's eloquent words in his description of Mastino II dei Scalizeri, in which he writes of that as—"surmounted by the figure of the Capitano del Popolo, spear in hand, riding on his war-horse; the horse and horseman riding with their faces towards the setting sun, as all in life must ever ride; the effigy below lying so that at the last day the beams of the day-star in the East may first meet its view, and awaken him that sleepeth here in peace?" '

idea, the R.H. side of the horse and man is comparatively dull and uninteresting;* and both heads are now turned away to look down into the N. side-aisle!

Please have this corrected so soon as you can, for it is prejudicing the Mont, as also the reputation of Stevens.

*and makes bad *lines of composn* to the Groups.'

Stannus had now told MacColl twice that Alfred Stevens had proposed that the statue should face away from the altar, and it seems strange that MacColl should take no notice of the man whom he had first looked upon as the fountain-head of information about the monument, and from whom he had bought Stevens's model. It turned out almost immediately that there was, in the view of the committee, something underhand going on behind the Dean and Chapter. John Tweed got to hear of it first and wrote hurriedly and confidentially to MacColl:[1]

'Have you seen the letter in ysdays D.T. & the enclosed letter from Macartney I received last night. I know he brought Stannus to the Cathedral and sent for Canon Scott Holland, why none of the other Canons. I will write him to say I wish the horse removed. He has had several people at the Cathedral and Harding has had to turn the Horse round for them . . . Only I feel strongly you should get quits with Macartney, its so low to go behind our backs and also that of the Dean and Chapter it means mischief. Is it not your Committee that employs him to design the pedestal. I leave it to your judgement to act, but I do say that it is

dangerous to work with a man like that, and Stepney should know his character. Somers Clarke was straight and acted as a gentleman . . .'

It would appear from the enclosure that Macartney was going behind the committee's back, for his letter, written on 26th January, thirteen days after that from Stannus to MacColl, implies that Stannus had only just heard of the matter.[2] MacColl's view prevailed and it was agreed that the statue should face eastwards, and there the position rested until John Belcher, A.R.A.,[3] wrote to *The Times* in October 1908. He wanted to know what the latest developments regarding the monument were. The Bishop of Stepney and the Dean and Chapter of St. Paul's decided not to answer this letter, but MacColl himself wrote to Belcher, and asked him to call at the Tate Gallery for a talk. Belcher, however, was in bed ill, so he wrote to MacColl that no reply had been sent to *The Times* by Stepney, nor anyone else. He felt that as the Wellington monument was not merely a public, but a national one, some information should be given as to what was being done towards its completion. He asked if MacColl could write something for publication to alleviate the anxiety not only for himself, but the others who were acting with him. This last statement was like a red rag to a bull; who was with Belcher—the Academy? So MacColl sent Belcher's letter to the Bishop of Stepney, whose chaplain told MacColl that the Bishop had been quite sure that there were others behind Belcher, and that he now had written to

---

[1] Undated, but the letter referred to was in the *Daily Telegraph* for 27th January 1908. It was signed under the pen-name of 'F.S.A.' The writer criticised the proposal to complete the monument 'by a young Chelsea sculptor . . . under circumstances which, owing to the secrecy for a long while kept, have been publicly characterised as "discreditable"'. He also stated that Stevens's model was not in a condition suitable for the purpose as it was only 'a sketch roughly thrown together to enable the sculptor to judge of the size. It was never a design.'

[2] 'Dear Tweed,
I have meant to have had a talk with Harding about the construction of the pedestal and support of the horse on Saturday. But he was taken ill on Friday and it may be some time before he is about. I can not do anything without him. I spoke to the B. of Stepney on Saturday about paying for the "sediment" and he is to call the Committee together to go into this matter. The D. & C. flatly declined to do or pay for anything. . . . The wordy warfare will begin in a few days. I expect Stannus is on the track.'

[3] John Belcher, R.A. (d. 1913).

The Times, but he did not wish to be drawn into any further controversy. Accordingly the following letter appeared on 9th November:

'. . . may I make two remarks on behalf of the Dean and Chapter of St. Paul's?

Firstly, as to the strength and stability of the monument, all the facts are well known to the Dean and Chapter, and have been carefully considered. Every care will be taken that the completion of the monument shall not affect its stability.

Secondly, in order that the public, and especially all who are interested in the work of Alfred Stevens, might have every opportunity of seeing the model of the equestrian figure and pediment, ample notice was given in the Press last December that it would be placed *in situ* in the Cathedral. It remained there open to public inspection for two months. No adverse criticisms were received. Further, before finally deciding as to the position of the figure and the design of the pediment, the Dean and Chapter had the opportunity of considering all the information which the late Mr. Stannus[1] was able to give, and all the available original drawings of Stevens. Their decision was based upon these materials. It was only made in May, five months after the model had been exposed to public inspection. It will be recognised that it is too late now to reopen a discussion for which full opportunity was given during these months.'

Belcher and others were not really satisfied with this answer. The Bishop had mentioned 'pediment' when presumably he meant pedestal. As, however, no mention before had been made about alterations to the pediment, this mistake started another hare. What was the decision made in May, asked Belcher, was it to omit the figure, raise it or reverse it? We do not know whether Belcher even had an answer.

Again, all was quiet for a few months until

Ernest George,[2] then President of the Royal Institute of British Architects, stated that he had been trying unavailingly to find out some information from the committee. He thus felt that it was his duty to draw to public attention the present condition of the monument, which was cracked and insecure, so that in his view it would be dangerous to put a statue weighing several tons on top, and also even to attempt to strengthen it for this purpose.

Harold Hodge informed MacColl[3] that he had written an answer to Ernest George who was, he thought, 'in league with the Academy'. There was to be a committee meeting the following week and he wanted to meet Tweed and MacColl to discuss the casting of the group.

Hodge's letter to *The Times* appeared on 20th April. In this he said that he had told the R.I.B.A. to wait for the next Wellington Committee meeting to be held shortly, after which they would get a reply. As he had said nothing about the dangerous state of the monument, *The Times* sent a reporter to St. Paul's Cathedral. There a spokesman for the Dean and Chapter stated that they knew all about the cracks, which had been pointed out by their Foreman of Works. These had been remedied and it was not foreseen that there would be any difficulty in strengthening the monument without altering its appearance in any way.

In spite of all the opposition the Wellington Monument Committee had experienced, the moment had come to cast the statue but at precisely this stage MacColl and Tweed fell out. Tweed had done what MacColl could not stomach, he had put a little of Tweed into the statue. The first indication of any disagreement between the two appeared in a letter to MacColl from Hodge written on 5th May 1909. Hodge wanted to meet MacColl before the next committee meeting, which was to be held on 11th May, as evidently MacColl had threatened

[1] Hugh Stannus had died on 18th August 1908.

[2] Sir Ernest George, R.A. (1839–1922), architect.
[3] 19th April 1909.

to resign from the committee if he could not get his own way. He went on:

'I should be immensely relieved if you and Tweed could be got into line. If you leave the Committee, you burst us up entirely; to say the least, you will give the Academy and all our opponents a leg up for which they will all be truly thankful to you. You know, old chap, we gave the work to Tweed on your recommendation. I was only too glad to follow your advice. If the Wellington collapses, the burden and odium will fall on me.'

If MacColl could not endorse the committee's view in everything then what he should do, was not to resign but to have recorded in the minutes that he dissented from it. If necessary Hodges would publish in *The Times* this minority view of MacColl's. He should remember that the alternative to Tweed's statue would *not* be a facsimile of Stevens's group. The Dean and Chapter would not agree to that, but turn instead to the Royal Academy scheme, which would undoubtedly be given to Brock.

What had Tweed done which was causing all the trouble? This comes out in a letter from MacColl to the sculptor. His model, in the view of MacColl 'lost something of the essential . . . of Stevens's design, viz. the turn of the arm of the Duke, and the neck of the horse, and the turn of the advanced foreleg. The projection of the . . . horse affects the silhouette both broad-side on, and looking from the East.' Tweed must consider modifying his model. As it stood at the moment MacColl could not agree to its passing as Stevens's design, which he had throughout insisted upon as a condition, and therefore would be forced to resign.

While this new argument was thus fermenting, Hodge was having difficulties about the new pedestal. It had been agreed to give the order for this to Somers Clarke, but a precise condition must be laid down, so that he did not produce only what he himself thought

fit.[1] What Hodge had in mind was the design which MacColl had approved.

Between May and August 1909 Somers Clarke and the committee conducted various experiments with the proposed new pedestal for the statue. Models were made which caused Somers Clarke to warn against the amount of money being spent, but as he said, no good results could be arrived at without at least some models. A decision was reached in July for a light metal frame to be placed inside the upper pedestal, so that most of the weight of the new statue would be taken by that, and not by the top of the monument itself. Work had progressed far enough by 5th August for Somers Clarke to write to MacColl as, if he was the committee member who had to be satisfied over the group, then presumably he had to agree to all the other related work. Clarke informed him that he had 'obtained an estimate from Messrs. Farmer & Brindley for the curved top to the upper Pediment, in marble of the same quality as that of the rest of the monument—this is of course essential. The curved surface carved with laurel leaves as on the model I have made, the estimate is £223. This alarms Mr. Hodge very much.

'I have also an estimate for the work smooth on its surface, i.e. without the laurel leaves. This estimate is £164. Are the laurel leaves essential? I think them very desirable and in accordance with the spirit of the design but, no doubt, there is no evidence to show that Stevens had proposed them.

'The large stone has been taken off the top of the monument. It weighed 12 cwt. The marble work would weigh about 15 cwt, so we do not in this matter add seriously to the load. I am, to-day, seeing the engineer about the metal frame to carry the horse.'

The relationship between MacColl and John

[1] The Cathedral Architect was not offering views about designs of the base of the statue. The Committee should offer suggestions for the Chapter (Chapter Minutes, 28th March 1908).

Tweed was now rapidly worsening. Tweed was not quite ready with the group at the beginning of October but wrote to say that he hoped shortly to be able to ask Hodge to call a committee meeting at his studio, so that the statue could then be sent to the caster. The slight alterations which had enraged MacColl earlier in the year when he had seen Tweed's work, had been reported by him at a committee meeting on 11th May. The Committee then instructed Hodge to tell Tweed to proceed with the casting as soon as the modifications in the model, specified by MacColl and approved by the committee, had been completed, but unfortunately the modifications were not set out in detail. In fact all that Tweed did was to alter the hoof of the right foreleg of the horse, as he says 'at Mr. MacColl's wish'.

The matter, however, did not come before the committee again. Hodge and the chairman discussed it but concluded that it would be better not to bring the subject up once more as (a) there was apparently no chance of agreement between MacColl and Tweed, (b) if Tweed was acting in bad faith, he would still not agree to make the modifications and the committee could not make him. The result would thus have been deadlock, which might have resulted in the whole project being abandoned, as it was felt that the committee should remain neutral in the argument. As Hodge said, heretically, it was not as if the alterations were vital.

MacColl, however, still wanted his own way. On 4th November he wrote again to Tweed:

'I have fortunately kept a copy of the letter in which, at your request, I enumerated the modifications in your model, I insisted upon if I was to remain a member of the Wellington Monument Committee. The letter was addressed to you on May 9th, 1909, and if you will refer to it you will find that it clearly specifies among the departures from Stevens's design, the line of the advanced foreleg of the horse. This disposes of the contention with which you astonished me on Tuesday, that you understood me to refer to the hoof only. I had already at great length at St. Paul's with the aid of the photos gone into the difference in the inclination of the leg in your model . . . and explained it fully at the same time to Hodge. As he recollects it was discussed again at your studio on May 11th, and with great reluctance you finally agreed to this as well as other changes. I reported accordingly to the committee the same evening. When I came down to view these modifications this last Thusday I at once noticed that the leg and hoof had not been altered and drew your attention to this. You again raised objections, and I again referred you to the change in the outline of S's design as shown in the photos. It was not until after lunch that you promised to make the alteration, adding "Well, if I do you must try to get me more money for the job". I replied that I would do what I could, though I could make no promise for the committee. We then parted on this understanding.

On Tuesday I discovered by chance that you had sent the model to the caster without altering leg and hoof. You offered, on my asking for an explanation, then to have the hoof put right, but denied that you had promised to alter the leg.

I had never contemplated or discussed with you, nor had you suggested to me a compromise upon what I specified in my letter and discussed with you in detail.

I therefore fail to understand the reason in your mind as to the leg when you made your promise and also your failure to carry out what you admit you agreed to on the Thursday with respect to the hoof.

PLATE 74. *The completed monument, seen from the south. Photograph:* Royal Commission on Historical Monuments (England).

These being the facts I am bound to maintain the view of your conduct that I impressed to you at the time.

Yours faithfully, D. S. MacColl.'

Gone was the friendly tone of all the previous letters between the two, and Tweed's reply four days later was curt and formal:

'Dear Sir,

I received your letter of the 4th and have sent it to the Secretary of the Wellington Statue Fund.

Yours truly, John Tweed.'

Tweed sent the letter from MacColl to Harold Hodge, stating that he declined to discuss the matter but asked that the committee might hear his 'account of Mr. MacColl's conduct'. Hodge told MacColl at the time that these letters would be put before the committee at their next meeting which Tweed would be invited to attend. As we have seen above, the chairman and Hodge eventually decided not to involve the committee. 'What an irony', wrote Hodge, 'that your personal recommendation of Tweed to the Committee should result in estrangement between you and him. But, of course, I know you did not then contemplate more than very slight work for the sculptor.'

It appears that in spite of MacColl's opposition from then onwards, the model was, in fact, cast without any further alterations being made by Tweed.

In July 1910 Somers Clarke was still occupied with the necessary architectural additions to the top of the monument, and was suggesting that yet another model be made[1]

and, now that the culmination of years of preparation was near at hand, Harold Hodge was busy trying to find the last five hundred pounds necessary finally to get the Duke to the top of the monument. All the City Companies were invited to subscribe[2] and soon almost all the money was to hand.

The sculpture was cast, raised to its position, and the Committee got ready for the unveiling ceremony. But even this was frustrated. Without consultation in any way with the Committee the Dean and Chapter of St. Paul's decided to announce that the completed

---

[1] 20th July 1910. Somers Clarke to MacColl:

'Perhaps the Committee's consideration of the question, whether the bronze keystone and festoons with a guilloche in the panel on the soffit of the carved pediment may be attested by the copies of Stevens drawings which I send herewith. I send the photograph marked A because it shows so clearly Stevens intentions as regard the carved top in marble. This is adopted by the Committee. The photo B seems clearly to be a part of the same mental impulse and here we have the festoons sketched and the keystone indicated. The photo C gives us the treatment of the soffit of the curved pediment in detail and also of the keystone bracket.

I have already in a report to the Committee, pointed out that the jointing of the marble arch is actually prepared for the keystone. The jointing we now see is without reason unless it were intended for the keystone.

It will be essential to have a model made, for experiments, for the keystone and the festoons—coloured bronze—also for the guilloche etc, and this, without adding another burden of money collecting on Mr. Hodges back. But I think I know where the money may be found.'

[2]   April 1911
WELLINGTON MONUMENT COMPLETION
FUND
To the Master, Wardens and Court of Assistants of the Worshipful Company of . . .

The Monument to the Duke of Wellington in St. Paul's Cathedral has never been completed although commenced nearly half a century ago. Accordingly a number of Citizens of London and others have privately raised a fund to provide for the casting and erection of the equestrian figure of the Duke according to the original design. The greater part of the money required has been collected and the work is nearly finished, but the Committee have been unable to raise the last five hundred pounds required to complete. In these circumstances, feeling that this is a national matter with a peculiar appeal to the City of London, as appurtenant to the Metropolitan Cathedral, they venture to ask the assistance of the Livery Guilds and Citizens to allow this memorial of one of Britain's greatest heroes and Statesmen to be finished without debt. We enclose a short financial Statement together with the contributors.

H. Scott Holland, Chairman.
(Canon of S. Paul's, Regius Professor of Divinity at Oxford.)
Gervase Beckett, Treasurer. (M.P. Whitby Division.)
Harold Hodge, (Editor of the Saturday Review) Hon. Sec.
D. S. MacColl, Keeper of the Wallace Collection.
Herbert Trench, (Director of the Haymarket Theatre.)

monument would be on view to the public on St. Paul's Day, 25th January 1912, and that there would not be any unveiling ceremony (Plate 74). The committee learned of these arrangements only by reading the newspapers which carried the announcement at too short a notice for a committee meeting to be summoned.

'Yes', Hodge told MacColl, 'the Dean and Chapter made fools of themselves, to put it

---

WELLINGTON MONUMENT COMPLETION FUND

RECEIPTS AND EXPENDITURE

Spent	£	s.	d.	*Received*	£	s.	d.
Mr. Tweed (Sculptor)	1,300	0	0	Subscriptions	1,817	7	0
Stevens' Model	50	0	0	Rebate on photographs of Group	4	4	0
Casters (bronze on pedestal)	68	0	0				
Pedestal (marble & steel frame)	228	1	1				
Mr. Wallace (Architect acting for Mr. Somers Clarke)	2	12	6				
Photographs	25	0	3				
Putting up in S. Paul's Cathedral facsimile of Stevens' model, Mr. Tweed's model, and the equestrian figure as finished in bronze	146	1	11				
Printing	1	5	0				
Balance given to S. Paul's Decoration Fund		10	3				
	1,821	11	0		1,821	11	0

CONTRIBUTORS TO THE WELLINGTON MONUMENT FUND

The Duke of Wellington
The Late Duke of Devonshire
The Duke of Marlborough
The Duke of Bedford
The Marquis of Anglesey
The Marquis of Londonderry
The Earl of Rosebery
Earl Curzon of Kedleston
Lord Rothschild
The Late Lord Masham
Lord Grimthorpe
Lord Montagu of Beaulieu
Lord Iveagh
Hon. Gervase Beckett, M.P.
Sir Samuel Scott, Bart.
Sir Julius Wernher, Bart.
Sir Lionel Phillips, Bart.
Sir Edgar Speyer, Bart.
Sir E. Durning Laurence, Bart.
F.M. Sir Evelyn Wood, V.C.
Sir Thomas Sutherland
Professor Scott Holland
Mr. R. S. Gundry, C.B.
Mr. J. F. Mason, M.P.

Mr. D. S. MacColl
Mr. John R. Clayton
Mr. E. Bayley
Mr. Herbert Cook
Mr. Lockett Agnew
Mr. Edward Huth
Mr. W. Alexander
Mr. Douglas Freshfield
Mr. Brinsley Fitzgerald
Mr. A B. Horne
Mr. C. W. Dyson Perrins
Mr. J. H. Fitzhenry
Mr. George Harwood
Mr. J. W. Harris
Mr. Ernest Hobson
Mr. Harold Hodge
Messrs. Carfax
The Corporation of London
The Mercers' Company
The Grocers' Company
The Fishmongers' Company
The Skinners' Company
Certain Sums per Mr. Herbert Trench

no more severely. It was a pity that our business happened to fall to Alexander. Was it not an irony that I should happen to be thrown on the low Church and latitudinous Canon? Both the high Churchmen (Lang and Scott-Holland) served us admirably. Of course, technically, the question of an unveiling ceremony or not is entirely for the Dean and Chapter; so, when Alexander mentioned it to me some time since, I could not protest. But I had not the smallest idea he meant to let the figure be public anything like so soon. If I had, I certainly should have taken some steps to prevent it. It is amusing to see how completely our old enemies have been silenced. I mean the Academy lot. They have taken their revenge by getting the Press to ignore the Committee. At least I think the Academy must be behind, I hope I made no mistake in our article last week. Owing to Alexander's action everything had to be done in a hurry.'

MacColl by March 1912 was still not able to forgive Tweed for daring to tamper with the work of the Master. He insisted that the following be inserted in the committee's minutes:

'Mr. MacColl desired the Committee to note that he did not accept responsibility for a departure from Stevens's design made by the sculptor Mr. Tweed in the line of the right foreleg of the horse. He had included a modification of Mr. Tweed's model in this respect in his report to the Committee of 11 May and the Committee had approved it. He had drawn up in a letter to the Secretary of 2 November 1909 a full statement of the case as between him and the sculptor; and he desired this letter to be entered on the record. Resolved that Mr. MacColl's disclaimer of responsibility to be noted and his letter to Mr. Hodge of 2 November and the subjoined extract from his letter to Mr. Tweed of 9 May 1909 be placed in the minutes. It is understood that Mr. Mac-Coll is under no obligation of any sort not to

make public his objection in this respect to Mr. Tweed's figure.'

Harold Hodge appended a further note in the minute book in fairness to John Tweed—'I was present at the meeting of Mr. MacColl and Mr. Tweed referred to in the above letter. Mr. Tweed did not admit that he had undertaken to make the modification in the right foreleg in the horse described by Mr. MacColl.'

A month after this, on 4th April, Hodge formally told MacColl:

'I am directed by the Wellington Monument Completion Fund Committee to inform you that the equestrian figure of the Duke of Wellington, designed by Mr. Tweed on the lines of Alfred Stevens's model, was put up in S. Paul's Cathedral on S. Paul's Day, the 25th January, 1912. All charges in respect to the undertaking have been fully met. I beg to enclose a copy of the names of the contributors together with a statement of receipts and expenditure.

I am also desired by the Committee to tender you their best thanks as expressed by the resolution passed at their final meeting of the 6 March, 1913, for your very kind contribution to this Fund. The work and object for which the Committee was formed being now fulfilled, a resolution that the Committee be dissolved was passed at the meeting referred to.'

Thus after nearly fifty-six years the story of the Wellington monument comes to an end. From the beginning until the final day it had been the object of suspicion, disagreement and argument. Nowadays it is largely ignored by visitors to the Cathedral who appear to prefer the marble groups of Bacon, Flaxman and Rossi.

*   *   *

Writers on Stevens and the Wellington monument have always taken the view that the sculptor was the victim of persecution by a philistine government department. However, it should be remembered that he received a large sum of public money and had produced almost nothing but a plaster model; time and time again he gave successive Commissioners of Works assurances that all was going well, and the monument would soon be finished, although at work instead on other projects, such as his major scheme for the redecoration of St. Paul's Cathedral. It is hardly surprising that, after some ten years or so of delay, the Office of Works at last lost patience and demanded more positive action. If the Office of Works had not taken a firm stand, in all probability the Wellington monument would have been yet another scheme which Stevens did not bring to fruition, and the finest work of sculpture produced in this country during the 19th century would have been lost.

X

The Competition Models

What became of the various models, successful in the competition, and which under the rules were retained by the government? In January 1860 they were all, with the exception of that by Stevens, in the Conference Room of the Houses of Parliament, but, as the space was needed, George Buckler of the Office of Works enquired where they could be safely put. On 24th January the Royal Institute of British Architects agreed to house them and put them on exhibition at 9, Conduit Street.

There they remained undisturbed for two years until E. J. Hähnel, who had been awarded the eighth premium, of £100, asked if his model could be sent on loan to the 1862 Exhibition at South Kensington. The Office of Works asked the R.I.B.A. to release this one model, which was subsequently exhibited as No. 914 in the German section of the Fine Art Department. It was back with the R.I.B.A. by 18th December 1862.

After a further thirteen years there, the secretary, Charles L. Eastlake, wrote on 14th October 1873 to the Office of Works to say that the models were so large that the Institute was finding it somewhat inconvenient to house them all, and wondered if they could be found another home. The South Kensington Museum was by this time well-established, so the authorities there were sounded to see if they would like the models for the new architectural gallery. Norman Macleod, for the Museum, replied on 29th October to say that the Museum authorities would be pleased to exhibit three of them. Three models duly arrived; however, they had to be labelled, so another letter went to the Office of Works asking for the sculptors' names. This request

was passed on to the R.I.B.A., but they had no idea of the names of the artists, nor could they find any record of them, and suggested instead that the various articles on the competition in 1857 to be found in *The Builder* might be consulted profitably. Eventually everything was sorted out; the sculptors of the models displayed at South Kensington being William Calder Marshall, Giovanni Dupré, and the collaborators Mariano Folcini and Ulisse Cambi.

When Stevens died in 1875, he had in his possession the competition model and, of course, the full-size models, as well as a mass of drawings and sculptured details.

On 19th July 1877, and the following day, there were two sales of his drawings and models, the first being held in his former studio; at this sale most of the material offered was connected with the Wellington monument. From an annotated sale catalogue reproduced in *Alfred Stevens* by K. R. Towndrow, we find that Hugh Stannus and James Gamble bought a high proportion of the Lots, as for example Lot 46:

'A pair of small-scale casts from model groups . . . "Valour and Cowardice" and "Truth and Falsehood" (£1. 16s.).'

or Lot 59:

'The original colossal-size plaster cast of model of proposed equestrian statue for Wellington Memorial . . . and wood profile (£5).'

There were, however, no bids at all for certain items:

'Lot. 76. A colossal finished plaster group of "Truth and Falsehood", portion of Wellington Memorial.

Lot 77. The companion group "Valour and Cowardice".

Lot 78. The ditto finished plaster model of sarcophagus and recumbent figure of Duke of Wellington.

Lot 81. Shield and Garter.'

These had remained in the possession of Alfred Pegler, Alfred Stevens's executor, who in 1876 began to make enquiries about their disposal and wrote to South Kensington inquiring if the museum would like the models for the monument. The Museum asked the Office of Works who the legal owner of these was, as the Museum thought it had been one of the conditions of the competition that the models of the prize-winners became government property. The Office of Works, on 22nd February 1876, replied that this was quite right, and Pegler also received a letter informing him of the true position.

Nevertheless, during the following year Pegler tried again, this time writing to the Office of Works to let them know that he intended to auction the models. Once again, James Fergusson was called in for advice, and his view was that he saw no objection to Pegler putting the full-size model up for sale, but sold, or otherwise, he should keep it in his possession until the completion of the monument itself, and a letter to this effect was sent to Pegler on 10th July 1877.

Pegler digested this news for a few months, and then, on 15th January 1878, asked the Office of Works to give him proof that the competition model was government property. He was told once again of the condition in the original competition. This was all very well, he countered, but could the Office of Works give him evidence that Alfred Stevens had ever

received the prize of £100? After some days of hurried searching the Office of Works officials found what they wanted; Stevens had been sent a draft for £100 on 21st October 1857, and he had cashed it on 26th October. Probably, suggested the Office, the best thing for Pegler to do with the model was to send it to South Kensington. On 15th March 1878, Leonard Collmann agreed that in his opinion this should be done, but there was a drawback, however, as Pegler had the (then unexecuted) crowning figure of the equestrian Duke. The First Commissioner of Works wrote to Pegler enquiring about this but, as has been shown, it became the property of Stannus and was stored at St. Paul's; by the 25th March 1878 all the other models had been delivered to South Kensington.

All was not over yet, however. On 5th January 1881, the R.I.B.A. wrote to the First Commissioner about the models in their charge in the Architectural Museum. They were anxious that they should be removed; so they were then moved into store at Somerset House. A few years later, in December 1885, South Kensington wanted to be relieved of the three on loan to them, so they too were placed in Somerset House. A report of 1899 stated that all the models were then in store, but were somewhat damaged. A search in the vaults of Somerset House in 1967 revealed nothing. One can only assume that the cumbersome plaster constructions had proved too fragile to survive over half a century of disregard and neglect.

Many drawings relating to the monument survive; there are several in the Victoria and Albert Museum, and others are to be found in the Tate Gallery, Royal Institute of British Architects, the Fitzwilliam Museum, Cambridge, the Ashmolean Museum, Oxford, the Walker Art Gallery, Liverpool, and the British Museum.

APPENDIX

Catalogue[1] of the Models Exhibited in Westminster Hall, 1857, with Criticisms from Contemporary Sources

1. 'The Wellington Star Monument', is a very curious production, and is the only one of its kind in the exhibition. It consists of a statue of the Duke (a very fair likeness), supported on a twisted column of Druid marble. This column springs from a pedestal surrounded by eight more twisted columns. The top of the pedestal is made to represent the summit of a castle, from between the embrasures of which appear several brass cannon, and on either side are figures of Peace and Justice. Round the basement are recorded the names of some of the Duke of Wellington's more prominent victories. This design is certainly very original, but is hardly, perhaps, suited to English taste. The modelling is very ably executed.

['Commencing at the entrance of the Hall with No. 1, we may remark that we are extremely slow to believe that this production is really the work of a sculptor, for assuredly nothing could well be conceived more absurd than the whole affair. The lower portion of it consists of eight twisted columns, surmounted by another of more bulky dimensions, crowned by an Ionic capital of most villainous design. On the abacus of this capital is placed a globe, on the top of which, on a square pedestal, stands the hero of a hundred fights, with a bended sword in his hand. To show the poverty of the inventive faculty displayed in this production, we may remark that at its base are two miniature casts of the noted lions of Canova, attached to the tomb of Pius VI in St. Peter's at Rome.' *The Building News*, 24th July 1857.]

['But on no supposition can we account for the exhibition of a work which first meets the eye (No. 1) in the collection. A production so completely destitute of art, it has never been our lot to encounter. This one work surely will not be described to an *artist*, British or Foreign.' *The Builder*, 1st August 1857.]

['. . . nothing more than a huge twisted spiral column of vulgar detail and proportions.' *The Ecclesiologist*, August 1857.]

['We wish any of our readers who may have seen it could help us to some solution of a very remarkable model in this collection, known as "The Star Monument",—but which we, ourselves, have already alluded to as "The Corkscrew Monument". Ours is the better name; because the star is no part of the design, and the corkscrews are its leading feature. The Duke stands on a large screw, which climbs out of the centre of a pedestal supported on eight smaller screws,—and the pedestal has a circular battlemented edge mounted with cannon. There are figures of Peace and Justice, and some other things; but all else is subsidiary to the corkscrews. Now, this work has given us great mental trouble, in the attempt to master the intention that underlies it. Whatever may be said for or against allegory, we question if sculpture can be canonically treated as a conundrum. We do not like to give up, however; and have wondered whether the author of this mystification could possibly mean to indicate that Wellington had uncorked bottled fame wherever he found it, and drunk off all the wine of glory at the cannon's mouth. The fact that the greater number of the Duke's victories were achieved in a wine-growing country, favours this solution. Still, we cannot feel quite certain that we have here done the work of Oedipus.' *The Art Journal*, August 1857.]

[1] *A Critical and Descriptive Catalogue of the Exhibition of Models for the Wellington Monument now on view in Westminster Hall*, published by H. G. Clarke & Co., 252, Strand, London, price Six-pence.

2. 'Mars.' Represents a colossal group. On the summit of a pedestal a beautiful figure of Britannia is seen crowning her hero with laurel. Round the pedestal are bas-reliefs, showing the portraits, of the size of life, of several of the Duke's most illustrious companions in arms. The artist, in the portraits he has inserted, does not propose them as likenesses, considering that those who should be put in, should be selected by the judges. This is a work of great merit, and will find many admirers.

['No. 2., with the motto "Mars", is composed of a red granite basement, surmounted by a circular pedestal, round which are bassi-relievi, at the base of which are two recumbent lions. On the top of the pedestal Britannia is represented crowning the hero with a bronze wreath.' *The Building News*, 31st July 1857.]

['. . . The principal interest of the composition would have to be looked for in the equestrian figures of his companions in arms surrounding the dado of the oval pedestal.' *The Builder*, 25th July 1857.]

3. 'To be, or not to be.' This design depicts the Duke at the end of his long career. He is standing on a pedestal, whilst a figure, representing the genius of Fame, calls him from mortal to immortal life. At the corners of the pedestal are named four of his principal victories—Vittoria, Waterloo, Seringapatam, and Assaye. An alto-relievo in front represents the result of the battle of Waterloo, and the one behind represents the capture of Seringapatam. At the corner of the pedestal are figures of Minerva, War, Peace and Prosperity. This work is evidently the work of a foreign artist and evinces great talent and originality of design, with the promise of perfect execution.

['No. 3 comprises an oblong moulded plinth in colored marble, on the die of which are lions in bas-relief, and at the corners picturesque figures. The pedestal is surmounted by a recumbent figure of Wellington, with a figure of Fame blowing a trumpet over him. On the ends of the pedestal are represented trophies of war.' *The Building News*, 31st July 1857.]

K

4. [Motto not quoted.][1] A very chaste and simple production will be much admired. It represents the Duke standing, holding a wreath of laurel; at his feet crouches the British lion; at the corners are female figures, one of which holds a shield, on which several of the Duke's victories are recorded.

['No. 4 is formed chiefly of colored marbles. On one side of the pedestal are the late Duke's arms, and on the other a wreath, enclosing a field marshal's cap, sword, and other emblems encircled in palm leaves. The plinth is surmounted by a pedestal with canted corners, the cornice of which is of pale colored marble. The sides of the pedestal are charged with faint allegorical groups in white marble . . .' *The Building News*, 31st July 1857.]

5. 'Through courage and circumspection to victory.' Certainly a very curious production. On the top of a pillar is a winged gilded female figure, holding in one hand an olive branch, typifying peace, and in the other a cornucopia, signifying plenty. Beneath is the duke, in the act of drawing his sword, supported on either side by two figures, one holding a laurel wreath and the other a shield containing the royal arms. At the base, is the Genius of History, writing his various victories and the principal deeds of his life.

['No. 5 is distinguished by a difference in its ground plan, having a minor pedestal on one side of it, which is surmounted by a Corinthian capital, on which is placed a gilded figure of Peace, holding in one hand a myrtle branch, and with the other supporting a cornucopia. On the larger pedestal Wellington is represented as a *Roman* general, supported on each side by female figures, which form a pyramidical group. At the base, in front is the genius of History inscribing the various victories of the military hero.' *The Building News*, 31st July 1857.]

6. 'Wellington fortes viri sapiensque.' A work of great beauty, but the introduction of different-coloured marbles somewhat mars the general effect. The foundation stone is to be of porphyry, over which there is a basement of bronze, profusely ornamented in bas reliefs with the arms of the

---

[1] No motto in the Office of Works list in the Public Record Office.

conquered nations. Upon this is raised another base, of an oval form, of Cyproline marble, upon which is to be placed whatever inscription may ultimately be determined by the judges. Four figures, representing Strength, Justice, Temperance, and Prudence, are at the corners; on the second base there are bas-reliefs representing Ireland instructing Wellington in science; Victory crowning the duke as Sir Arthur Wellesley, on the taking of Mysore; the Peninsular campaign; and the entrance of Wellesley into Paris. Upon this last base a sarcophagus is placed, upon which the principal group stands, which represents Wellington giving back his sword to Britannia, who is in the act of crowning the spirit of the duke. On the left an Angel of Peace invites him to heaven, and History, on the right, is recording his varied exploits.

Altogether this is a work of great merit; but some, from the introduction of so much colour, may think it has somewhat of a meretricious appearance.

['In the model No. 6 we have a departure from the usual oblong form, as the pedestal above its base assumes an elliptical form, and is covered with a continuous series of emblematic war trophies, intended to be executed in bronze.' *The Building News*, 31st July 1857.]

['. . . There is little art of sculpture or architecture in the composition, though it is one which has some pretension by its dimensions and mass.' *The Builder*, 1 August 1857.]

7. ['Beatus ille qui merente palmam onusque tulerit.'] A work of great power and imagination. The artist has sought to represent the Duke in his later rather than his earlier days. He proposes to have a colossal statue of the duke in the costume of Sword Bearer, and holding the Sword of State before the Queen, as was his duty on the appearance of her Majesty in the House of Lords, and as was the case a few months before his death. The likeness of the duke is very good, and forcibly brings back the remembrance of what he was in his latter days. The statue is placed on a massive pedestal, on which are bas-reliefs, each representing a remarkable episode in the duke's life. One shows the late hero on the field of Waterloo, and

the other delivering his famous speech in the House of Lords, on moving the second reading of the Catholic Emancipation Bill. Around the pedestal are allegorical groups, one representing Britannia, who brings a wreath to the tomb of her hero. Fame is depicted as proclaiming with her trumpet the immortal, glorious deeds of the dead. Another group represents a Chelsea pensioner taking his children to the conqueror's tomb, and points out to his grandson a Grenadier whom he desires him to emulate. Altogether this is a charming work; all the details are carried out with marvellous precision.

['No. 7 . . . is intended to be constructed of red and gray granite and marble, and is chiefly distinguishable for being surmounted by a colossal statue of the Duke, holding in front of him an enormous sword. Around the pedestal are the usual stock allegorical figures of Britannia, Fame, &c.' *The Building News*, 31st July 1857.]

['. . . represents the Duke in a posture of decrepit crouching beadledom—bearing the great sword of state.' *The Ecclesiologist*, August 1857.]

['. . . a mere statue of the Duke as the State-sword bearer, with whatever accessories or figures around the base, would not satisfy the national object, or the other conditions.' *The Builder*, 25th July 1857.]

['. . . Is like many of the models, better in its accessory figures than as to its principal figure and centre in the composition.' *The Builder*, 1st August 1857.]

8. [No motto quoted.][1] A full-length figure of the Duke standing on a pedestal.

9.   'Uno de' due
D'un' illustre vittoria andra superbo;
Il cimento e comune, ed avvien spesso
Che morte incontra chi di darla ha speme.'

A beautifully executed model. It is composed of two parts, one inferior, the other superior. The inferior comprises a pedestal, on which are two bas reliefs, one representing Wellington, urging his companions on to victory, and to plant the British flag on some ramparts which are seen in the distance: and the other shows Wellington at the Congress of Vienna, when the news has just arrived

[1] 'Pro Patria' in the Office of Works list.

of the escape of his powerful rival from Elba. The group on the top of the pedestal represents the Duke crowned by the Genius of Victory, whilst the Genius of War has grasped his arm, in which he holds his field-marshal's baton, and urges him on to further deeds of daring and self-devotion. Four figures, representing History, Fame, Diplomacy, and Peace, support the superior pedestal.

['. . . a foreign production . . . and displays less merit than is to be found in several English works. There are, as in other cases, tolerably good sedent figures on the lower pedestal, but the principal figures are almost absurd.' *The Builder*, 1st August 1857.]

10. 'Arno.' An Italian work of great power and beauty. The monument rests on a quadrilateral base, on the four sides of which are bas-reliefs, representing the principal events in the life of the Duke. On the base is elevated a cornice, at the angles of which are seated allegorical figures of Science, Temperance, Constancy, and Protective Force. Above rises the principal group; Wellington clothed in a mantle, attended by Victory and Peace.

['The author . . . a foreigner, believes that the monument should be simple in its main lines, and he, therefore, gives architectural details in which we see only poverty of thought. Wellington is habited in the toga, and is led by the hand of Victory— Peace kneeling.' *The Builder*, 1st August 1857.]

The sculptor, Cavaliere Giovanni Dupré of Florence was awarded the 4th Premium of £200. (Plate 20.)
Subsequent reviews were:

'This design has many points of novelty. The plan of the tomb is oblong, with projecting squares at the angles. On the four faces are reliefs of scenes in the Duke's military and civil career: the submission of the Mahrattas, the battles of Vittoria and Waterloo; and the introduction of the Duke to Sir Robert Peel by the Prince of Wales! At the angles are four groups, each an adult figure with a child: Military Science with the Genius of War; Temperance with the Genius of Frugality; Constancy with the Genius of Patriotism; and Valour

protecting Weakness. On the summit of the tomb, Wellington is seen taking Victory by the hand, and Peace stands on the other side; but this is a composition of overloaded allegory verging on absurdity, and clumsy combination of the real and ideal, the sublime and the ridiculous. Yet the design has its graceful points apart from the conceits which we have considered entitled only to censure: it is beautifully modelled.' *The Illustrated London News*, 12th September 1857.

'The fourth prize, £200, is given to a work in which figure as impersonations those airy conceptions, Temperance, Constancy, and Protective Force. Science, too, sits in this monument for her portrait; but that is more possible, as an affair of costume. This is an Italian work . . . On the four sides of a quadrilateral base are represented in bas-relief some leading events in the life of the Duke. At the angles of a raised cornice are the embodied invisibilities named; and above all rises a group composed of Wellington clad in a toga, led by Victory, and knelt to by Peace. The work builds up well, and has considerable merit: but it should not have received a prize till many others in this hall had been so distinguished.' *The Art Journal*, September 1857.

'In no ground can we discover why the fourth premium was given to the design (10) by Cav. Giovanni Dupré, of Florence. The apotheosis of Wellington is represented at the top of the monument,—the duke habited in a toga or drapery, being led by the hand by Victory; whilst Peace, kneeling, is placed on the left. At the angles of the pedestal are seated figures, intended to represent the principal virtues of the deceased, each with an attendant genius in the form of a youth. The pedestal is decorated with *relievos*. The mouldings and general architectural features are of very inferior character.' *The Builder*, 29th August 1857.

'In the design of M. Dupré the structural part is, proportionately to the subject, too large. The whole rises well up to the arch; but the base is too high and tomb-like.
It aims largely, too largely, at allegorical display, having not only four *corner* groups of that character, but the *crowning* group itself includes two allegorical figures, besides a statue intended for

the Duke. For history it has four large bas-reliefs. The groups at the four corners are ably modelled; but their meaning is not easily seized. Indeed without a description they would not be intelligible. The bas-reliefs are in composition too violent, and their subjects are ill-chosen.

In the upper group there is a total want of counterpoise, owing to one of the allegorical companions of the Duke being seated whilst the other stands, thus injuring the effect of the central figure. This figure, sadly reduced in pre-eminence by the others, exhibits the outrageous fault of being dressed in a classical costume. Its action is too dramatic, and therefore *completely uncharacteristic* of the Duke. The resulting form, with the straight depending lines of the drapery, cut by others running from the left shoulder to the elbow and wrist, is awkward and disagreeable in the extreme. The meaning of the group is obscure, or, if anything, suggestive of some incident in the life of *Marc Antony* rather than of *Wellington*. This model should certainly have changed places with one of the £100 prizes.' *On the Designs for the Wellington Monument*, 1857.[1]

11. ['Non a caso e virtu angi e bel l'arte.'] A work from Rome of much beauty and merit, but it is a work absolutely architectural—a building designed for erection over the vault—making use of sculpture only in five statues, which are placed in niches, and are therefore very subordinate to it. There is a distinction between a memorial or monument and a monumental tomb, which, we say should be observed. The details of this work are beautifully designed in the style of the Renaissance, and deserve examination as illustrating the real character of the style, as to which, from the indefinite use of the term there has been much confusion of ideas of late.

['The model No. 11 may be likened to a triumphal arch with its apertures closed, and surmounted by a bold group of sculpture, covered by an elliptical

---

[1] *On the Designs for the Wellington Monument* by 'One of the People', published by Chapman and Hall, Piccadilly, was a pamphlet in which the author criticised the prize-winning models, and which came to the conclusion that Thornycroft was the only one of the competitors who had produced a worthwhile design.

dome, on which is a sort of crown. One side of this building is perforated by three niches, the centre one of which is on a large scale, and filled on its internal surface with coloured marbles in mosaic. It contains a statue of the Duke who is busily engaged in nursing an unwieldy heap of unnecessary drapery. The internal surfaces of the minor niches on each side are treated in a similar manner, and are filled with winged female figures. The sides of the model are divided vertically by pilasters, on the faces of which is elaborate foliage of the *cinquecento* period, very cleverly executed, but much too elaborate to be effective, as placed in a large building like St. Paul's. The work is elevated on a plinth of colored marble, the same material being dotted about the plain surfaces of the structure throughout.' *The Building News*, 31st July 1857.]

['. . . the Renaissance tomb . . .' *The Builder*, 1st August 1857.]

['. . . a gigantic wedding cake with a coronal above, such as might be the vagary of an insane pastry-cook.' *The Ecclesiologist*, August 1857.]

12.   'Tis not my profit doth lead my honour
       My honour it.' *Shakspear*.
We are most pleased with the admirable work which is placed next. In this the architecture element is indeed prominent; but figure sculpture is also freely introduced, and by its treatment at once claims attention. The architectural details and ornaments also are novel and suggestive. The principal mass consists of a superstructure of sculpture, well combined with the architectural details, and supported by an arch highly enriched with carved ornament on the face, and colour on the soffit, and spanning a bronze lid of a sarcophagus, on the ends of which are seated figures. One of these is a mourner, and the other appears to be recording the great deeds of the deceased. *In the podium*, colour marbles are introduced in panels. A statue surmounts the whole.

In the British Museum is a pamphlet, printed in Florence, 1857, entitled *Description of the model of a monument to be erected to the Duke of Wellington in St. Paul's Cathedral*, in which is inserted a photograph. (Plate 21.) This was sent 'All'

Egregio Signore Il Signor Antonio Panizzi Bibliotecario in Capo al Museo Britannico pegli Autori Il Suo devotissimo Servo V. De Tivoli', and was received (according to a date-stamp) on 11th July 1857, that is, during the Westminster Hall exhibition.

The author states that:

'We have made the tomb as it were the foundation of the whole work, both for philosophical and oesthetic reasons. In it rest (or are supposed to rest) the ashes of the Hero. The lid of the tomb alone is seen, oesthetic considerations requiring it to be to a certain extent buried in the ground. It lies beneath a vault formed like a mortuary niche and adorned with gold stars on a ground of lapislazuli. Seated on the lid of the tomb, on one side is *History* writing the deeds of the Hero, on the other *Political Science* holding in her hand the volume of Grotius's *De jure belli et pacis*.

The presence of this figure indicates that the great Soldier aided his country and Europe not with the sword only, but with his talent as a Statesman.

Beneath the outer arch of the mortuary niche are placed, in a semicircle, garlands of oak and laurel, each containing the name of one of Wellington's great victories. At the four corners, as if guarding the tomb which lies beneath, are the statues of four Genii, bearing allusion to War: *Valour, Reason, Battle*, and *Strategy*. In the compartment above that just described, and in the centre of the monument, is placed a group of three female figures, *Victory, Justice*, and *Peace*, with their respective emblems, indicating that from the decisive victory of Waterloo Europe obtained peace, and with it justice, and the re-establishment of the political balance of the world.

On the opposite side is placed a group representing *England, Ireland*, and *Scotland* lamenting the Hero's death. Ireland, as the birthplace of Wellington, exhibits a deeper sorrow than the other two. Seated in a line with these on either side are *Prudence* on the right, and *Firmness* on the left, thus embodying the principal virtues of the English Hero. Below these statues are two Bassi-relievi, one representing Wellington *receiving the supreme command of the Armed Powers*, and the other portraying the great Soldier at the *battle of Waterloo*.

At the summit of the monument, upon a base adorned with military trophies having reference to his victories, stands the Statue of the Duke.'

The author continues by saying that if any parts of the design were not considered suitable, the sculptors would change them if the committee of judges desired:

'As, for example, the Artists, in representing *Political Science* in the abstract . . . have figured her as wrapped in a mantle, but should the Committee prefer that this statue should represent the bold, loyal and true hearted policy of the great Soldier of Waterloo, they could make her as about to withdraw the mantle with one hand from her lips.'

At the end of the publication are:

'Estimates of the principal expenses . . . concerned under the supposition that the workmanship of the marble, squaring, ornaments &., should be executed in Tuscany, where greater facilities and cheapness of labour are to be found than in any other part of Europe.

	Sterl.
Cost of the rough statuary marble of the best quality from the quarries at Carrara, Porta Santa, and Granito	1860
Workmanship and squaring of the various parts forming the monument.	1400
Carving of the various architectural works.	1000
Sculpture of all the ornaments, friezes &.	1650
Background of the vault in Lapislazuli with stars of gilt bronze.	300
Cover of the bier, with cushion and crown, cast in bronze, gilding, &.	511

Statues
of the finest quality of Carrara Marble

For the four Genii at the corners of the monument.	1680
For the four seated statues.	1800
For the two groups.	4000
For the crowning statue of the Duke in marble or bronze.	950
For the two bas-reliefs.	650

Other Expenses

Packing and transport from Tuscany to London.	700

Work for erecting it in the Cathedral of S. Paul all expenses included.   800

Salary of the Architect for the design of the monument, for the models, and the development to the true size of the component parts, for the general direction and supervision, till its complete termination and erection; travelling expenses at home and to London.   2600
                                                                      ———
                                                    Total sterl. 19,901'

['In No. 12 we have the architectural element prevailing to a very great extent. It consists of a great heavy mass of constructive masonry, highly decorated with ornamental carvings, with the addition of statuary of the usual emblematic class, and a colossal figure of the great general on its summit. The basement is formed of architectural panelling, over which is a very heavy arch contrived to receive a sarcophagus.' *The Building News*, 31st July 1857.]

['In No. 12 . . . we regard the *architecture* as tending to undue prominence. There is, however, so much that is clever and good in the details, conjoined with much that is beautiful in the groups of three figures, and in the single figures, that we should regret to lose sight of the design with the closing of the exhibition. With all the demerits, the Wellington Monument, if erected from this design, would, we think be a fine work of art, and an advance in memorial sculpture in our country. The ornament in the tympanum over the arch, on each face, formed of trophies and a coat of arms, is unequal to the rest of the work.' *The Builder*, 1st August 1857.]

['. . . shows some academic aptitude.' *The Ecclesiologist*, August 1857.]

This design was awarded the 5th premium of £100, and was by Mariano Folcini and Ulisse Cambi of Florence. (Plate 22.)
Subsequent reviews were:

'The award to the Florentines adopts an arch under an arch.' *The Art Journal*, September 1857.

'This is another group, wherein the allegorical virtues, Valour, Strategy, Victory, Justice, Peace, Prudence, Firmness, &c., England, Scotland, and Ireland, and a long list of victories, enact the principal characters, and make up another elaborate work of over-loaded allegory. The design is Renaissance, of an indifferent type, with some attempt at coloured decoration and architectural effect. The artist's own illustration of "Political Science is wrapped in a Cloak" almost provokes a smile, yet it approaches reality.' *The Illustrated London News*, 12th September 1857.

'The mixed architectural and sculptural composition of Messrs. Folcini and Cambi is very pleasing in its effect, and I believe is acknowledged by skilled judges to have much merit, considered as a combination of architecture and sculpture. Its quantity is grand; its form and outline square and perpendicular; and, if not somewhat too heavy below or too narrow in its single figure above, it is well adjusted to the arch and to the adjacent architectural lines and masses. But its effect is too ornate for the subject, and for the site.

Its allegorical figures are well composed, chastely designed, and beautifully executed, but somewhat scattered and overdone. The historical part is perplexing rather than illustrative, and consists only of bas-reliefs at once too many and too diffuse. The principal figure is not *in any way* like the Duke.

The great fault, however, is its *exotic style*, and its *total want* of character and individual fitness for a monument of the Duke. Indeed, as one gazes at it, he *fades* from one's recollections; and the chief feeling it excites is one of admiration at the cleverness of the associated designs.' 'One of the People.'[1]

13. 'Death makes no conquest of this conqueror;
    For now he lives in fame though not in life.'
                                        Richard III.
    Presents a striking contrast to the model immediately adjoining.
    It is a pretty conception, and evinces great talent, but is scarcely in accordance with the subject. The extensive introduction of gilding and colours

---

[1] *Op. cit.*

scarcely seems in keeping with a national monument. The materials of the above design are to consist of different-coloured marbles, copper gilt, mozaics of lapis lazuli and Brazilian pebbles. The design itself consists of a domed shrine open on both sides, in which approached by steps is a sarcophagus, richly ornamented. On the sarcophagus reclines a statue of the duke. The dome and sides of the shrine are highly decorated and coloured. At each of the corners of the shrine are well-executed figures, representing Valour, Prudence, Justice, and Truth.

['No. 13 displays an entire departure from the general form of those which we have previously described, and exhibits an illustration of polychromatic application. Its general platform is necessarily oblong, on which is constructed an open enshrined dome, the supporting piers of which are rounded externally, and covered with bassi-relievi; over these are figures of Justitia, Prudentia, Veritas, and Fortitudo. Within the shrine is a recumbent statue resting on an elaborately worked tomb, the sides of which are divided vertically by porphyry columns, between which are subjects in relief, gilded. The internal surface of the dome is tastefully colored, and intended to be inlaid with various kinds of marble.' *The Building News*, 31st July 1857.]

['. . . the work, we fancy, of one who is not a regular sculptor—is almost the only one that has the merit of attempting to make use of mosaic coloured marbles and such-like polychromatic materials. His modelled figures, however, are inferior, and the top of the design is fatally bad. Still his feeling is good, and he seems to us to deserve a prize.' *The Ecclesiologist*, August 1857.]

['. . . the coloured and gilded shrine over a recumbent figure and tomb, has the motto from *Richard III* . . . There are some good details in this work, but much injured in effect by the want of sufficient care in putting on the colouring and gold.' *The Builder*, 1st August 1857.

'. . . the beautiful forms of allegorical representation by the author . . . where Justice, instead of the scales, holds a weight in each hand, and Truth is placed beside a sundial.' *The Builder*, 15th August 1857.]

14. [No motto given.][1] In the design the ancient and religious idea of a monumental tomb has been strictly adhered to; the Great Duke is represented as resting after his labour, awaiting in Christian hope, the Day of Resurrection.

['No. 14 is neither Greek, Roman, nor Byzantine. It consists of a Mediaeval sort of tomb, surrounded by eight arches, the columns of which have very rude and ill-proportioned capitals and bases resting on a plain-moulded plinth. It would be difficult to conceive how £5,000 could be expended on this design instead of £20,000, the sum at command.' *The Building News*, 31st July 1857.]

['. . . a good thought—a high tomb under a kind of Italian shrine. But the occasion deserved something better.' *The Ecclesiologist*, August 1857.]

15. 'Great in War and Peace.' It has a good sedent figure on a pedestal, which, of course, would have to be placed transversely to the line of the nave.

16. [No motto given.][2] In the centre is a tomb, on the top of which are two medallions of the duke. In front is a figure of Clio, the Muse of History, at her side is a cupid who holds in his hands wreaths of immortelles. On the right is a figure of Eternity, and on the left that of Hercules, representing Power. Behind is a group of Victory consoling Britannia for the loss of her Hero. Above the medallions, is a figure of Fame or Immortality sounding his great deeds.

['No. 16 . . . is made up of five figures of the allegorical class, supporting a cornice, which is surmounted by a figure of Fame standing on one leg and blowing a trumpet at a tremendous rate. On one side of the pedestal is an extremely woolly-looking figure, which has already scratched on it "Arthur, Duke of Wellington". On each side of the figure are a couple of short columns with capitals.' *The Building News*, 31st July 1857.]

['. . . with the device of three crosses, is a curious design, which is all pedestal, except that there is a

---

[1] A device of the Greek letter, delta, in the Office of Works list at the Public Record Office.
[2] A device of three Maltese crosses, in the Office of Works list.

figure of Fame on a pedestal of much lower size, on the lower pedestal. This lower one is decorated with arches and columns, and relievos of lumpy figures, in marble and bronze.' *The Builder*, 1st August 1857.]

17. ['Spero Meliora.'] A massive tomb, on which a figure of the Duke in bronze is reclining. The corners of the tomb are supported by groups of some of the most celebrated men in English history, such as Alfred, Cromwell, Shakespere, Milton, Drake, &c. On either side of the tomb are bas reliefs, one representing the birth of our Saviour, and the other the resurrection. It does not appear quite clear what peculiar idea the author of this design wishes to enforce. The figures, however, are most admirable.

['. . . presents the Duke as "a central figure in English history", &c. This the artist accomplishes by having a recumbent figure in bronze on a pedestal, around which stand figures of some of the principal "celebrities".' *The Builder*, 1st August 1857.]

['. . . is thoughtfully conceived. There is a recumbent effigy surrounded by representative Englishmen.' *The Ecclesiologist*, August 1857.]

18. 'I know of but one art.' A fine piece of architectural splendour, most admirable in its restrained richness, and well studied in its light and shade. Erected in a provincial square, it would be the pride and crown of the place. The bronze statue high in the air—the open arch below—the pillars—the crown—the crushed figure of War squeezed under his shield—are full of spontaneousness and originality.

['No. 18 is essentially architectural, and is carried to a great height. It is in three stages, the first being raised on an enriched basement, and is made up of twelve isolated columns, which support an entablature having an enriched frieze, over which is a semicircular-headed arch, the soffit of which is elaborately panelled. Over this arch the next stage is supported by four moulded columns. Against the ends of this stage are groups of figures that would puzzle a conjuror to make out what they are intended to represent; they may be Satan reproving Sin, or the Death of the Dragon of

Wantley, or anything else you may choose to name. Still, reaching beyond these nondescripts, on a plain entablature, and to crown the whole, on an enriched pedestal, sits the great Duke, on, we presume, Pegasus.' *The Building News*, 31st July 1857.]

['. . . the only attempt at an Arabesque reproduction of the great late Elizabethan tombs. The effigy is recumbent; the composition is elaborate and grandiose; the pile is surmounted, according to precedent, by a small mounted effigy. But this design wants recasting and chastening, and its demonology is intrusive and unintelligible.' *The Ecclesiologist*, August 1857.]

['. . . is a model for an Elizabethan kind of monument, for bronze, with a recumbent figure and an equestrian statue at the summit. It would reach, we think, to not less than 40 feet in height. There is some vigour in the groups, which are introduced at the ends, of Truth overcoming Fraud or Falsehood, and of "Valour with Cowardice at her feet".' *The Builder*, 1st August 1857.]

This design, by Alfred Stevens, was placed sixth in the competition and was awarded a £100 premium. (Plate 23.)

Subsequent criticisms were:

'Mr. Alfred Stevens's model would be far too lofty for the cathedral. The equestrian statue would, we think, reach nearly to the crown of the arch.' *The Builder*, 29th August 1857.

'. . . is one of the loftiest designs in the competition. An open arch rises on a picturesque cluster of twelve columns, supporting a rich pedestal, high above which stands the bronze statue of the Duke. Two groups of sculpture at the sides represent Truth crushing Fraud, and Valour quelling Cowardice; the two vanquished figures being flung out from the pile with a boldness and terrific spirit. Still, this monument is in the main architectural; it is in three stages—the first an enriched basement made up of twelve insulated columns which support an entablature bearing an enriched frieze, from which rises a semi-circular-headed arch, the soffit of which is elaborately panelled. Over this arch the next stage is supported by four moulded columns; and from the ends of this stage are flung the strange figures we have referred to. Above this stage, on a plain entablature, but enriched pedestal, is an equestrian statue of the great Duke. If, however, the monument is to be placed beneath one of the arches of St. Paul's Cathedral, this design—arch within arch—will be objectionable. The decoration of this monument is very elaborate, but we do not admire the selection or arrangement of the objects upon the sides of the sort of altar-tomb upon which is the recumbent figure of Wellington.' *The Illustrated London News*, 12th September 1857.

'. . . the award . . . is unquestionably a mistake. Of no possible principle of judgment can we understand how this work came to be singled out from such a collection as this.' *The Art Journal*, September 1857.

'. . . the least worthy of the nine, is that of Mr. Stevens. Built up in stories, of disjointed members intended for quite other purposes, reminding one somewhat of the curiously and painfully raised fabrics sometimes seen on the floor of a nursery, with a formal altar tomb inserted below, an equestrian figure at the top, and certain violently composed figures projecting midway from its sides; its uninteresting materials put together with scarcely so much design as to satisfy the requirements of constructive security, entirely destitute of dignity and repose, exciting no feeling in common with the character and associations of the Duke, it towers up so high an architectural pile, as would completely block up the recipient archway, and would, if erected, constitute the heaviest inconsistent, and least suggestive structure that could well be conceived for such a purpose.' 'One of the People.'[1]

19. [No motto given.][2] A great work. It is intended to depict the Duke in a twofold character, viz., that of a warrior and a statesman. He is represented standing on a rock, with a sword in one hand a scroll in the other. On one side is a figure of Victory rising with her wreath to crown her favourite, and on the other a figure of Fame. In the centre are beautiful figures of Peace and Plenty. War is represented by two male figures; one, with

[1] *Op. cit.*
[2] 'Try On' in the Office of Works list, but erased.

a broken sword, looking upon another figure bowed down with fear and despair. At the foot of this extremely well-executed group are figures representing Legislation and History, and at the back of the group, is a figure of Britannia mourning over her departed hero. This design will inevitably attract special notice.

['In No. 19 the architectural element is nearly ignored, being only applied to a pedestal supporting a composition, which is admirably modelled. The basement is of the usual description, except that it is varied by circular corners, on which are statues, emblematic of Industry, Commerce, Europe and Asia—the two latter of which as typical of the hero's military triumphs. On one side of the pedestal is a bassi-relievi sketch of the battle of Waterloo, and on the other that of Assaye. On one of the ends is represented the Duke's coat of arms, and on the other the different honorary orders bestowed upon him, surrounded by colours. Around the upper portions of the composition are grouped figures, emblematic of History, Legislation, War, and Fame, with Britannia mourning for her hero, the whole being surmounted by a statue of Wellington.' *The Building News*, 31st July 1857.]

20. 'Finis coronat opus.' A colossal figure of the Great Duke standing on a pedestal; on the base are figures of Ireland, India, Europe, and Great Britain. It is a work of considerable merit, and shows experience and a certainty of treatment.

['. . . is probably the best of the simple statuesque monuments. Wellington stands on a plain pedestal, round which are good figures of Europe, Great Britain, India, and Ireland.' *The Builder*, 1st August 1857.]

This was the work of Matthew Noble, and gained the 7th Premium of £100. (Plate 24.)
Reports after the announcement included:

'In this model the principal figure is a sketch for a colossal statue of Wellington in the matured vigour of life, and is intended to indicate both his civil and military character; the military character being denoted by the sword, and the six volumes of the Wellington despatches; and the civil by the State document in his hand, in reference to which the Duke is represented as speaking in the House of Lords. The accessory figures in the design—which, like the statue, would be coloured—are ideal, and have been chosen as admitting, when duly carried out, a higher artistic effect and a more comprehensive meaning than accessory figures of another class, would permit. These figures are personifications of Ireland, India, Europe, and Great Britain. Ireland, the birthplace of the hero-statesman, is personified as rejoicing in having contributed to the annals of the United Kingdom a name so illustrious. India is represented resting upon the laws of England; while she holds the Institutes of Menu, and is contemplating the Indian deeds of Wellington, and the good which has resulted from them. Europe with the sword sheathed, and in the calm enjoyment of restored peace, is acknowledging the pre-eminent services of Wellington in bringing about that blessing. Great Britain, triumphant, yet unelated and dignified, is also grateful to the wise, upright, and victorious Wellington for all the aid he rendered to increase her power and honour among the nations of the world. The material would be the best Carrara marble for the whole of the monument. By uniting simplicity with colossal proportions and effective treatment of the figures, Mr. Noble has aimed with success at a certain grandeur in keeping with the character of Wellington and the magnitude of St. Paul's Cathedral. This is the able work of a sculptor whose best works are his statues and busts of the great hero.' *The Illustrated London News*, 29th August 1857.

'A work of great sculpture qualities is No. 20 from the hand of Mr. Matthew Noble . . . The grand Art-feature of simplicity made it always a relief to pause beside this model after a travel amid the extravagances of the exhibition. The figures are five only in number, and all designed to be coloured. They represent the Duke standing on a pedestal, on whose base are personations of Ireland, India, Europe, and Great Britain, Wellington is represented as in the mature vigour of life; his military character being indicated by the sword and the volumes of the Wellington Despatches, and his civil by a state document which he holds in his hand. The character of the whole work is that of mass and firmness; and the figures stand well and nobly on their pedestals, and are

serious and majestic in their sentiment and bearing. Of the class to which it belongs, there is nothing finer than this work in the hall.' *The Art Journal*, September 1857.

'Mr. Noble has the Duke in a . . . lifelike garb, perched on a short shaft. At the corners of this are the actors who perform the parts of Ireland, India, Europe and Great Britain.' *The Building News*, 4th September 1857.

'The design of Mr. Noble possesses a certain aim of simplicity, which, however, fails to secure its anticipated effect of breadth or grandeur; for it displays singularly little power as a composition. It is weak in mass, and inadequately fills its arch. Its base, or architectural part, is far too plain, and the general outline of the whole too tapering or pyramidal. Its principal figure is disjointed from those below, which are rather *dis*posed than *com*posed around that.

Instead of proper allegory, there is the personification of four different territories. There is not a particle of historical character, or fact. The Duke, habited and accoutred as a soldier, is, nevertheless, supposed to be addressing the House of Lords. This and the remaining figures, with their drawnout proportions as to length, their undecided and weak modelling, and their confused draperies, complete a group feeble in artistic power, poor in effect, and, I cannot but think, wholly unequal to the subject and unworthy of the site.' 'One of the People.'[1]

21.   'A design in clay resembles life,
        A stucco-copy resembles death.
        The execution in marble, however, is the
            resurrection of the works of art.'

A figure of the Duke standing on a pedestal, represents him in the moment after the battle of Waterloo. He stands upright, his right foot leaning on a piece of Artillery, and following with his eye the flying enemy, he is putting back his victorious sword into its sheath. At the front of the pedestal sits Britannia, holding the trident with her right hand. At the four corners of the monument, stand allegorical female figures representing War and Peace, and Wisdom and Truth.

[1] *Op. cit.*

['No. 21 consists of a colossal statute of Wellington standing on a pedestal with canted corners, round which are four figures of War, Peace, Wisdom and Strength, and in the front a large sitting image of Britannia, holding on her left arm a circular shield, on which is inscribed the word "Wellington". Taken individually, the whole of these figures are most admirably modelled. The chief statue is extremely fine.' *The Building News*, 31st July 1857.]

['It consists of a group of six figures on pedestals. The latter, we may remark, exhibits one of the mistakes which we have often found, the mouldings giving the appearance of badly designed joiner's work. The figures of Wisdom, Strength, War, and Peace, with Britannia in front, have considerable merit.' *The Builder*, 1st August 1857.]

This design was awarded the eighth premium, £100, and was the work of Ernst Julius Hähnel, of Dresden. (Plate 25.) Comment after the announcement included:

'21 Consists of a colossal statue of Wellington sheathing his sword; it stands on a pedestal with canted corners, round which are four figures of War, Peace, Wisdom and Strength; and in the front a large sitting image of Britannia, holding on her left arm a circular shield inscribed "Wellington". The several figures are finely modelled; the chief statue especially. The design has fewer objectionable features than three or four of the other prize models; but it is scarcely sufficiently monumental in character, and the figure of Britannia is more commonplace to an English eye than to its foreign artist.' *The Illustrated London News*, 12th September 1857.

'. . . we shall say no more than that it represents the Duke in the act of sheathing his sword after victory, with his foot planted on a gun, that Britannia sits by the pedestal in front, and that on detached pedestals at the four corners are allegorical figures representing Wisdom and Strength; and War and Peace.' *The Art Journal*, September 1857.

'Somewhat like to Mr. Noble's, but having its peculiar or distinctive characteristics, is the design of Herr Hähnel. These two models, indeed, more than any other two, invite a comparison; but the Dresden professor decidedly outweighs his English competitor.

Both the quantity and outline of the entire group are more agreeable; the *one*, owing to the larger dimensions of the central figure; and the *other*, to the greater squareness of the composition. This latter effect is attained by the better distribution of the lower mass, owing to the additional figure in front, to the perpendicular and widely-set corner figures, and likewise to the closer proximity of the central figure to the level of the heads of the others. The artist has taken care to correct the originally too open order of his corner figures, by connecting their pedestals to the central mass. On the whole, it harmonizes well with the vertical sides of the arch.

The impersonation of Britannia, and the four allegorical figures of War, Peace, Wisdom, and Strength, are beautifully designed; and the central figure is powerfully conceived; The draperies of all are remarkable for intelligent arrangement; and the execution is unsurpassed in the whole collection. There is, however, one marked defect in the arrangement of the composition; and that is, that the pedestal on which the Duke stands is set quite back in the group, so that although the striking advantage of *relief* by projecting masses is secured *in front*, this is accomplished at the sacrifice of the hinder view, which is equally important in the Cathedral. It is, in fact, a three and not a four-sided monument. In addition to this, there is something disturbing and displeasing in the *three* different sizes adopted in the figures; and the central figure, if executed in large, would be disagreeably preponderant.

The fundamental objections to this design are, however, of still greater moment. Its almost classical purity of style and beauty of finish cannot redeem its want of English feeling, historical illustration, and of actual adaption to the characteristics of the Duke. It would fail therefore in creating any national interest; and as the only realistic portion of the design, the central figure, is obviously so unlike the man, it would never serve, even in this mere personal matter, to elucidate and hand down to posterity the chief subject and object of the design.

Nevertheless its admirable technicalities render it worthy of a far higher position amongst the prize-models than has been accorded to it.' 'One of the People.'[1]

22. 'Di quell'umile Italia.' *Dante*. A square tomb, above which, on a pedestal stands a figure of the Duke. At the corners are four seated allegorical figures.

['No. 22 has a large basement of lavender colour, divided vertically by gilded divisions of the shape of those sometimes used in the front of church organs; over this basement is an octagonal pedestal, on which is a colossal image of the Duke.' *The Building News*, 31st July 1857.]

['. . . architectural, but of a style as yet unheard of; the columns are nothing but nine-pounders standing on their narrow ends, like so many street posts.' *The Ecclesiologist*, August 1857.]

['. . . has a figure of the Duke, on a pedestal, round which are sedent figures of Britannia and India, and two others. This part of the monument has some merit of treatment; though no greater invention than just the moderate quantity, which, as it will have been apparent from our notices, is to be observed in a considerable proportion of the models. The sculpture in No. 22, however, is placed on a high pedestal of most tasteless character. It has a Doric entablature, with cannon in place of columns; and cannon balls are heaped around. All these "decorative" features have a profuse application of gilding. We have no evidence certainly in this competition that good art is to be procured necessarily from the continent, . . . we can look to Italy only to feel how low she has fallen . . .' *The Builder*, 1st August 1857.]

23. 'A tomb and an Apotheosis.' Fame crowning a figure of the Duke.

['The pedestal of No. 23 is rectangular at its basement, and recedes in its upwards tendency to the pyramidical form, ending in a circular platform, on which stands the Duke, crowned by a winged Victory, attended by cupids. At each end of the pedestal are seated figures.' *The Building News*, 31st July 1857.]

24. 'Jacta est alea.' A square pedestal on the sides of which are inscribed the principal victories of the Duke, supports a full-length figure of his Grace, and at each corner is a seated life guardsman. On the principal sides of the base of the monument are bas-reliefs of Waterloo and Badajos.

['No. 24 is worked on the principle of being entirely composed of gray granite and bronze; and is very simple and plain in its appointments. The sides of its pedestal are curved, and on one side of them is a sketch of the battle of Badajoz, and on the other that of Waterloo.' *The Building News*, 31st July 1857.]

25. [No motto quoted.][2] Represents the Duke standing on a rock, surrounded by female figures, intended to portray Wisdom, Prudence, Valour, and Justice. Britannia is crowning her favourite son, and a figure of Peace looks on with an approving smile. Below, in a niche in the pedestal, there are admirably executed figures, viz., Fame bidding Time to take note of Waterloo. At either corner are soldiers of different branches of the service.

['In No. 25 the artist relies on marble only as the vehicle of his thoughts. The pedestal of this work is, in great measure, architectural, with a niche in each of its sides filled with emblematical figures, and four soldiers at the corners. On the summit of this model, on a rock, stands the hero of Waterloo, accompanied by the usual allegorical fraternity.' *The Building News*, 31st July 1857.]

26. 'I have done my duty.' The principal group in this design represents the Duke of Wellington at the close of his long and brilliant career, calmly resigning himself to Immortality, with his right hand placed on his heart, affirming 'I have done my duty.'

The Architectural portion of this design represents a Mausoleum with bronze doors closed, and four lions at the base also in bronze, the pilasters enriched with festoons of oak, laurel and palm, on the back and sides are intended basso relievos of the Battles of Assaye, Waterloo, and the triumphal entry into Madrid.

[1] *Op. cit.*

[2] 'Jacta est alea' in the Office of Works list, and is presumably by the same sculptor as No. 24.

The group on the right with scroll represents Duty and Honour, and that on the left Wisdom and Valour. On the opposite corners are Peace, and an aged Minstrel supposed to be recording his various exploits.

['No. 26 has two bronze casts of lions guarding a doorway leading to a tomb, on the top of which is an image of Wellington, leaning his head against an angel.' *The Building News*, 31st July 1857.]

['—a tomb and figures, open to several objections which we offered to works of the class, and to those in which unity of thought was not observed, is clearly double the scale intended for the models, and ought to have been excluded, considering that in other cases models with accessories which would have over-stepped the limits of the space shown on the lithographed plan, were denuded of their additions before the opening of the exhibition.' *The Builder*, 1st August 1857.]

['. . . is an architectural speluncar tomb of non-descript floral style, with coarse closed doors;—a very old man, guarded by a winged female, at the top, and posture-making virtues looking up at him from the four corners.' *The Ecclesiologist*, August 1857.]

27. 'Immer strebe zum ganzen.' A base composed of Peterhead granite on which are *bassi relievi* representing the Battles of Waterloo and Assaye, and the orders of the Garter and Bath, supports a pillar inscribed with his various victories, on which is a figure of the Great Duke as he appeared at Waterloo. At the corners are seated figures representing Victory, Valour, History, and Peace.

['No. 27 has a pedestal made up generally of a frame work of red granite, the sides of which are charged with bas-relief representations of battle scenes and military trophies. Some of the mouldings are in bronze. From the centre of the pedestal springs a gray granite shaft, with a statue of Wellington on its summit; at the base of the pedestal are four emblematic figures in bronze.' *The Building News*, 31st July 1857.]

['. . . the commonplace treatment of the statue with four sedent figures on a lower pedestal, is much redeemed by the good proportions of the monument and its parts, and by the attitudes and effect of the figures individually. The lower pedestal of Peterhead granite has mouldings and relievos in bronze. This monument would reach to a height of about 34 feet. There seems to be considerable differences of opinion, amongst the authors of the works of the better class—whether a low monument or one coming to above the springing of the arch, would be best suited to the building. Experiments might be tried at very slight outlay, in the Cathedral. We hear that one or more models were accompanied by an enclosing arch. This was not thought proper to have exhibited.' *The Builder*, 1st August 1857.]

One of four models, chosen as the most suitable by *The Athenaeum*, 1st August 1857.

28. [No motto given.][1] The Duke is here represented with his foot on the globe, and surrounded with standards inscribed with his several victories, is presented by Britannia with a laurel crown. At one side is the British Lion and on the other a despairing figure of Despotism.

29. [No motto given.][2] An equestrian figure of the Duke. On his right are figures of Victory and Peace, and on the left War and History. In front is seated Britannia, and behind is a group of Ireland and Scotland.

['No. 29 consists of an allegorical family stuck about a rock, on the summit of which is an equestrian statue of the Duke.' *The Building News*, 31st July 1857.]

['. . . apparently by the author of No. 16 . . . has an equestrian statue of Wellington in bronze, planted on a rock. In the lower portion of the monument are a number of figures—to be in part marble, and in part bronze.' *The Builder*, 1st August 1857.]

30. [No motto given.][3] Represents her Majesty Queen Victoria mourning the memory of the Counsellor, the Hero, and the Friend.

['In No. 30 a female figure rests against a pedestal surmounted by a large urn.' *The Building News*, 31st July 1857.]

[1] 'Je donne à César', *etc.*, Office of Works list.
[2] A seal, with a dog and scroll, *loc. cit.*
[3] 'Amor Patriae et gratitudo Regalis', *ibid.*

['. . . the Queen, scantily clothed, weeps over a shield with the Duke's profile.' *The Ecclesiologist*, August 1857.]

['. . . her Majesty is represented mourning. A draped urn, and the British Lion are amongst the accessories. We should scarcely do our duty were we to pass by these miserable pretences for *sculpture.*' *The Builder*, 1st August 1857.]

['No. 30 is distinguished by its simplicity. Her Majesty the Queen rests her arm upon a tomb, and bears a shield embossed with a medallion of the Duke. The elegiac intention is conveyed by the extremely lachrymose aspect of the Queen, and that of a small lion who reflects her grief, and looks intensely demure, proper, and ridiculous.—Again we say, let there be an end of unlimited competition, which mocks the earnestness of a nation with things like these.' *The Art Journal*, September 1857.]

31. [No motto given.] The Duke is here represented as laid in state, attended by Britannia, at the foot of the monument are two lions.

['The misfortune is that attempts—such, for example, as No. 31, where Wellington is laid out on a draped car drawn by lions, and attended by Britannia, attract attention—as though the object of a visit to Westminster Hall, were to be tickled with such puerilities, and not to have the more intellectual and dignified sense impressed by the works which may be found there,—such as are real works of art, if still sometimes showing that British sculpture is, like architecture, in a peculiar stage of transition—yet one which is hopeful as to the future.' *The Builder*, 1st August 1857.]

['. . . our readers may look at No. 31; in which, so far as we understand it (because in this and some other instances we are not exactly sure of our readings), the substance of the work is fact, and the accessories only are allegorical . . . There is some little confusion even in the facts. The Duke lies, as it seems to us, in his clothes, on a couch spread on his funeral car, and is wheeled, as we suppose, to his grave, on castors. The allegory comes in with the castors, which are British lions:— and more quaint and conceited-looking little lions there are not in all Westminster Hall. Britannia is

by their side, as a walking mourner. There is a bas-relief on the panel of the car, but we have not been able to read it. The only thing in it that we can distinctly make out, is a very excellent piece of matter-of-fact. The Duke of Wellington is riding on horseback through the sea, and holding his sword well up to prevent its getting wet.' *The Art Journal*, September 1857.]

['. . . the old Duke is slipping, in a most uncomfortable way, off an uneven couch.' *The Ecclesiologist*, September 1857.]

32. 'Alpha.' Wellington attended by Peace and War. Peace proclaiming to Europe that through the Victories of her Hero, Britannia is still triumphant. The pillar is supported by figures; and below, through heavy marble waves, ploughs the car of Britannia, surrounded by sea-nymphs. [By E. H. Baily, R.A.]

['We have no hesitation, however in selecting Nos. 13, 27, 35 and 32 both by the same hand, and 56, as the best designs in point of mere ability.' *The Athenaeum*, 25th July 1857.]

['. . . one of two works by the same author, which surely cannot deserve what has been said of them . . .' *The Builder*, 1st August 1847.]

['The choice, in our humble judgment, lies between the models marked 32, 35 (variations of the same idea—apparently by the same hand), 56, and 27. We must add, however, that in marking these figures as superior to the rest, we take into account not merely the sculptural ability displayed in modelling, but also the fitness of ideas and the probabilities of effect when the works shall be represented on a grander scale. We must also add, that, in our opinion, any one of these works could be profitably executed for 10,000 l.' *The Athenaeum*, 1st August 1857.]

['. . . in which allegory is employed in a manner more recondite, and expressed in a composition of more rich and elaborate beauty. Throughout this composition, also, the double character of the Duke is enforced. Around the base of the monument, through the marble waves of that allegorical sea which represents at once the seat and the symbol of the British empire, sweeps the car of

Britannia, attended by the sea deities, in a procession that no other sculptor, since Flaxman, could have modelled. The idea, of course, is, to picture the foundations of that power for whose maintenance the life of the hero was spent in the field and in the senate. Then, the peace that he purchased with the battles that he fought is allegorically expressed above. Round the rock-pedestal that rises out of the sea are grouped, in an ascending arrangement which likewise carries up the eye to the crowning statue of the great Duke, a series of figures, in whose action Peace is made to proclaim to Europe, that, through the victories of her hero, Britannia is still triumphant. The base of this monument wants greater breadth; and would doubtless have it, if carried out on the great scale, which the limitations of size for the models forbade . . . as a piece of modelling, it unquestionably excels every other work in the exhibition.' *The Art Journal*, September 1857.]

33. 'Nameless.' Four seated caryatides representing Courage, Military Service, Prudence, and Valour, support banners on which is elevated a statue of the Duke, behind whom is an equestrian figure of Britannia crowning the Hero with Laurel. At their right is the British Lion.

['. . . a curious production wanting alike structural character and good architectural detail. What serves for platform to the principal group is composed of a number of flags borne by seated figures at the angles of the pedestal. On this somewhat unstructural base stands Wellington, to whom a figure habited as a king is doing homage; and Britannia on horseback holds a flag over the Duke.

The author seems to be a Frenchman. Curiously enough, he has written the name "Britannia" upside down.' *The Builder*, 8th August 1857.]

34. 'Rem magni animi a gressus.' A lofty gothic tomb, on the base of which are *bassi relievi*, within is seen the sarcophagus of the Duke, and above is placed a figure of the Hero.

['No. 34 is—we are ashamed to say—the only quasi-Pointed design in the whole collection. It is meant to be Italian-Pointed, but every spark of grace or beauty or even fitness has escaped the unlucky composer.' *The Ecclesiologist*, September 1857.]

['. . . is an imitation of a Gothic monument, with a recumbent figure. There are small groups of figures at the angles of the piers, and a figure of Wellington at the top, in what we can best describe as "a fighting attitude".' *The Builder*, 8th August 1857.]

35. 'Alpha.' Queen, Lords and Commons. Wellington stands on a low pillar, at the base of which the four estates of the realm mourn: the wigged and robed figures are well designed and have a significancy of grief about them. [By E. H. Baily, R.A.]

['In casting our eyes round the models in Westminster Hall, we come at once upon a work which may serve as an illustration to what we have said [about allegory]. This work was numbered 35 in the Exhibition and represents as its leading theme the Estates of the Realm mourning for the great Duke. Here, of course, is a summary expression for the national pride and national regret, if it can be rendered monumentally. The Queen offers no difficulty. She is an Estate in herself, and appears in her own person. The Lords and the Commons are severally corporations and must appear symbolically if they appear at all. But the symbols which present themselves are at once familiar and dignified,—and lend themselves well to monumental composition. The Lords appear in their Chancellor,—who, by the constitutional, and perfectly understood, theory, *does* embody in his person the collective dignity and prerogative of their house:—and the Commons are similarly impersonated, in their own house and here, by their Speaker. Here, then, we have allegory doing its work in language so direct that it is scarcely allegorical, and so comprehensive that it sweeps into its purview the whole figure of national lament. The fact of the Duke's double figure as warrior and statesman is even suggested in this union of the Estates; to be marked more emphatically by the figures of Peace and War uniting in the tribute to his memory. Peace and War as personations belong, of course, to the classic idea; but they are, nevertheless, of that class of accepted allegorical figures, which are generally understood,—and so obviously carry on the idea here, that they unmistakeably express themselves. Thus, in a few grand epic phrases, the entire subject is expressed:—the Duke's fame divided into its two several parts, and a nation, for its double sake, in the attitude of mourning at his tomb. The breadth of scope is obtained by the utmost simplicity of character; and the unity of thought leaves out no part of the subject which was necessary to its fulness. Amid things of far greater show and pretension, a work like this, which effects its object by means so sculpturally direct, was very likely to have been overlooked by the crowds; but should not have been so by any competent judges, were it only on the grounds of its modelling. The Chancellor and the Speaker, with Peace and War, form the figures at the four angles of the pedestal. Raised, in a centre, above the figures of the Chancellor and the Speaker, so as to bring the three Estates in front, sits the Queen; and her raised arm carries on the eye, and the thought, to the Duke, standing monumentally on the summit of a low pillar which rises out of the centre of the pedestal. The back and the front sides of the pedestal show in bas-relief the first and last fights of the hero,—Assaye, and Waterloo: and the sides are enriched with shields, coronets, and cornucopias. The varieties of costume have grown into rich sculpture incidents in the modeller's hands:—and these five figures, all detached, and carried out on the great scale ultimately intended, would make a noble, and beautiful monument beneath the arch in St. Paul's.' *The Art Journal*, September 1857.]

['. . . There is, doubtless, something to admire in the separate figures in this latter work. But the idea, again, like others, is not removed from *commonplace*; and further, the endeavour to express the raising a monument, as part of the real monument, were better, we believe, not made.' *The Builder*, 1st August 1857.]

36. Perhaps, of all the designs the one which is most touching and affecting to the feelings, is one constructed by an artist who has as his motto the simple words, 'Past [*sic*] away.' It represents a mausoleum, on the top of which is a beautifully-executed statue of the Duke, supported by two figures reclining, one holding a wreath of laurel. The mausoleum, within which is a marble sarcophagus, has brazen gates, exquisitely designed

and executed, on which, on medallions, are depicted the principal epochs of the Duke's life. On one side of the gate there is an angel, charmingly modelled, who with one hand is closing the gate, and with the other places a finger on her lips, as if hushing all to silence, and whispering the words, 'Passed away'; outside, and guarding the gate, reclines a British Lion. The design truly portrays the words of the artist, 'The angel of Death completes the tale. The gates are closed, the warrior and statesman has passed away, and History writes his deeds.' A finer production has not been brought forth for many a day, and the author, whoever he may be, may well be proud of his work.

['No. 36 represents a small Egyptian mausoleum, having the large distinguishing cavetto as its cornice, which supports a dwarf circular pedestal, on which stands a statue of Wellington. A female figure is closing the gate of the sepulchre. The gates are of bronze, and contain in them circular panels, within which are bassi-relievi, commemorative of incidents in the hero's career.' *The Building News*, 31st July 1857.]

['. . . is good of its sort; but yet it might in all ways be better. A British Lion guards the closed bronze gates of a rock tomb, and an angel, with finger on her lips, points to it. Above is a standing effigy of Wellington, and behind History is writing his deeds. Wretchedly commonplace is all this, and—as is the case almost universally—wholly irreligious; but still the modelling is good.' *The Ecclesiologist*, September 1857.]

['. . . This design will probably be that which will tell with the public. The prominent feature is unquestionably a fine conception: probably in those qualities of art which it has, it is not surpassed by any other work in the collection; and simplicity of treatment, and intelligibility, by no means necessitate poverty of thought. But we question whether as a whole, the monument does not offend against the unity of aim for which we have contended. Like the tablet by Marochetti, lately placed in St. Paul's Cathedral, and which exhibits a representation of a monument in the actual monument, the work here before us, mixes up different *motives* in its expression,—or confuses the objects of actual *fac-simile*, and imitation in art.' *The Builder*, 25th July 1857.]

['We still look upon works of this sort, as being the best of them erroneous in principle. The spectator is asked to take upon trust that the body of the deceased is within the sarcophagus and tomb. He knows this to be false; that the whole thing is a pretence and make-believe: and the chance is that he goes away less impressed than it was the artist's object that he should be. There are two sorts of imitation—that which alone the true artist would attempt—and that where the object is less art than mimicry or deception. The two kinds of so-called *art* are here mixed up. In No. 36, there is certainly much to admire in the action of the figure closing the gate, and in the group at the summit; and the simplicity of the sculpturesque features is commendable. The *relievos* on the bronze gates, it is proposed should illustrate "the remarkable events military and political from 1790". In the group of objects at the back of the tomb, the coronet and shield are strangely represented, as being about equal in diameter.' *The Builder*, 8th August 1857.]

Edgar G. Papworth was the author of the design, for which he received the third premium of £300. (Plate 26.) After the announcement of this, the critics wrote:

'This design consists of a tomb, shaped like the pylon of an Egyptian temple, at the bronze gates of which stands the Angel of Death, with a finger on his lips. The Angel is by far the finest figure in the composition. Opposite the figure is a couching lion, and on the other side is represented History, who has opposite her a pile made up of a coronet, a robe, a buckler, and a sword. The Duke is represented standing, in a military cloak. The gates, and the details throughout, are cleverly managed; and the design deservedly attracted a large share of public attention at the exhibition.' *The Illustrated London News*, 12th September 1857.

'If the public verdict be worth anything in a matter like this, there should be much Art-virtue in a work which was numbered 36 in this exhibition, and contributed by Mr. Edgar G. Papworth. The judges are of the opinion of the public,—and have awarded to it their third prize of £300: and we are of the opinion of the judges,—with something of a difference. It is probable, that if the distribution of these awards had rested with us, we should have

assigned to this model pretty nearly the place which it now occupies with reference to the exhibition generally:—with reference to the works only which are actually chosen as prizes, we should have placed it better. The character is eminently solemn and sepulchral, and the sepulchral view is expressed with great poetic beauty. Working for a church and for a tomb, the sculptor has kept conscientiously in view the dead Presences in which he wrought—Death and Religion,—and made his art the minister of both. No passages of triumph disturb the awful shadows of the place,—no sculpture phrases affect to evade the authority of the great destroyer. The body to death, and the great memory to fame,—is the moral here written, in characters distinct and beautiful, by Art. By the grave to which the mortal that has "passed away" is solemnly committed, the rescued Immortality is handed over to the keeping of History. No better test could be afforded of the value of the thought here embodied, than the way in which the mind was affected by the sense of monumental fitness when it came suddenly on this work from some of the *louder* ones, so to speak, that preceded it up the long sculptural aisles. The silence of the grave was at once felt to be here,—but out of it "a still small voice" speaking clearly to posterity. Here, is thought,—thought solemn, poetic, and unborrowed,—and allegory speaking a language at once sweet, subdued, and majestic. The design is as follows:—

On the summit of a lofty mausoleum stands the figure of the great Duke, with his robe gathered round his breast. Two figures, male and female, are grouped reclining at his feet, and may be considered as representing the genius of War, and that of Peace. The Duke's sword-point reversed, and resting on the ground, may be taken to indicate that period in his life in which he is passing from the first to the last; while, amid the other touching the morals of the work, it is felt also as faintly shadowing out that final rest from his labours which this monument is the record. By the tall bronze gates of the mausoleum, which are imitated from the famous Ghiberti gates, at Florence, and intended to be covered in all their panels with the sculptured events of the Duke's life, stands the Angel of the Grave—calm, serene, and beautiful. Her finger is on her lip, to indicate the eternal

L

silence, and her outstretched hand is closing the gates for ever against the world. Through the narrow opening is seen the marble sarcophagus of the Duke; and opposite to the angel, the lion of England sits watching by his tomb. At the back of the monument History—a finely-modelled figure—has taken up her office where it properly belongs, and commences the keeping of the great record whose incidents have just been closed on the other side.' *The Art Journal*, September 1857.

'In Mr. Papworth's design there *is* a leading sentiment, strikingly expressed; but this is not specially commemorative or distinctive of the Duke. It is rather indicative of the common fate of all men, famous and obscure, high and low, weak and great. It suggests chiefly that the Duke died,—a fact unnecessary and improper to be recorded here, but so patently recorded, as to destroy any pleasure one might have in contemplating the living figure with which, on some unknown principle of art, the sculptor has surmounted a sepulchre.

As a design, however, it is defective: *first*, because its long pyramidal outline would combine unpleasingly with the equally long vertical lines of the arch; and, *secondly*, because, if carried out in the required dimensions, its chief masses are so simple that it would form merely a cyclopean mass of masonry, embellished with some attractive gatework in bronze. These are the features which would rivet the eye and attention; and their undue proportions would not only injure the rest, but instead of adorning would damage the surrounding architecture.' 'One of the People.'[1]

37. ['*To Καδηκον*.'] Is a very simple, but remarkably chaste, design. The Duke is represented as holding a sword of state. The pedestal is surrounded by groups of figures charmingly executed, and the basement is richly ornamented with bas-reliefs, representing some of the principal epochs in the late Duke's extraordinarily varied life.

['In No. 37 . . . a figure of Wellington, holding the sword of state, is placed on a circular pedestal. Round this are grouped some capital allegorical figures; and on the lower pedestal two *alto-relievos* are shown, which though very roughly modelled, are remarkable—The one, the battle of Waterloo, for the fire and spirit, which is expressed in *the charge*; and the other, apparently the entry into Madrid, for the grace and beauty of the composition.' *The Builder*, 8th August 1857.]

38. 'Cincinnatus.' This design forms a pedestal, upon which is placed a statue of the Duke, who is supposed to be surveying the scene of his last great effort. The pedestal also serves the purpose of forming a mausoleum, in which he is represented as reclining on a sarcophagus; the walls of the mausoleum being covered with the portraits of some of his most illustrious companions in arms.

['In No. 38 . . . most of the errors we have been remarking upon, as inconsistent with the intention in sculpture, are accumulated. We have first a representation of a tomb (on which is a recumbent effigy of the Duke), next a building enclosing the tomb; and on this, a group including the statue of the Duke—who is supposed to be surveying the field of Waterloo. The sides of the pedestal or building have bronze gates, which are the best part of the design, and internally around the walls are statues of the Duke's companions in arms, and a number of flags. The angles of the pedestal are cut away for the insertion of figures (we can hardly call them cariatides), just in the manner which is condemned in buildings—where the same artifice is resorted to, merely for the insertion of columns not required for the structure; and the cornice overhangs at these angles in a very unsightly manner. We could not quote a better instance to show the desirableness of architectural criticism on the exhibition, and the necessity for architecture itself—that is, good architecture—as an element in the design of works in monumental sculpture.' *The Builder*, 8th August 1857.]

39. [No motto given.][2] The Duke is represented on the field of battle: at the corner are statues of his generals, and on the base is a supposed representation of his monument mourned by his companions.

['No. 39 has around the die of its pedestal no fewer than eighteen figures of military officers and men

---

[1] *Op. cit.*

[2] Illegible in the Office of Works list.

weeping on three of its sides, and a very vigor-ously-executed bas-relief on the other. Above this, at each corner, is the figure of a field marshal, and on the central sub-pedestal is placed the statue of Wellington, surrounded at the base by can-non and soldiers in forcible action. It will thus be seen that this model is essentially of a military character.' *The Building News*, 31st July 1857.]

['. . . a work of a foreigner, is defective in the structural and architectural elements: and it also exhibits the error of the representative sculpture in making beauty of form, of secondary importance—except as regards outline and general grouping. Wellington at the summit of the monument is shown as though in action; near him are guns and artillerymen; and round a pedestal of poor design, are statues of generals; whilst a lower pedestal exhibits an ancient sarcophagus, and figures in the attitude of mourners.' *The Builder*, 8th August 1857.]

40. 'New England.' A statue of the Duke attended by his generals, above a figure of Victory. At the back of the monument is a statue of Napoleon at St. Helena.

['. . . is not creditable to the country from which it would appear to have come. Wellington stands with his generals about him; and over his head, on a large ball marked "Waterloo", and to which the duke seems in dangerous proximity, stands the figure of Victory. At the back of the monument, Napoleon is represented.' *The Builder*, 8th August 1857.]

41. 'The man whose exploits and labours have been recovering for many people peace and liberty, deserves to be crowned with immortal honour.'
A very elaborate and ornamental work.

['Among the designs which carry out the sculptur-esque as well as architectonic principles that should be always observed, and which also convey the idea of a certain lavish devotion of art required by the importance of the subject, we have marked No. 41, which appears to be the work of a foreigner. The grouping of the whole is excellent, and the architectural details of the base are sub-ordinate to the sculpturesque element; and are novel and

good—whilst not those of an ordinary pedestal.' *The Builder*, 25th July 1857.]

['No. 41 exhibits a most profuse combination of architectural and sculptural art. It is carried up to a considerable altitude in three stages, its second one being essentially architectural, and overloaded with mouldings, cornices, and bassi-relievi of coats of arms, figures, and other emblems, which form as a whole, one of the most ornate productions of its class in the whole collection. The upper portion of the composition is composed of Wellington, supported by a female figure resting against an obelisk, on the summit of which is a statue of Britannia.' *The Building News*, 7th August 1857.]

42. 'Aut nunquam tentes, aut perspice.' A design of great boldness and vigour. It represents the Duke when in the zenith of his power. He is stand-ing on a pedestal, above which is a figure of Britannia pointing to her hero, and claiming him as her own. Fame is represented as recording his glorious deeds. The grouping of the figures in this design are excellent. The model is sure to be much admired.

['. . . there is a figure of the Duke on a pedestal; and the latter is inscribed with the name "Wellington", to which Fame is pointing. Why should the artist not have seen the necessity which art is ever under, of doing something fresh? It does not follow that we are to have eccentricity and *bizarrerie*.' *The Builder*, 8th August 1857.]

43. 'Semper nomen obitur.' A very able produc-tion. Above, the Duke is represented as ordering the advance of the British flag; beneath, an angel of victory is rising to crown the conqueror, and two seraphs below are holding up a celestial crown for his acceptance. On the base are allegorical figures of Peace and Order.

44. 'Outes.' This design will find a host of admirers for its chasteness and simplicity, and for the manner in which the figures are executed. It is intended to illustrate the Duke's great and high love of duty—one of the strongest characteristics of his character. He is represented as going forth at the bidding of Britannia (a fine figure at the top of the monument)

to fight her battles. On either side of the Duke are figures emblematic of War and Victory.

['No. 44 consists of an oblong pedestal with circular ends, on the outer edge of which two winged figures are sitting very uncomfortably, and in some danger of falling to the ground. On the central portion of the pedestal is a statue emblematic of War.' *The Building News*, 7th August 1857.]

['. . . includes some allegorical figures, half-seated and flying, and exhibits the tendency to commonplace, and the imitation of a dramatic action.' *The Builder*, 8th August 1857.]

45. [No motto given.] Wellington standing on a rock, attended by the British Lion and Peace.

['In No. 45 the pedestal is proposed to be constructed of gray granite, with statuary marble bassi-relievi on the sides, over which are emblematic figures, surmounted by Wellington and the everlasting lion, mounted on a circular cippus.' *The Building News*, 7th August 1857.]

['. . . the sculptor has sought to produce effect by the contrast of white marble with the grey granite of his pedestals—a method of treatment which, though it may have been practically exemplified in a large number of the mural tablets in our cathedrals, and though it may once have had the sanction of Chantrey, judging from his recommendation of a *leaden wash* on the stonework of Westminster Abbey, as a background—is open to many doubts. Wellington here stands on a rock, placed on a circular pedestal; which itself stands on one of oblong form, bearing seated figures and enriched with *relievos*.' *The Builder*, 8th August 1857.]

46. 'Britannia and her Colonies.' Four lions support a pediment on which stand allegorical figures. The whole surmounted by a statue of the Duke.

['. . . with a statue of the duke, and figures representing Britannia and her colonies, becomes ridiculous from the pedestal formed of lions, colossal in proportion to the figures above.' *The Builder*, 8th August 1857.]

47. 'England's Pride.' The *alto relievo* represents the Duke on the field of Waterloo. Above is a full length statue of the Duke.

['. . . is likened by the *Times* [and *The Ecclesiologist*, August 1857] to Punch's show; and the resemblance to that particular form of *dramatic art* must have been apparent to many before they read our contemporary's notice. Besides, the *alto-relievo* is so managed, that one of the horses is shown as having only three legs.' *The Builder*, 8th August 1857.]

48. 'Du Courage.' The design consists of a sarcophagus, placed beneath a triumphal arch in honour of the illustrious dead. On the summit of the arch is a statue of the Duke in the act of sheathing his sword at the conclusion of the war when the objects for which he had contended were obtained.

['No. 48 is simply an architectural triumphal arch.' *The Building News*, 7th August 1857.]

['. . . exhibits architectural features prominently, under the idea of unison with the building, but at the same time misconceives architectural as well as sculpturesque principles. An arch, with pilasters and entablature, as though a reduced copy from one of the *bays* of the nave, supports a statue of the Duke. Beneath is a sarcophagus, covered by a pall, the ends of which are raised by figures of Duty, Truth, Peace, and Religion. The pedestal displays a number of *relievos*, which, being in low relief, seem in their treatment to trench too much on the province of pictorial and landscape art. One of them is a view of Walmer Castle, showing the sun setting.' *The Builder*, 8th August 1857.]

49. 'Victory and Peace.' Is noticeable for its combination of figure sculpture around a central stem, or support; but here the design, though it has considerable beauty, has not the same merit as those works where curved lines are less used in the structural part; and it seems better fitted for objects of small dimensions.

['No. 49 is a design of great power and originality. The sitting figure of Fame at one end of it is equal in conception to anything ever produced of the energetic class by John Martin the painter, Giovanni de Bologna, or Buonarotti, in vigorous power of treatment. The corresponding figure of

History at the other end of the work deserves nearly equal praise; it is extremely fine. The whole production, although only a sketch, and consequently coarse in execution, is a masterpiece of plastic art.' *The Building News*, 7th August 1857.]

[In its first report on the exhibition *The Builder* quoted the remarks above from the catalogue; on 8th August 1857 it commented 'No. 49 . . . would have appeared more to deserve what we said of its general character—which, however, we thought suitable to objects of small dimensions—had the lion, which is introduced at the base, appeared less uncomfortable. A figure of Wellington is, of course, the main feature. The figures with out-stretched arms, holding wreaths, form the best part of the design.']

50. One of the simplest and most honest designs in the Hall. It is a plain tomb surmounted by an equestrian statue, while below Hill, Lynedoch and other of the great Peninsular Generals stand as mourners. This is a work of a sensible, clear, manly, honest mind, and is a good, wearable, useful design; but the horse renders it unfit for a church. Once admit horses, and we shall turn St. Paul's into a perfect Tattersall's. Even the angels, with crowns below, do not save it. For a market-place or a square this would be worth carrying out. The figures are well executed, and there is a careful conscientious care in expression, which makes us respect this sculptor even in failure when we read the absurd flatulent descriptions that some sculptors have sent in. [By William Calder Marshall, R.A.]

['No. 50 consists of a gray granite pedestal, on which is placed an equestrian statue of the Duke; round the pedestal are figures of the ordinary kind.' *The Building News*, 7th August 1857.]

['Nos. 50 and 80, by same author, each having the motto from Shakespeare—

"Most greatly liv'd
This star of England, fortune made his sword,"—

have bronze sculpture and pedestals of gray granite. Bronze was, we believe, preferred by the artist, on the ground that marble cannot be preserved in a sightly state in St. Paul's, where the monuments are generally covered with dust, and are frequently broken. We should be scarcely ready to admit that advantages in point of artistic effect, would attend either the general, or the partial use, in prominent positions, of bronze. In the one case, a deadly sombre effect would pervade the edifice—far different to the "dim religious light," which may be really wanting to the building, could impart to it; in the other case, in place of the architectural uniformity in the arcades, and the beauty of perspective *gradation* which results, spaces would be dotted out, at irregular distances, which would wholly mar the architectonic effect, as designed. But No. 50 and 80 . . . are very remarkable for the beauty and technical skill which are exhibited in the separate figures and in the modelling; though they nevertheless exemplify the observations which we have made, as to the absence of other requisites in the works of some of our best sculptors. In No. 50, passing over the question raised by some, whether an equestrian statue would be desirable in the Cathedral, there is little that is really monumental, or that touches the feelings through the presence of a poetic ingredient. The work is a simple representation of Wellington, with figures of his generals in front of the pedestal; excepting that at each end of the monument is a figure holding an olive branch; and these features are perhaps the best parts of the composition. The pedestal is blank and tasteless. This model it is right to say, as No. 80 also, was accompanied with four figures besides those spoken of—intended to stand in re-entering angles of the architecture of the building, and which would probably have had much value in the grouping. These figures, however, were not allowed to be exhibited . . .' *The Builder*, 8th August 1857.]

51. A Corinthian column, on the summit of which is a statue of Victory; in front the Duke is attended by Britain, and Europe, who is offering him a wreath.

['No. 51 is made up of a pedestal of black and gold marble, surmounted by a group leaning against an Italian Ionic pillar, on the top of which is a gilded figure of Victory.' *The Building News*, 7th August 1857.]

[' "Waterloo" includes a figure of Wellington with allegorical figures, and an Ionic column supporting a gilded Victory. This composition is placed on a black pedestal, decorated with a profusion of gilding to festoons and *relievos*.' *The Builder*, 8th August 1857.]

52. 'Glory and Immortality.' The Duke, his left foot planted on a cannon, is being crowned by Britannia.

53. 'Power.' In a recess is seen the Duke writing his dispatches, and above a full-length statue.

['No. 53 is a copy in bronze of the well-known print of Wellington writing his dispatches.' *The Building News*, 7th August 1857.]

['. . . exhibits anything but the characteristic of "Power" which is its motto. It is the proscenium of a show, in which a *relievo* is copied from a well-known engraving of the Duke in his study.' *The Builder*, 8th August 1857.]

54. 'Multum in parvo.' The Duke seated, attended by Victory. On each side of the pedestal are allegorical figures and bas-reliefs.

['. . . is in some respects better designated by its motto; but the *multum* is the abundance of details rather than the higher *much* which may be expressed in small cubicae or superficial compass. Wellington is here a sedent figure, and, the irreverent would say, looks as if he were being patted on the head by Victory. The pedestal is covered with *relievos*; and it has at the angles crouching figures which are the best features. The busts above them are as much out of place, as the one pediment over another that is condemned in architecture.' *The Builder*, 8th August 1857.]

55. An equestrian statue in advance of a group of allegorical figures and a pedestal, with a Victory at the summit.

['No. 55 departs from the usual rectangular plan of the pedestal, it being square at one end and has a supplementary block attached to it, on which the hero is riding jauntily on a very ill-proportioned horse, which, by its length of neck and other glaring characteristics of bad proportions, completely outrages nature. This conjoined pedestal is surrounded with figures of military men, and on

the summit of its principal portion is perched a figure of Victory on a colored ball.' *The Building News*, 7th August 1857.]

[' "*Τον δη τοι καεος εσται οσον τ εγικιδναται ηως*" . . . It includes an equestrian statue on a double pedestal, and a still more lofty arrangement of pedestals with allegorical figures, and a Victory at the summit. The dados of the pedestals generally are enriched with *relievos* of processions. The artist deserves praise for his recognition of many of the *desiderata* of monumental sculpture, inclusive of good architectural detail.' *The Builder*, 8th August 1857.]

56. 'Avon' is a work of considerable merit. Here the Duke is seated aloft, in an attitude of repose—as resting from his labours. And below him are seated allegorical figures of Order, Energy, &c.—rather too subtle essences of the mind to be imprisoned in any form. In Energy we only see a lady with a large walking-stick, and in Veneration a demure woman with a crown on a cushion.

['No. 56—On the centre of the pedestal of this work the Duke is represented as he appeared in the close of his life, and embodies a consummate likeness of the aged warrior and statesman as we saw him three months before his death, and is replete with nature as drawing to its close, in the "sear and yellow leaf" of its withering existence. The four subsidiary statues are most favorable examples of the sculptor's skill; and the architecture of the pedestals is subdued, chaste, and unobtrusive.' *The Building News*, 7th August 1857.]

['In No. 56, "Avon"—where there is an excellent seated figure of Wellington, and figures, also sedent, of Devotion, Energy, Order, and Decision—the architectural detail of the chief pedestal is not equal to the demand; and the monument would, we think, be even better without the modillon cornice. We may be better accustomed to it in buildings; but, whilst requiring architecture in monuments, we require also new design in ornament, from the artist—the sculptor—whose promise it should be specially to supply it. The titles "Devotion," "Energy," &c. are written below the figures, otherwise the allegory in the case of some of them, might be what is called "far-fetched".' *The Builder*, 8th August 1857.]

W. F. Woodington was awarded the second prize of £500. (Plate 27.) Afterwards the *Illustrated London News*, 29th August 1857, commented that it was a work of great merit, representing the Duke resting from his labours, 'the artist preferring to symbolize the character of the man rather than the achievements of the hero: this view appearing more suitable to the sacred edifice in which the monument is to be erected. The points of character which Mr. Woodington has selected, as being most distinctively those of the great Duke, are—Devotion, Energy, Order and Decision. In the three former have been adopted the recognised form of emblem; Decision is represented as in the act of affixing the seal. The figures are admirably modelled.

'Mr. Woodington has placed the attributes or allegory on a lower stage, that the ideal may not be mixed with the real; it was desirable to poetise as little as possible, so that the whole might preserve simplicity, another feature of the Duke.

'In the architectural structure the style of St. Paul's Cathedral has been adhered to. Although the figures would be, according to the present scale, very large, yet, being distinctive and within the arch, they would harmonize. The artist's attempt throughout has been to make the work simple and solemn.'

'The second premium has been awarded to Mr. Woodington for a model which, under the circumstances, is paltry. Except that Wellington has a coat to his back, everything has been done to make the whole concern classical, and to enlist the classical sympathy of the judges . . . Mr. Woodington has very ingeniously seated the Duke in a curule chair, wrapped in a cloak round his waist and legs, and so dealt with the coat that a not over observant spectator will believe that the Duke wears some kind of a toga of recondite form.' *The Building News*, 4th September 1857.

The Art Journal, in September 1857, thought that 'this group, according to our judgment, has many great artistic qualities of its own, and many properties which rob it of essential fitness for this particular purpose. The Duke is seated aloft, in a chair, in an attitude of meditation, reviewing to himself, as it should seem, the events of his life; and at the angles of his tomb are seated, severally, impersonations of the virtues which the sculptor conceives to have been its guiding spirits. These are, Energy, Decision, Devotion, and Order. Now, as a variety in treatment, after that monotony of treatment which . . . must be a consequence of excellence itself, we dare say the judges were not sorry to come on this model; but that it would have been taken as satisfying the conditions of a Wellington monument if it had been presented alone, we cannot persuade ourselves. In the first place, it sinks all notice of the Duke's military character,—which scarcely becomes the record of a great soldier; and in the second place, the treatment is philosophic, not religious,—and in so far, less suited to a church. The air and attitude of the Duke are those of an ancient sage. Then, the four virtues attributed are really essences far too subtle for impersonation; and it is quite certain that no visitor could name the figures but for the gilt letters that direct him. Equally certain is it, that some of them might change places, without rendering it necessary to shift these letters. Noble shapes, beyond doubt, they are,—greatly conceived, and beautifully executed; and the work has the one grand Art-grace of simplicity. But the whole monument is an abstraction, and it has no moral to suggest and no story to tell.'

'One of the People', biased in favour of Thornycroft, considered that 'Mr. Woodington's design produces at once a decidedly favourable impression. Its large and simple masses, and its careful execution, struck the eye forcibly and agreeably immediately on entering Westminster Hall; and in its present position, relatively to its encompassing arch, it still retains its pleasing character. Its simplicity of construction, its few, large, and well-arranged masses, the compactness of the entire composition, and, especially as compared with the models already examined, the solidity of the upper part, attained by the sitting figure, added to a certain neatness and definition in the execution, all tend to produce this effect. So, too, the fine square lines and surfaces of the base and pedestal powerfully aid the allegorical figures, the composition of which, if examined individually, is somewhat stiff.

If, however, this design were executed in large, the constructive part, especially the base, would appear far too plain, and would suggest both space and opportunity lost. Even in its sculptural masses there is too much mere surface to bear the effects of expansion on a larger scale. The very quality it now has *in small*, would detract from it when carried out; and it would destroy the adjacent architecture, at the same time that it would lose in interest itself.

The absence of all historical matter is here complete, and of course intentional on the part of the artist, who has sought to direct attention solely to the *character* of the Duke. But it must be doubted how far it is possible, clearly and unmistakably, without appended titles, to typify in sculpture, Devotion and Energy, much less Order and Decision. These figures, indeed, are not strikingly suggestive of their meaning; and as to the central figure, it certainly is not a soldier, much less the Duke, at any period of his life. It might be a statesman or a poet, but it is more like a philosopher than either. It is not even *generically* of the soldier form and bearing, and has no pretension to *individual* character.

'Besides, therefore, having so little in it for a large composition, this design, though undoubtedly meritorious, fails to express its allegory, or to represent its principal personage distinctly; and, avoiding history and fact, would possess but little interest as a national or characteristic memorial of the great Duke.'

57. 'Studens.' A very beautifully executed design. The front represents the Duke in meditation, and reversing his baton in token of peace. Figures emblematical of Peace and War are on either side of the hero. Beneath is the Genius of History recording his 'deeds of high emprize', and on either side are figures representing Belgium resting on her sword, and Spain wounded, holding a British sword, her own being broken. At the back are two gates opening into a mausoleum; above the gates is a figure of Britannia, mourning her departed hero, and on each side of her are figures representing India and Portugal. The workmanship is masterly in the extreme. [By John Bell.]

['Nos. 57 and 60 are evidently by the same hand,

and are works of considerable merit, but in them the architectural detail is decidedly too obtrusive.' *The Building News*, 7th August 1857.]

58. 'Right, faithful, true he was in deed and word,
    But of his cheere did seem too solemn sad,
    Yet nothing did he dread, but ever was y-drad.'
              Faerie Queene, Canto I.

A black marble sarcophagus supported on pillars, on the lid of which rests an effigy of the Duke. At each corner kneeling soldiers.

['No. 58 simply represents a sort of parallel black coffin, supported by six lumpy Lombardic-looking columns, with capitals of ugly design. At each corner is a soldier, as a sort of pall-bearer, holding colors. On the top of the coffin there is a recumbent image of the Duke.' *The Building News*, 7th August 1857.]

59. 'God's providence.' This group is intended to represent the homage of the three United Kingdoms to their great Hero. Three warriors, English, Scotch and Irish, hold up together the National flag, which is surmounted by the Goddess of Victory. The wreath of laurels in her left hand appears to crown the hero, while the palm of peace in her right is emblematic of the blessings obtained through his valour. The Duke with a Marshal's baton in his right hand points with his left to heaven, as if making a modest disclaimer expressed in the words on the basement, 'God's providence, and your bravery, Britons.'

['No. 59 is pyramidical in its general form, on a canted basement. The aim of the artist appears to have been to represent the homage of England, Ireland and Scotland to the great hero, which is accomplished by three figures of soldiers holding up together the national flag, surmounted by a gilded figure of Victory. In the lower portion of the group is a statue of Wellington.' *The Building News*, 7th August 1857.]

60. 'Studens.' Evidently by the same artist as No. 57. The design is very similar, the only marked difference being in the character of the base. The workmanship is alike beautiful. [By John Bell.]

['Nos. 57 and 60, marked "Studens", are by the

same hand, and very nearly resemble one another. The chief difference may be expressed by our saying that No. 60 has at the back of the monument, a door, or the representation of one, to a tomb; and that the end of a sarcophagus is carved on the front of the same monument; whilst in the other work, the sarcophagus form is marked by incised lines. It will be observed that No. 60, assuming that there is not an obvious and "practicable" entrance, or descent, would not observe principles which we have endeavoured to mark out—namely, that where there is no actual tomb, none should be indicated, but that the work should be strictly *monumental*. The end of the sarcophagus may be approved of as simply emblematical—not placed there in the manner of mimicry or deception; the *indication* of the form by incised lines, however, would, according to our view, be preferable. In other respects, the design, treating it as the same, in each—for, so it is, with slight interchange of figures—deserves particular commendation. Whilst it is admirable in the technical sculpturesque requisites—especially in the modelling of the figures, and the arrangement of the whole group of the Duke, with Peace and War, which surmounts the monument—structural disposition is attended to, and the allegorical figures or personifications of countries in the lower part of the monument, are introduced with recognition of the principles for which we have contended. Inscriptions also play their part. The only detraction from the merit of the work in certain particulars, arises from the detail—as of the mouldings. This is somewhat inelegant and wanting in novelty. On the base is inscribed: "Flere et meminisse relictum est".' *The Builder*, 8th August 1857.]

['There are also two models of remarkable ability, No. 57 and 60,—or, rather, they should be spoken of as one, for they are the same design with variations—by Mr. Bell; of whom, too, no notice is taken by the commissioners. The principal objection which we have to these works is, their massive character, and the solid way in which they would fill up the assigned arch; but the modelling is of great excellence. The design is sepulchral, and so far appropriate to a cathedral for locality; and the front of the sepulchre has the figure of Wellington reversing his baton in sign of peace:—thus

presenting him, as most other models here naturally do, at the Janus point, between figures of War on the one side and Peace on the other. These figures form the principal group, and are composed in a pyramid. On a lower base are six figures, forming also pyramids, back and front. In the front central niche is History recording, and in the back Britannia mourning. There are other figures on the angles, different in the different models. The works are not very easy to describe; but it is, at any rate, incredible how these should have escaped the eyes of the judges when certain of the prizes were given away.' *The Art Journal*, September 1857.]

61. 'The path of duty is the way to glory.' Intended to express in stone the Biography of the Duke of Wellington. We have here the Duke at six different periods of his eventual life.

First —As a child playing with a toy cannon, 1772.

Second—As a soldier intent on the study of fortifications: showing the patient industry by which he was qualified for his future work, secure of ultimate success, long afterwards manifested at Torres Vedras, 1786.

Third —As a young soldier in the first flush of youthful valour, 1800.

Fourth—As the victorious general penning his dispatch on the field of battle, 1816.

Fifth —As the statesman, having exchanged the toils of war for the equally severe task of serving his country in the senate and cabinet, 1852.

Sixth —The field marshal and Commander-in-Chief, watching over the interests of British arms throughout the world.

['In No. 61 is taken up the Shakesperian idea of the seven ages of man, not, however, worked out very successfully. First we have the child playing with a cannon, then the scholar, afterwards the young soldier, then the victorious general, the field marshal, and statesman. This work is intended by its author to be entirely of Carrara marble.' *The Building News*, 7th August 1857.]

62. 'In God and the Britons I hope.' A square

pedestal supports a figure of the Duke, sur-mounted by allegorical figures; on the basement, bas-reliefs.

['No. 62—In this model the figures rest upon blocks of colored marble, and in panels on the sides of the pedestal are subjects in bassi-relievi.' *The Building News*, 7th August 1857.]

['. . . appears to be a foreign production. There is some design about the pedestal, which is composed of coloured materials; but the proportions of the sculpture appear defective.' *The Builder*, 8th August 1857.]

63. 'Let us guard our honour in art as in arms.' The Duke is represented seated: around him are Victory, Peace, Science, and Industry. The attitude of the Duke is meditative. The gallantry and devotion of his companions in arms dwell in his memory; their statues in bronze proudly guard his monument, and his soldiers of every arm form a procession round its base. [By Thomas Thorny-croft] (Plate 28).

['The basement of No. 63 is of granite, above which are bas-reliefs continued all round of a military character, and on a sort of sub-plinth are eight figures, which want appropriate connexion. In the upper group of which this work is composed the Duke is represented sitting and around him are figures emblematic of Victory, Peace, Science and Industry. In the lower relief, gilded, the most brilliant episodes of the hero's life are embodied.' *The Building News*, 7th August 1857.]

['. . . is quite wanting in the architectural element . . . Wellington and his generals are rep-resented in bronze.' *The Builder*, 8th August 1857.]

After the announcement of the awards in which No. 63 received £100, *The Builder*, 29th August 1857, stated that it had passed over Thornycroft's design with a very short notice. 'It is so entirely wanting in all the architectonic elements, that we marvel that it should have been thought deserving of preference. But, with the greatest defects in some of the requisites of monumental sculpture, it combines considerable beauty in the merely sculpturesque features. The Duke is seated on a camp-stool, with a lower group of figures of

Victory, Peace, Science, and Industry. These are raised on a misshapen pedestal, decorated with *relievos* in bronze, an upper range of them being gilded. The pedestal is surrounded by bronze figures of the Duke's companions in arms. At the base of the pedestal, the contrast between the colossal lions' heads at the angles and the small scale of the *rilievos* is very objectionable.'

'Mr. Thornycroft's model shows the best thought of the whole four [singled out in 'Architectural Projects in the Metropolis'] but it is not well carried out; nevertheless, by knocking off the allegorical figures, it would be much more credit-able as a national monument than the other three although Wellington is seated in an ungainly attitude on a kind of camp or curule chair. At the base of the monument are eight of Wellington's generals in various uniforms, but unhappily Mr. Thornycroft has kept on some of them the cocked hat and cocks' feathers of the staff. In others the hussar and dragoon uniforms come in well. At the top of the pedestal are four reliefs; on the four sides of the pedestal are the names of his victories; on the base a procession of the soldiers of all arms commemorates the various regiments who fought under him; and there are likewise eight small re-liefs. On the truncated corners of the base are four lions' heads, which are very ugly, and should be struck off. The material of the statues is bronze.

Mr. Thornycroft should be allowed to alter the top of his monument, to take away Victory, Peace, Science, and Industry, who are not wanted there, to put the Duke in an upright attitude, and to take the hats off the generals, and then the whole would pass muster.' *The Building News*, 4th September 1857.

The Art Journal, September 1857, thought that Thornycroft's was a 'very striking production. It differs in treatment from most of the other models in the hall; and had, we dare say, its air of originality to recommend it to the judges, in addition to its own great intrinsic merit. Nevertheless, the leading incident has in all probability been suggested by the Prussian sculptor Rauch's monument to Frederick the Great. Here, as in Mr. Woodington's work, the Duke is seated, and musing; and around him, as supporters, are allegorical figures of

Victory, Peace, Science, and Industry. A series of bas-reliefs present a variety of incidents in the career over which his thoughts appear to be travelling. As in the monument to Frederick, bronze statues of the companions-in-arms who helped to make that career illustrious support him; and soldiers of all the arms which he commanded meet in a procession around the base of the monument. We believe, the public are well content that this work should have a prize.—But the public will, we also believe, travel no further with the judges,—and here, at all events, we ourselves part company from them.'

'One of the People,' however, had come down in favour of Thornycroft, and his pamphlet *On the Designs* explained his choice at great length:

'Mr. Thornycroft is the only candidate who (we cannot escape from the conviction) has taken a firm grasp of the requirements of the subject, the occasion, and the site, and who has produced, thereby, a decidedly original composition. His design, though seen most disadvantageously amidst a crowd of others, grows upon the spectator, and, when placed in juxtaposition with its eight competitors, and surrounded by its intended quantities and lines, seems more and more to satisfy both the mind and the eye.

Its great and distinctive characters are these: It is *truly individual*, being applicable to the Duke, and to the Duke only. It aims chiefly at giving expression to *real fact*, *contemporary associations*, and *national events*. It includes a larger amount than any other design of the historical element, not omitting, however, altogether, clear and well-known allegory.

At the bottom, as if the foundation of all, it shows every kind of arm in our military service, infantry, artillery, and cavalry, to which the Duke gave a unity or organisation, and with which he worked. Above this, are the Generals whom he reared, employed, and honoured. As the evidence of his successful career, are four great events in his life—triumphs and honours,—in India, in the Peninsula, in Central Europe, and in his own Country. Cut off from this, his soldier life, he is seen above in mature age, surrounded by Victory and Peace, Science and Industry, contemplating

the progress of the latter as the happy issue of the former.

There is a story in stone and metal, containing more well-selected and well-arranged matter than any of the other models, and applicable to none other than the Duke of Wellington. It abounds in human interest, represented by and appealing to us in a profusion of human forms.

The entire conception, so practical, is handled practically, and in quite an English, modern, and unconventional spirit. Its English character strongly contrasts with the exotic feeling displayed in many designs in the general collection in Westminster Hall. The *popular* and the *aristocratic* element in our constitution here find themselves both represented;—the one in the procession of troops,—the other in the persons of the Commanders; so that both peasant and peer can say, "WE were the companions with whom he fought: *these* formed the strength, and *those* contributed the genius of his army". But not only does this design realise to use, persons, events and things, associated exclusively with the Duke's career, but, if carried out with the detail admissible on its intended scale, it would hand down to future generations of our countrymen the characters, costume, and military weapons and accoutrements of its own epoch. Thus it would continually grow in interest as ages passed on, until it might become, in its way, as instructive, entertaining, and valuable, as are the Nineveh marbles in theirs.

The allegorical portion of the monument, simple and intelligible, is after all equal in amount to Mr. Woodington's entire composition. It is clearly detached, and not commingled with the rest, serves to enforce and supplement the bold and largely treated realistic portion of the design, and abundantly satisfied the demands of the ideal in such a work. How, then, it must now be asked, has the thoughtful and earnest purpose of the artist been carried out?

In the first place, the composition is admirably suited to the surrounding architectural lines. Its solidity of mass and squareness of line (which, when contrasted with the varied and broken lines of the designs surrounding it in Westminster Hall, gave it rather a formal aspect) harmonise perfectly with the heavy and vertically lined masses of the closely adjacent pillars. Its height is so studied, that the arch is amply, but not over-filled; and the principal group is well placed, occupying as it were the lower portion of an imaginary circle corresponding with the curve of the arch above. Its geometric, four-sided, and equally balanced mass, is the best adapted to produce an agreeable form from whatever quarter it is viewed; and, although, as already mentioned, it may at first sight strike the eye as in this respect formal, it is the only one really *suited* to the intended site. Moreover, this general squareness, simplicity of mass, and strict attention to counterpoise, give it an air of sedateness, repose, and grandeur, fitted to a Cathedral, and perfectly in keeping with a soldier's character, especially of such a soldier as was the Duke. At the same time, it leaves the spectator's eye undisturbed, as it would be and is by the more broken and fragmentary composition exhibited in several of the other designs.

In reference to the details of this design, it may in the first place be pointed out, that the belt around the base, formed by the various troops, is a happy and legitimate adaption of a most interesting element of classical design, namely, the procession of a frieze; and it would afford great scope for variety and richness of treatment, with its men and horses, carriages, cannon and accoutrements.

The eight full-length figures of the Generals (how much more liberal and valuable than *four* figures, the number prevalent in most of the designs!), give a remarkably rich and imposing effect to the next member of the composition, especially in the corner or perspective views, in which five, or even six, of the eight Generals are more or less visible. *Individually portraits*, these figures are posed with much variety and feeling, and are modelled with great vigour; whilst, *collectively*, they clothe the pedestal, and lead up the eye along agreeable lines and masses to the corner allegorical figures above, and thence to the culminating mass of the sitting Duke. From the richness and variety of their costume and accoutrements, these eight important figures are most admirably adapted to bronze.

The subject of the four bas-reliefs above, as is rendered necessary by their position, are lighter and more open in composition than the endless military procession below. They are felicitously selected for artistic purposes, as well as for biographical and historical illustration; and whilst free from violence and bloodshed, afford great opportunities for development on a larger scale.

The composition and modelling of the allegorical figures are careful, and full of agreeable lines from whatever point of view they are seen; the draperies of these and the central figure are well studied and intelligible.

The Duke himself, bareheaded and seated, is placed in a dignified, unostentatious, and contemplative attitude. He is at once perceived to be the principal personage of the composition, and when it is remembered that, more completely perhaps than any other general of great renown, he outlived the warlike epoch of his existence, and long filled a more peaceful but equally honoured position, his elevation and distinction of attitude from the subjacent figures in the composition is a happy idea, alike in harmony with the senatorial character of his later services to his country, and with that widespread feeling of respect and reverence which he commanded in his old age.

But do no faults or blemishes strike the critic's eye? Is all quite perfect? It would be equally presumptuous to give a negative answer to the first, as a positive reply to the second question.

I cannot detect, however, in this design any radical faults, nor do I see in it one particle of convention, affectation, violence, pettiness, or anything offensive to propriety and good taste, or to the feelings of any class of people.

On the whole, more thoughtful than its competitors in conception, more intelligent in plan, suited thoroughly to architecture, entirely characteristic and individual, deriving its interest essentially from human impersonation, its different figures composed and put together with knowledge, and the whole carried out with decision of manner and vigour of execution, there is doubtless still room for minor but important modifications.

The bronze processional composition below might be inlaid in the base, and the General's feet would thus be detached from it, and rest on the stone. These eight figures themselves, now seeming somewhat crushed by the projecting mass above, would be greatly enhanced in value if the central shaft of the pedestal were slightly increased in height. Instead of the four shields, each containing the Duke's arms, I would suggest that the arms and cyphers of the four Sovereigns, in whose reigns the Duke lived, should here be placed. Not that I condemn the repetition now existing, any more than I would that of the lions' heads below, for this is evidently part of the geometric problem to be worked out; but the change recommended would add to the interest of the monument as an historical record. In particular, however, I would prefer that the upper group should be slightly reduced in the size of its component figures, of the central one especially. I believe, also, that the front and back of the pedestal supporting the Duke's campstool should be flat, not rounded surfaces. Others might suggest further changes.

If, however, we imagine the entire design carefully and highly wrought and receiving the benefit of those last touches which always soften down and beautify an original design, I feel confident that this striking and original work of Mr. Thornycroft would take a very high place in the chronicles of British art.

It must not escape notice, that there is a more decided and masterly use made in Mr. Thornycroft's model, of differences of material and variety of colour, than in any other of the designs in which this has been attempted, whether in the prize models or in the general collection in Westminster Hall. This use of colour is a novel and even hazardous experiment, but it is here an essential element of the plan, and, it must be confessed, is employed with appropriateness of purpose and sobriety of effect. The lower part, where *force* resides, is of bronze and dark stone; next is bronze, relieved by a light marble; then the triumphs, in gold and white; and, lastly, the allegory and chief figure in Carrara marble. I feel, perhaps, here, that another slight change would be an advantage— viz., to substitute bronze (with or without relief in gold) for the chromatic decoration in the four shields.

It is impossible to take a parting glance at the nine competing models, or indeed to carry back the memory to the combined efforts displayed in the entire exhibition, without once more experiencing, in all the force of contrast a peculiar pleasure derived from the real and practical character of Mr. Thornycroft's design.

He has, like Rauch in his celebrated monument of Frederick the Great, sought for his materials in

historical facts and personages. He has concentrated in one rich and powerful group, the human and material agencies by the employment of which the great personage here the object of national worship, himself attained his high and brilliant ends, and rendered his name for ever illustrious in British story. My self-imposed task is now accomplished. I cannot lay down my pen, however, without recommending, as both desirable and fair, that the nine prize models, at present in the Palace at Westminster, should, for a short time, be open to general inspection as they now stand, when public opinion would perhaps assume some definite shape, and the judgment of "many" would revise or sanction the individual criticisms of

"ONE OF THE PEOPLE."'

64. 'Virtute et Viris Virtutis.' Is composed of two bodies, the first being the base of the tomb. On this base are bas-reliefs, and on the extremities brass gates, which open to a commemorative enclosure. At the angles are figures—one representing a British soldier, another England, a third History, and a fourth an Angel pointing to heaven, and invoking immortality and happiness to the departed hero. The interior of the pedestal is to contain the Duke's coronet and sword, on a raised dais, together with his marshal's baton and hat.

['In No. 64 we have the admixture of black, white, and gray marble, together with gilding in the moulded portions of the pedestal. The statuary attached to this production is poor and paltry in the extreme.' *The Building News*, 7th August 1857.]

['. . . is a building of black and coloured marbles, and it contains the duke's hat and a gigantic coronet. Need we say more.' *The Builder*, 8th August 1857.]

['One competitor (No. 64) makes the enshrined coronet and insignia of the deceased hero the great object of popular veneration.' *The Ecclesiologist*, August 1857.]

65. 'Roma.' Has some good details of ornament, and generally an architectonic arrangement. On the summit of the monument is the statue of

Wellington, supported on either side by figures representing Peace and War.

['No. 65—In this model the designer has departed from the usual hackneyed form of pedestal, and thrown throughout the whole composition a large amount of elaborate architectural detail, in the French Renaissance style. The lower basement is divided vertically by figures of children standing in pairs, over which is an inner block, at the corners of which are seated female figures, and in the centre a circular pillar, the cornice of which is of bold projection, and embellished with trusses, between which are lions' heads. On the summit of this pillar stands the Duke (in Hessian boots), supported by statues of Peace and War.' *The Building News*, 7th August 1857.]

['. . . has a poorly-modelled figure of the Duke; but we were induced to notice if for the general attention to architectonic principles, and the novelty which is attempted in the details of the circular pedestal, and the lower one of oblong form. Resting on the latter, are sedent figures on each side, holding a circular tablet, and in the lower pedestal are boys with festoons, and medallions with the names of great battles.' *The Builder*, 8th August 1857.]

66. 'Virtute prudentis Victor', is a very chaste production. Wellington is represented in the act of returning his sword to Justice, which he had so well used in the cause of his country. On either side are attendant genii, with celestial and terrestrial coronets. Other groups illustrate Victory as the result of wisdom and valour. [By Joseph Durham and John Lawlor.[1]]

['No. 66—In this composition the architectural element is, in a great measure, ignored. It consists of an oblong box with canted corners, on the sides of which are faintly curved niches, in one of which is a group of figures; at each end of the pedestal are winged female statues, and on the summit Wellington is represented between two emblematic figures of the classical school.' *The Building News*, 7th August 1857.]

[1] John Lawlor (1820–1901), an Irishman who had worked in London for John Thomas. He carved the group Mechanics' for the Albert Memorial.

['. . . a work which would have deserved a more prominent place than it now occupies in these notices, it has, indeed, such excellence as is seldom found in monumental sculpture. It is true that architectural *detail* is not elaborated; but architectonic principle is attended to, as in the general grouping and mass; the group stands upon a proper moulded base; and the sculpture, which is beautifully modelled, tells its story—and that a thrilling and full one—yet has a pervading character of simplicity. A plain marble slab, slightly diminishing, with a shallow niche on each side, forms the background to the principal allegorical sculpture; and it supports a group of Wellington in civil costume, returning his sword to Justice—Britannia on the other side. The group in front of the slab represent Victory the result of Valour and Wisdom, and at the back of the group, Religion, Liberty, and Peace. At the ends are angels with the terrestrial and celestial coronets. There is no extravagance of action here, nothing but what is within the limits of the sculptor's art; and nothing but what tells the more, for not attempting to go beyond that art. Neither is there Pagan association of ideas, nor use of allegory in any manner but that which can be readily understood.' *The Builder*, 8th August 1857.]

['The model No. 66 is understood to be the joint work of Messrs. Durham and Lawlor. It is not in the published list of prize works chosen by the judges,—but we find it in ours. It is too much broken into groups for epic treatment; but the groups are all well designed, and very ably modelled, and the whole looks massive and monumental. In the leading group,—which is another version, less obviously treated, of the double character,—Wellington is in the act of surrendering the sword to Justice which is needed no longer for war. Two other groups may be said to keep the same moral. In one, Victory is shown as the result of Valour,—in the other, as the result of Wisdom. Attendant genii on either side bear crowns such as the earth yields, and such as the heavens reserve. The eye comes to the repose and harmony of this work again and again, when wearied with the clever multiplicity in so many places around it.' *The Art Journal*, September 1857.]

67. 'Arma virumque cano.' At each angle of the base are figures embodying War, Fortitude, Temperance, and Peace, combined with a sarcophagus, containing inverted torches and wreaths, emblematic of death and eternity. In eight panels on the base are *basso-relievos*, representing some of the principal works of long life. This base is divided by a door and a tablet, with drapery suspended. Surmounting the whole is a seated figure of the Duke, in the Costume of a Field Marshal, in repose.

68. 'Integrita.' Its author says:—'In this design the aim has been to make an architectural mass, in harmony with the structure and position in which the monument is to be placed, and to embody the chief features in the character and principal incidents in the life of the warrior and the statesman.' It is a great building of a dome form, expressly designed to correspond with the architecture of St. Paul's. It is a little meretricious with its gilt angels, but has much merit.

'Integrita' was the pseudonym used by John Thomas, and his design was undoubtedly the favourite of *The Builder* which devoted much space to it and even made a full page wood-engraving (Plate 29) of it—apart from the prize-winners it seems the only other model to have been illustrated in a journal. On 1st August 1857, *The Builder* stated that 'The eminently valuable characteristics of No. 68 . . . are to be found in the conception of the sculpture, which is poetical and allegorical. When this part of the design is looked into for a few minutes, and the expression of thought is gathered, the architectural element is no longer seen unduly prominent, whilst the idea of the building with no interior, like that once called by the strange name of the Lanthorn of Demosthenes, vanished. Perhaps the comparison was not likely to have occurred to anyone but the architect; and there is no resemblance between the model and the monument at Athens, excepting in their both being circular as to the general plan, and being without apertures, for entrance or light. The model, the author says, "is left to tell its own tale": no written "argument", or description is offered. In the allegorical intention of the sculpture, the leading thought is clear and beautiful. This is expressed by the figure of Peace (represented

with a rayant crown, and wings tinged with gold) on the *domed covering*, as we called it, of the monument, but on what is rather designed to represent the globe, over which the light of Peace is diffused in golden rays from the spot whereon she descends. The domical or globular feature is encircled by the cornice which terminates the structure of the monument, and which is of novel character, enriched with lions' heads, and inscribed with the names of Wellington's chief victories. The main portion of the monument is divided into four fronts or compartments by winged figures on pedestals, and by sedent figures below; and the whole is elevated on an appropriate pedestal, enriched, like other parts of the work, with relievos and inscriptions, carrying out the general illustration of peace and war, and the commemoration of Wellington in his two great spheres of action. The principal front has a statue of the Duke. Towards the head, two of the winged figures extend their arms, holding gilt wreaths, whilst in the other hand, each sustains a sword. The pedestals are inscribed with the words "Honour" and "Duty". The corresponding figures in the opposite front have the attributes of Peace and under them are inscribed "Firmness", and "Truth". On this side of the monument, in place of the statue of the Duke, there is a seated figure of Justice. Below it is an *alto-rilievo* of Wellington addressing the House of Lords, whilst in the corresponding position on the front is a finely-executed representation, in a similar character of relief, of the battle of Waterloo. Below this is a simple panel, with a work in low relief, expressive of the simultaneous announcement of Victory and Peace. In the corresponding panel at the back, Commerce and Industry with Mechanical Science, are represented in active operation. This sort of contrast and variety as to the sides of the monument, and as to the sort of rilievo, is observed throughout. Thus, at the ends, one of the rilievos represents the field after the battle, and the opposite one reapers at work. One of the sedent figures at the angles, that of War, is finely conceived, and the allusion to letting "loose the dogs of war" is well expressed. The thinking figure under which is written, "The prudent are crowned with knowledge", is excellent in design and treatment. An inscription in a prominent position gives the words in the Duke's despatch of the 19th June, 1815,—"Believe me, nothing except a battle lost, can be half so melancholy as a battle won." On the whole, we consider this work has more of the poetical requisites of monumental sculpture than any other in the collection. It might, perhaps, have been better had the architectural or rather structural element been subsidiary instead of prominent. The winged and seated figures, however, are not quite so plain in their personification as we should have desired them; though now they excite thought—like those on the Portland Vase, to which have been given one or two different renderings. The meaning of some of the figures is obscured rather than popularised by the inscriptions under them; and these might well be reconsidered. To be understood, a work of art into which allegory enters, must have its personified virtues or qualities, such as may stand marked in a character; it should not attempt minute psychical definitions. Also, to be understood, the language of the allegory must be strictly logical. We are not certain that the author of No. 68 does not intend distinct personifications of Integrity and Truth. The design, however, as we have shown, has great merit.'

['No. 68—The basement is varied from the formal rectangular plan by having segmental sides and octagonal corners, over the latter of which are emblematic sedent figures. On one of the segmental sides of the pedestal is a bas-relief of the battle of Waterloo, and on the other the Duke is represented addressing the House of Lords. The upper portion of the pedestal assumes a circular form, in which is a niche, having a statue of Wellington as a modern military officer, and on circular pedestals are statues of Firmness, Truth, Duty, and Honor. The upper portion of the pedestal is surmounted by a cornice of novel design, around which are inscribed the principal battles in which Wellington was personally engaged. This cornice is crowned by a dome, on which stands a figure of Peace, with partially gilded wings. This model is proposed by its author to be carried out entirely of Sicilian and Carrara marble, the former to be applied to the architectural portions.' *The Building News*, 7th August 1857.]

Some weeks later, on 19th September, *The Builder* published the design of John Thomas's model, and again, gave quite a lot of space to it; altogether, in fact, *The Builder* gave it more prominence than any other design. 'The author of the design which we engrave, Mr. John Thomas, claims to have prepared it in strict accordance with the plans, elevations, and perspective views of the locality of the proposed monument, together with the printed conditions issued by the Chief Commissioner of Works. Not foreseeing that the judges, in giving their decision, would themselves ignore the instructions of the Board of Works, the sculptor studied the position which they had determined for the erection of the monument, little thinking they would expressly declare in making their award, that they had not taken into consideration the all-important question of site. Had all the artists allowed themselves this liberty, their designs would have probably been different in nearly every case, and the author of No. 68 would, in all probability, have taken a different view of his subject, had he not felt bound to consider it quite as much as an architectural as in a sculptural point of view, in order that his design might harmonise with the edifice, of which it was intended to form a part . . .'

69. 'Adsic Fortuna.' A figure of the Duke habited as a Roman General, attended by Victory.

['. . . one of those which boldly clothes Wellington in a toga. The speciality of this design is a trumpet-blowing angel, apparently flying loose in front of the pedestal, as Ariel might be managed in Mr. Kean's *Tempest*.' *The Ecclesiologist*, August 1857.]

70. 'Quod potior perfeci.' A design conceived from Collin's 'Ode to the Brave:'

'Here sleep the brave, who seek to rest,
By all their country's wishes blest.'

The design consists of a mausoleum, outside of which is a laurel wreath; in the centre there is a medallion of the Duke, which a figure of Fame is intently scanning, and inscribing his name on her tablets.

71. 'Pro Patria.' It represents a Doric tomb

decorated with sculpture, above which are placed figures of Victory, Peace, Wisdom, and History, the whole surmounted by a figure of the Duke, holding in his right hand the marshal's baton. At the angles of the base are four standing figures, intended to represent the three kingdoms and the English colonies.

['In No. 71 we have architectural forms in a great measure predominating. It is composed of a circular Greek-Doric temple, surmounted by four figures sitting at right angles to it, resting against a cippus, on which stands an extremely queer-looking image of the Duke. On square dwarf pedestals at the lower portion of the pedestal are female statues.' *The Building News*, 7th August 1857.]

['. . . a simple figure of the Duke, with the usual accessories of figures, allegorical and statuesque, on a general quadrilateral plan in several stages. A portion of the pedestal, however, takes the form of a circular building with a Doric order—the intercolumns filled up.' *The Builder*, 15th August 1857.]

72. 'Justice.' Wellington, standing on a low pedestal, is represented sheathing his sword, attended by Victory and Britannia.

['No. 72 . . . entirely beneath critical remark.' *The Building News*, 7th August 1857.]

[' "Justice" is noticeable as having some attention given to the monumental requirements in grouping—in which the pedestal of coloured materials takes part—but the sculpture is defective.' *The Builder*, 15th August 1857.]

['. . . a bathotic attempt at an imitation of Michelangelo.' *The Ecclesiologist*, August 1857.]

73. 'Non desperabo.' Wellington is here represented as the aged soldier and scholar, attending to the instruction of Wisdom, and as rewarded by Fortune.

['. . . memorable for parcel-gilding. Every figure, and there are many, has somewhere or other something or other—a chaplet, a star, a wing, or a coronet—which is gilt.' *The Ecclesiologist*, August 1857.]

M

['No. 73 . . . entirely beneath critical remark.' *The Building News*, 7th August 1857.]

['. . . I cannot but think that the lesson the Duke's monument should teach may well be founded upon the motto of his own coat of arms—*Virtutis fortuna comes.*

These were the ideas which suggested my own design, and which I endeavoured to carry out in the following manner: 1st. I have a plain Sicilian base deep enough to raise the second base into a position of safety for the sculpture. 2ndly. The second base is of less depth, having base and cornice mouldings, and in the two sides are instructive bas-reliefs of Peace and War; that of War being indicative of the Duke's character and career; and on the ends are spaces for the names of his chief victories. Upon the corners of the second base stand allegorical figures of the four great estates of the nation—Christianity, Law, Commerce and the Fine Arts; for as the Duke was a man of the nation, the nation should be represented as doing him honour. There are also symbols of the four chief accidents of a nation—Peace, War, Life and Death—all so introduced as to constitute a chaste and orderly arrangement. 3rdly. On the top of a central oval pedestal stands the aged Duke, with a sword and book, indicative of the soldier and scholar. At his right hand is a figure of Wisdom, and on his left is Fortune. In attending to the instruction of wisdom he is represented as rewarded by Fortune. These allegorical figures do not diminish the apparent importance of the principal figure, but rather increase it. On the front of the oval pedestal are figures of angels bearing a shield with the inscription; and on the back are the Duke's arms and honors. I really think that . . . my design is as suitable to the case as any one exhibited. It is not quite so high as Mr. Marshall's (being about 17 feet), but might be made higher than it is, and the figures increased in size upon the same base. It has this advantage: the figures are spread openly upon the base, and there are three figures on the top of the pedestal forming a pyramidal whole without any nakedness . . .' Letter in *The Building News*, 9th October 1857, from the sculptor D. Hewlett, of 4 Gloucester Terrace, Vauxhall Bridge.]

74. 'Death has no conquest o'er this Conqueror.'

Standing on a sarcophagus, the Duke is receiving from Immortality a wreath of Amaranth or Immortal life. Round the base are groups of allegorical figures.

['No. 74 . . . entirely beneath critical remark.' *The Building News*, 7th August 1857.]

75. 'Hope.' A statue of Wellington surrounded by emblematical figures of Britannia, the God of War at rest, with History recording the deeds of the hero to a youth; and at the back a figure of Erin, representing Ireland, the birth-place of the Duke of Wellington. At the corners are a Life Guardsman, a Scotch Highlander, and two Irish Soldiers.

['No. 75, with the motto "Hope", rests on a gray granite basement, at the corners of which are figures of soldiers very creditably modelled. On the top of the pedestal is a statue of Wellington, surrounded by sedent figures of Britannia, the God of War, and History recording the deeds of the hero.' *The Building News*, 7th August 1857.]

['. . . has a statue of Wellington, and allegorical figures of Britannia, Mars seated in front, History reciting the deeds of Wellington to a youth, and a figure representing Ireland. The figures of soldiers are at the angles of the pedestal.' *The Builder*, 15th August 1857.]

76. ['A & Ω.'] A work not without merit, fails in grouping—by the use of two pedestals not well combined, but rather on the principle of design sometimes adopted in Birmingham manufactures, where a portion of one antique work is thought good anywise conjoined to any other.

['No. 76—The basement is of the usual rectangular shape, and the pedestal is decorated with some clever bassi-relievi, all of a classical character. The pedestal is surmounted by a statue of the Duke laid lengthwise, Mediaeval fashion.' *The Building News*, 7th August 1857.]

['. . . there is merit in the ornaments and *rilievos*; though the excessively architectural character, the representation of a tomb, the grouping of the tiers of pedestals, and the Pagan idea of a recumbent figure on a sarcophagus at the summit of the

monument, may all be objected to.' *The Builder*, 15th August 1857.]

This design by John Gibson, R.A., was described by him in *The Biography of John Gibson, R.A.*, by T. Matthews, 1911, pp. 219 and 220:

'The design for a monument to His Grace the Duke of Wellington, appropriate to a Place of Worship.

The base of the Tomb is a parallelogram, upon which is an octagonal Pedestal, supporting a sarcophagus, upon which is the figure of the Duke. All the subjects represented upon the Tomb are intended to illustrate one great and sublime moral—that all human greatness must terminate in death, and that at the sound of the last trumpet, the dead shall rise again to eternal life.

Description of the subjects.
The Duke is represented lying in death, enveloped in his mantle and with his sword.

Bassi-relievi.
Upon the upper part of the Tomb are all the victories of the warrior assembled together; they are led on by Fame, in procession, chanting to the glory of their Hero.

Upon the base is the return of Peace in triumph, amidst a rejoicing people. Victory brings Peace back in her own chariot drawn by four horses, and she is followed by Plenty, Science, Commerce, and Agriculture: the latter turns round and offers her pruning-hook to a soldier who is in the act of breaking his lance. An old veteran meets his daughter. Upon the other side of the Tomb is the door, having upon the one side Faith, and on the other Hope. Upon the two ends of the Tomb are medallions of the Duke at two periods of his life.

Statues.
Returning to the front, on the right of the Tomb, is Military Glory, bearing the British standard crowned with laurel; on the left stands History, meditating upon the exploits of the hero. From History we come to the Angel of Death, with the reversed torch in his hand, and he is crowned with poppies. From Death we come to the Angel of Life. "The Angel of the Lord", waiting intently for the divine signal from above, when, by the

blast of his trumpet, slumbering generations shall wake to life eternal. "A & Ω." When I was in England, I submitted the above ideas in words to a friend whom I consider the Best judge in the country, a man of highly cultivated mind. After meditating a little upon the subject, he said, "It's a grand conception." When I returned to Rome, I put my thoughts, as written above, into plastic form, and my model met with the approbation of the best native judges here. I sent it to the competition, but its great simplicity, among the numerous florid, confused and ignorant abuses of allegory, attracted no notice from those gentlemen who were appointed as judges.

My friend, whose judgment I think so highly of, and is considered such by the high in station there, decided not to give any opinion upon any of the models there. I believe it was from the fear of bringing himself under the vengeance of those papers in the interest of the artists in London. When I saw that curious collection, I soon perceived that not one of the celebrated sculptors of Europe had sent any design; but when I observed my own model there, I liked it more than ever.'

77. [No motto quoted.][1] A column on which is inscribed his principal victories, is surmounted by a statue of the Duke.

78. 'Deeds not Words.' A recumbent effigy of the Duke placed beneath an arch, on the top of which Victory is laying a laurel wreath. At the corners are figures of Truth, Valour, Duty, and Loyalty.

['No. 78 is an oblong-arched tomb, within which the old Duke is laid full length; at the corners are figures emblematic of Truth, Loyalty, Duty and Valour. On the sides of the pedestal, beneath the recumbent hero, are some bas-reliefs, meant to represent the battles of Waterloo and Assaye.' *The Building News*, 7th August 1857.]

['. . . has a recumbent figure under a low arch, destitute of architectural detail. The arch supports a kneeling figure of Victory, laying a laurel wreath.' *The Builder*, 15th August 1857.]

79. 'Faire sans dire.' This is a most elaborate and well-executed work. The Duke is represented on

[1] The Greek letter delta in the Office of Works list.

M*

the top of a pedestal, giving his orders for a charge. Victory and Peace on either side are crossing his path with the palm and olive branch. Below them are figures emblematic of Europe, Asia, Africa, and America, entwining themselves with festoons of the rose, shamrock, and thistle, representing the union of Great Britain with foreign powers, which he caused by his brilliant victories. At the back of these figures, beautifully modelled, is one of the Duke, in a sitting position, contemplating the wants and prosperity of his country. Between figures of Justice and Plenty, on either side, are figures representing England, Scotland, and Ireland; he bears a duke's coronet, the highest honour England had to bestow, and beneath is a bas-relief representing the decisive charge at Waterloo.

['The model No. 79 is composed of a plain pedestal, on which is raised a pyramidical composition representing what is called "Wellington serving his country in peace", and over his head four cupids are stuck about holding festoons of flowers. Further up, and hoisted aloft, is another statue of our hero, supported by a female figure on each side.' *The Building News*, 7th August 1857.]

['The Author . . . has tried to solve one difficulty in the portraiture of Wellington by showing him twice, at different periods in his career.' *The Builder*, 15th August 1857.]

80. 'Most greatly liv'd
    This star of England: fortune made his sword.'
                                    Henry V.
For bronze, chiefly remarkable for its modelling. The design represents Wellington, between Peace and War. The allegorical figures are Valour, Wisdom, Duty, and their result – Peace. The Horrors of War are represented by a Mother, with a child in her arms, discovering the dead body of her husband, slaughtered by invaders. On the other side, Commerce and Agriculture are rejoicing at the restoration of peace.

['In the work No. 80, the artist proposes to construct the monument of granite, bronze, and colored marble. It consists of a basement of gray granite, on which stands a superstructure of red Aberdeen granite, around which are emblematic figures in bronze of Peace, Valour, Wisdom and

Duty; and on the sides bas-relief representations of scenes from the battles in which the warrior was engaged. The pedestal is surmounted by a statue of the Duke.' *The Building News*, 7th August 1857.]

This model was unnoticed by any other reviewer except for *The Builder* which noted only that it was remarkable for its modelling. It received, however, the first prize of £700, and was by William Calder Marshall, R.A. After the awards, it naturally received more prominence. (Plate 30).

'. . . a highly meritorious composition. It is intended to represent Wellington between Peace and War . . .' *Illustrated London News*, 29th August 1857.

'As the designs are now recorded in the *Illustrated News*, they are accessible to all in town and country, and the sight of them will cause dismay at such a sum of £700 being given to Mr. W. Calder Marshall, and at the prospect of such a paltry performance figuring as the master sculpture work of this generation . . .

Mr. W. C. Marshall is an artist of great ability. His half-naked figure nicknamed Valour, and his draped figure nicknamed Peace, are well-balanced and well-designed. His sitting statues of Peace and War are neatly grouped: but what do they mean, and who wants them? How much in this design commemorates Wellington—a statue, and bas-reliefs of Assaye, Badajoz, and Waterloo, and Wellington receiving the thanks of the House of Commons . . .

Mr. Marshall has made use of the soldiery as corner figures at the angles of the arch at St. Paul's. Very fittingly a soldier of the 33rd—the Duke's regiment—is one of these.

Mr. Marshall proposes as his materials granite and bronze, which would be lasting and give variety, but we cannot see why he should avoid gilding. Colored marbles, bronzes of various tints, and gilding, give effect to some of the models, and it is to be hoped that the opportunity of introducing these varied materials into St. Paul's will not be neglected.' *The Building News*, 4th September 1857.

'. . . whose place in this award there will most

certainly be differences of opinion, though it is a work of talent beyond doubt. We had ourselves marked it for a prize—but will not say *where*, further than that it was not where we find it in this judicial report. The design is the accustomed one . . . Here then we have *two* figures of Peace . . . Peace as a subordinate, and Peace as a result. This is a fault in construction . . . There are bas-reliefs representing the siege of Badajoz, and the Duke receiving the thanks of the House of Commons; and on the base are the battles of Assaye and Waterloo. It is proposed by the sculptor that statues representing the Grenadier Guards, the Life Guards, the artillery, and the infantry shall be placed at the angles supporting the arch under which the monument is to stand:—and the model which Mr. Marshall originally sent in included a segment of the cathedral arch, showing these figures. But this addition enlarged the dimensions beyond the limits permitted by the specification; and, under the strict application of Sir Benjamin Hall's own rule, the sculptor was, we believe, required either to withdraw his model as an infringement, or to sacrifice that part of his design which made it so. The portion abandoned is an important feature in the effect, and we hear it talked of now as a constituent of the design to which the judges have given their first prize. If they *have* taken the arch and its figures into account, and have permitted to Mr. Marshall the benefit of this forfeited portion of his plan, then they have directly contravened the expressed intentions of the First Commissioner of Public Works, and mistaken their trust in a far more serious sense than that to which we before alluded. If it be so, it will be necessary that the sculptors who were candidates shall bestir themselves at once in the matter, and that the award, so far as the first prize of £700, shall be re-opened. The matter is serious, and affects the good faith of the whole proceeding.' *The Art Journal*, September 1857.

'We give this week an illustration of the design for the Wellington Monument which, in the late competition at Westminster Hall, gained the first premium of £700. This was the work of the eminent sculptor, Mr. William Calder Marshall, R.A.

Considering this design as an architectural

detail, and in reference to its position in the Cathedral of St. Paul's, of which it will form a component part, we have thought it right to represent it within the arch of the nave appropriated as the site (Plate 31), in order that it may be more carefully examined by our readers. The authorities, it will be remembered, have designated an arch in the nave as the site, with the view that the monument shall be more conspicuously seen; and of this situation a plan and elevation were, previous to the competition, prepared and published. The monument has, therefore, to be regarded not simply as a sculptural effort, but as an architectural production.

Mr. Marshall's object in the competition has been to represent Wellington between Peace and War—an idea, we must say, of little logical value, and illogically carried out. Wellington is portrayed by his own statue, a figure well-conceived, representing him in his military undress, sufficiently picturesque for the fancy of the sculptor, and truthful enough for the public spectator. The warrior leans on his sword. This statue is the best part of the composition; indeed, the only part which is worth anything for the purpose, as the other figures, beautifully treated, are irrelevant.

Peace and War are played by four allegorical figures at the base of the statue of Wellington. Valour—a naked Roman, or Greek, or Persian warrior, with a waistcloth for modesty's sake—and Peace—a young woman in ancient foreign drapery—look towards the nave. Wisdom and Duty—both figures of the conventional classic type—look towards the aisle. At the sides are other seated groups. Between Valour and Wisdom, strangely enough, are the horrors of war portrayed by a young mother, in dishevelled attire, with her babe in her arms, discovering the body of her husband, a Greek or barbarian soldier, slaughtered by invaders. In what way this designates the horrors of war in connexion with Wellington it is difficult to make out. Between Peace and Duty, on the other side, is an allegorical group of Commerce and Agriculture, who are said to be rejoicing at the restoration of Peace, though no one can make that from their countenances; and it so happens that Commerce and Agriculture in England did not rejoice at the restoration of Peace, but on the contrary, through many of their members, mourned the loss of war prices. For anything we know, Commerce and Agriculture are rejoicing at the continuance of War.

These figures are beautifully treated, picturesquely grouped, and admirably balanced, but the ideas attributed to them are puerile, and fail to be carried out. The monument of Wellington is therefore burdened with un-English trumpery.

Mr. Marshall has, however, in some degree, provided for the history of Wellington. On the pedestal are bas-reliefs of the Siege of Badajoz, and Wellington receiving the thanks of the House of Commons; and on the base others of the Battles of Assaye and Waterloo. The pedestal bas-reliefs are not well chosen, but the others refer to events of importance.

One notion of Mr. Marshall's is to place at the four angles of the piers of the arch a soldier, representing the Grenadier Guards, Life Guards, Artillery, and the 33rd (Duke of Wellington's Regiment), being four arms of the service, the men standing as at a military funeral. The object of this is to give a novelty of effect, and to connect the monument with the architecture. The figures likewise become representative of the history of the period. Perhaps it would be better if Mr. Marshall were to remove his four allegorical figures from the pedestal, and to place soldiers there, representing the several nations who served under him. There might be a Sepoy, a Spaniard, a Portuguese, and a Hollander. For his seated groups, if he wants such figures, he might have, for instance, a Spanish mother embracing her babe, and a Hindoo engaged in works of peace. These figures would not be altogether satisfactory, but they would have more meaning than those now introduced, *a propos* of nothing.

The group would be pleasing in the Cathedral, and not discordant with the ornate character of the order . . . For the time the introduction of one monument will make this arch unsymmetrical with the other arches, but this is only temporary, as the other arches will, in due course, be made the receptacles of monuments . . .' *The Building News*, 25th September 1857.

'Of Mr. Marshall's design, to which the highest prize has been awarded, I must nevertheless claim to speak without reserve. Having examined it again and again, I come to the conclusion that it has gained its place by exhibiting a pleasing conventionality of style, and satisfying the demands of a peculiar standard of taste, *not* by manifesting originality of thought, power of composition, or perfection of modelling and execution.

When seen beneath its model arch it instantly strikes the eye as being deficient in height, and, at its upper part, in quantity; therefore, in its general effect, it loses rather than gains compared with its appearance in Westminster Hall.

Its base is most decidedly too large; the outline of the part next above in the composition is pyramidal; and this again is surmounted by the almost vertical mass of the central figure. Hence the lateral contours actually *bend in* at the feet of the Duke, forming a very weak outline against the verticals of the adjacent pillars, and likewise condemning the upper figure unquestionably to an unmistakeable feebleness. It affords, perhaps, amongst the several designs here criticised, the most striking instances of the general principle already mentioned, that beneath a *massive circular* arch a *single standing figure* is necessarily less advantageous in effect than a sitting one. In this instance, at least, all dignity and grandeur are wanting; and it would seem almost easy to snap the statue from its pedestal. Still further, in looking only to the general effect, the rounded ends of the base are very commonplace and clumsy, would compose badly with the sides of the neighbouring piers, and would actually look heavier than properly managed flat surfaces.

Finally, there is a marked want of balance between the two lateral projecting groups, which makes the composition still weaker in effect.

Here again, as in Dupré's design, the allegorical part of the subject predominates:—Valour, Wisdom, Duty, and Peace; the horrors of War, with Commerce and Agriculture. Now this style of art, with all its boasted superiority, leads to—what? To a design appealing essentially to abstract notions, special to no epoch, to no nation, and to no individual. It teaches nothing, leaves a great gap in the spectator's mind unoccupied, will excite no patriotic pride or emulation, and ill consorts with the simple and practical character of the Duke.

A monument thus designed may fit a warrior's

memory; but it might be any great and successful soldier's; and certainly it is neither English nor Wellingtonian.

The nature of some of the allegorical figures here employed, has given to the artist an opportunity of introducing the *nude human form* to a greater extent than in any of the competing designs; and to this fact (besides its harmonising with conventional practice and orthodox ideas) he owes, if not his high place in the prize-list, at least an undeniably pleasing roundness and attractive richness in his detailed contours and forms. But this kind of art may be out of place. What has *so much* allegory to do with the Duke of Wellington, the simplest and plainest hero that the English people ever knew? What has he to do with Valour, as here abstractedly represented by a naked figure reposing in no very valiant attitude, with his bared thorax and limbs, his scanty costume, and his classical helmet and sword? Minerva, too, as Wisdom! How ill matched that divinity seems with a new-made allegory founded on the *Essentially human* quality of duty! Again, why should Wellington's monument, in particular, be rendered painful by the representation of a merely afflicting incident of war—a slaughtered man, lamented by a widow and her orphan?

Why, moreover, are we not spared the actual representation of bloodshed in the solemn aisles of a Christian temple?

The conventional or orthodox treatment of the subject here displayed, together with the advantages connected with the employment of the nude, have, I repeat, apparently raised this design to its high place; but, with every desire to do it justice, I conclude, that it is neither sufficiently *realistic* nor *characteristic*:—that, being chiefly allegorical, it is, in its own path, deficient in originality, expression, and artistic power;—that it contains many blemishes, and finally, is very inferior to Hahnel's, Woodington's, and Thornycroft's.' 'One of the People.'[1]

81. [No motto quoted.][2] The hero and his charger are represented as on the field of Battle.

['No. 81 is made up of a low oblong pedestal, on which is standing a very tame horse, against which

---

[1] *Op. cit.*   [2] 'England's Pride.'

the hero of Waterloo is leaning in the most commonplace manner.' *The Building News*, 7th August 1857.]

['No. 81 is a gigantic horse—Copenhagen, we suppose, with Wellington standing moodily by his side.' *The Ecclesiologist*, August 1857.]

['. . . without the help of allegory little can be done in this matter. Those of our readers who think otherwise we refer to No. 81;—in which there is a fine and satisfactory contempt of the ideal. Here, the national monument is reduced to portraiture, and divided in equal halves between two celebrities, —the Duke of Wellington and his horse Copenhagen. It is not easy to say *which* the artist who deals thus in facts considers the leading fact, the chief or the charger. The Duke is on foot, and so is the horse; and one stands beside the other: that is all.' *The Art Journal*, September 1857.]

82. 'Virtutis fortuna comes.' A statue of the Duke bearing in his hand a laurel branch. At the sides allegorical figures of Victory.

['No. 82 is worked out in colored materials, gilding, and statuary marble. Its basement, unlike any other in the exhibition, is octangular at each end, and one of its sides filled with a gilded bas-relief; the other has the Duke's coat of arms in very bold relief, which is also gilded. Over these are three figures, intended to be carried out in statuary marble. The whole is surmounted by a statue of Wellington, holding in one hand a sword and in the other an olive branch.' *The Building News*, 7th August 1857.]

['. . . a statue of Wellington designed to be placed on a tall pedestal of elaborate character; but which

forms a marked background to the figures, without contributing to the monumental effect.' *The Builder*, 15th August 1857.]

83. [No motto quoted.] A granite sarcophagus of archaic form, in the superstructure, with figures reclining on it, or grouped around, supports a group representing the Duke accompanied by allegorical statues of Victory and Peace.

['In No. 83, which is the last in the collection, the artist has taken his general idea from the celebrated tombs of Juliana and Lorenzo de Medici, at Florence, by Michael Angelo. Resting on each end of the sarcophagus, however, instead of nude figures, the sculptor has put recumbent statues of soldiers. On the upper pedestal is a full-length figure of Wellington holding an enormous sword. On the lower basement is a statue of Britannia and her attendant lion, backed by colors, and on each side figures emblematic of Military Art and Science.' *The Building News*, 7th August 1857.]

['Studiis et rebus honestis' . . . a sarcophagus as a leading feature of the structural part—the sculptor seems to have had Michelangelo's Medici monuments in his mind. The recumbent figures here, are on one side a soldier of Assaye, and on the other a Highlander of Waterloo; the principal group is a figure of Wellington crowned by Victory, and attended by Peace; and below are Britannia seated, and figures of Military and Civil Science. The architectural and sculptural elements are here well combined, and the general grouping is good. The pedestal, sarcophagus, and similar portions are of red granite; and gilt inscriptions are introduced.' *The Builder*, 15th August 1857.]

Index

Dd. 147345 K12